nascitur exiguus, vires acquirit eundo

LONCROSS PRESS

CARLISTS!

A Message for Our Times

**The Eyewitness Account
of a
Twelvemonth Spent with the Carlist Army of
Zumalacarregui, 1834-5**

by

C. F. Henningsen

Introduced and Annotated by

Henry von Blumenthal

1

Charles Frederick Henningsen was born in Brussels in 1815 to a Danish father and an Irish mother and grew up in Brussels. At 15 he had a poem published in London. At 16 he witnessed the Belgian revolution and published an eyewitness account of it. His family fled to London. Convinced of the justice of the legitimist movements, he enlisted in the Carlist army at the age of 19 at was promoted to captain within a year. After the death of Zumalacarregui he wrote up his experiences of his year serving under him while still on campaign with the Carlist army. His book caused a sensation when it was published early in 1836, and was quoted in parliamentary debates. He continued to fight with the Carlists until October 1837, when he left the Carlist army but was almost immediately captured by the Liberals, inhumanely imprisoned and only released on parole after an international outcry.

His love of adventure soon outran his political ideals and he lost his philosophical north. He fought in Circassia against the Russians, with Kossuth against the Habsburgs and for President Walker of Nicaragua, who made him a major-general. By this time he had come under radical and masonic influences.

He became an American citizen and fought as a colonel in the Confederate Army. His wife, Wilhelmina, founded a hospital. He was a prolific writer. He died in poverty in 1877, supported by friends such as the notorious Confederate freemason Albert Pike.

Henry von Blumenthal was born in 1961. He was educated at Westminster School and Christ Church, Oxford, where he read Theology. For ten years he worked in the City for oriental stockbrokers. From 1996-2000 he lived in Moscow as an advisor to the City of Moscow on its debt; for a year after that he worked in Bulgaria for the government of the ex-King Simeon II as an advisor on Capital Markets. Since 2001 he has lived with his wife and two children in Luxembourg, where he is Deputy Dean of the EIB Institute spending increasing time in San Sebastian..

Also published by Longcross Press is his *Seven Stories for Christmas* and *The Companion to British History* by his late father Charles Arnold-Baker, of which he is the editor.

CARLISTS!

A Message for Our Times

The Eyewitness Account
of a
Twelvemonth Spent with the Carlist Army of
Zumalacarregui, 1834-5

by

C. F. Henningsen

Introduced and Annotated by
Henry von Blumenthal

nascitur exiguus, vires acquirit eundo

LONGCROSS PRESS
2021

3

LONGCROSS PRESS

Published by Longcross Press
Lameschmillen, L 3316, Luxembourg

Copyright © Henry von Blumenthal, 2021

ISBN 978-99959-54-14-7

First published in 1836 by John Murray as *The Most Striking Events of a Twelvemonth's Campaign with Zumalacarregui in Navarre and the Basque Provinces.*

INTRODUCTION

The fraud of liberalism is always and everywhere the same. One way to appreciate this is to look at instances where all the fury it possesses was thrown into a fight which was then forgotten – or buried – after its triumph. I beg the reader not to be deterred by the apparent distance of Don Carlos' cause or that it may now seem finickety and irrelevant: it is deeply relevant because the Carlists saw liberalism in all its hydra-headed horror, and rejected not just a facet of it, but all its facets. We must do the same today. Judge for yourself, if the following does not resonate with the events of our times:-

An international coalition of right-minded powers set aside their differences to dismantle the evil empire which had dominated much of Europe under Bonaparte in the name of liberty and revolution. But as soon as this was achieved, those who had all along sympathised with the regime and its ideas regrouped and began, to use a phrase coined more than a century later, a long march through the institutions. They called themselves liberals and hid behind the claim that they stood for the liberty of the many. They often repeated, as they still do, noble-sounding catchphrases, we would call them soundbites, about freedom and liberty, but then as now these slogans were not applied to their opponents. There was an unofficial press blackout, internationally observed by all but the most disinterested papers, on reports which supported the Carlist case.

As they advanced their ideology, the liberals seemed to have an instinctive feel for an opportunity. In Spain, it was the weakness of Queen Christina, the dying King Ferdinand VII's wife, for her daughter Isabella, whom she wanted to become Queen at any cost in money, arms or principles. If there is one thing that differentiates a conservative from a liberal, it is the former's respect and the latter's contempt for the rules of the game. The existing rules barred women from the throne, so the rightful successor to the sonless Ferdinand was his brother Don Carlos. This may offend modern sensibilities but the point is that those were the rules as they stood. It was not for the beneficiary of a change in rules to make such a change. The liberals seized the opportunity with both hands. They offered to help move the goalposts by changing the succession laws, in return for other changes to their liking.

Isabella was typical of the sort of uncritical, vaguely conservative person who doesn't understand that a principle is a principle. She was therefore a gift to the liberals, a "useful idiot" in Marx's phrase, who were happy to see her enjoy her moment of bliss as her daughter was declared Princess of Asturias (i.e. future Queen), knowing that thereby the whole principle of monarchy – hereditary succession according to the rules, for better or worse – had been discarded and it was only a matter of time before a republic would dawn. As one of her own liberal army officers put it in a letter to the *Morning Post*:

> We have no confidence in the Queen. She was Royalist to please King Ferdinand, she was Revolutionary to please and serve herself; she was anti-Revolutionary to please the Government of Lord Grey, she was Liberal again when the wind set that way in England and France a few weeks ago, and now she will turn back again to Zea and his Party, or to any other party, if the Duke of Wellington will but recognize her. You will then ask me, perhaps, "Why do I serve her?" My answer is, because I am a soldier, and because I think that in the course of time some revolution to overthrow her and establish a democratical government may take place.

Disinheriting Don Carlos was not just a dynastic issue or even a matter of theoretical legitimacy. It happened on this occasion that practically all the issues which have always divided right from left came into focus in this single question. The principled stand taken by Don Carlos and his supporters was applied not merely to his succession rights but to everyone's rights. All over Spain different communities had acquired various local rights, which the liberals wanted to do away with, since centralism is ever the warcry of the Left. In particular, the four Basque-speaking provinces had a vast number of local rights called *fueros* which had been acquired over the centuries. These included the right not to be conscripted, and many regulations concerning local trade, which were very annoying to big business. This brings us to another aspect of that struggle, all too familiar today, which is that the same people who most loudly proclaimed their concern for the downtrodden were those who were cashing in for themselves. In the big towns of the Basque provinces there was considerable support for the liberal cause, not because of its concern for the poor but, on the contrary because it furthered the opportunities to make money. Unrestricted free trade was of great interest to the businessmen of San Sebastian and Bilbao, who reached deep into the pockets of British traders, the Chinese of their day. The plethora of *fueros* which protected the rural poor from exploitative pricing was an obstacle to their dreams of wealth.

In Britain, the cry went up to support the Liberal government in Spain. Not coincidentally, the loudest calls to support Queen Christina and her daughter were those who had notes of hand from her government and interests in Basque ore and manufactures. Demands for intervention were only resisted by Wellington and others who had fought in Spain two decades before and knew the ordinary people well. A tremendous publicity campaign was mounted in which it was said that the liberals represented the aspirations of the many against the backward and oppressive few; that the Carlists were hopelessly outnumbered and could easily be crushed and that no decent Spaniard could possibly support them. From the beginning the liberals executed Carlist prisoners as traitors, but when the Carlists responded in kind they were denounced as savages and the instigators of the practice. In one egregious example (among many) of Liberal disinformation, at Ormaiztegui General Zumalacarregui, with a force of 2,000, routed an army of 8,000 liberals commanded by their best generals. These then had the bells of San Sebastian rung out to proclaim a victory while the courier who brought the truth was shut in prison before he could reveal it.

That this liberal posturing was simply humbug was obvious to the young Henningsen and it shines through in both his conscious and unconscious remarks. Unconciously, he refers to the Carlists frequently as the Royalists, which would seem odd when speaking about a dynastic struggle if it were not clear that the liberal aim was not a liberal Monarchy but the overthrow of monarchy altogether. He frequently drops the phrase "so-called" or "*soi-disant*" when referring to liberals, and it is easy to see why.

Consciously, he points out the absurdity of claiming, on the one hand, that the liberals enjoyed the overwhelming support of the Spanish while, on the other, demanding that the foreign powers intervene to prop up the government. He denounces the lies and manipulation of the press. In a striking passage on the British intervention, he writes:

The public were led to believe that the majority of the nation was in favour of the will by which Ferdinand, in violation of the established law, altered the succession to the throne, on condition of its being surrounded by *soi-disant* liberal institutions. On that consent hinged the rights of Isabella and the exclusion of Don Carlos. There was evidently no right, according to their own reasoning, without this majority; but, according to their statements, the majority of the people were in favour of government, which had also the army of 120,000 men, all the strong places, and all the *materiel* of the kingdom. How is it possible, if all this were true, that they should need the aid of strangers? ... If the majority were in favour of the Queen's government, it could have no need of auxiliaries - holding, as it does, every resource - and least of all such auxiliaries as have been sent them. If it be not so, the right of the Queen is at once destroyed, on their own principles, and it is a crying injustice to take any part against Don Carlos; for it is, then, clearly for the sake of lucre only[1].

How the stockholders - those I mean who are innocently blind - can still give faith, as they do, to the statements of those papers which have so palpably

---

[1] In the House of Lords, Wellington remarked "it did unfortunately happen that certain parties in this country had been connected with the Spanish finances; and it was important to those parties that red coats should make their appearance in Spain, and that the name of Great Britain and of the British Legion should be mixed up in the operations of the war."

8

betrayed and deceived them, exceeds my comprehension. Let anyone take all the numbers of the greater part of these oracles for the last two years past, and they will find it repeatedly reported, that when the question first began to be agitated in England, "the Carlist faction, or rather the armed bands, represented as desolating parts of the kingdom, did not exist." Although they had never existed, we were subsequently informed that they were entirely destroyed.

Supporters of Don Carlos at first feared to step forward. When Zumalacarregui came on the scene, he found only 800 men willing to take up arms. But he communicated his personal courage and confidence so well that by the time of his death two years later he had an organised army in the field of 28,000 which was poised to take Madrid. Had he lived, Don Carlos would have been installed as king. But at this point foreign troops intervened and the Carlist supply lines were cut.

Ultimately the Carlists lost their struggle, and the liberals installed the military dictatorship of Espartero, but of course, the principles for which they fought, including the fundamental principle that principles actually exist, are still worth fighting for: rights, duties, respect for established laws, customs and procedures. They were not just fighting for some principles, but for principle itself. It is therefore no accident that they were deeply loyal to the fundamentals of the Catholic religion, as are Carlists today, for traditional Catholicism stands for nothing if not the cause of Objective Truth.

This leads me to pose the question: where is the Carlism of our own day? Where is our Don Carlos, our Zumalacarregui? Who will overcome the daunting alliance between big business, big tech, the big social media platforms and the great powers, ranged against honesty and principle?

Henry von Blumenthal,
San Sebastian,
St. George's Day, 2021

Henningsen's drawing from life of General Zumalacarregui.
His successor, General Eraso, as
ked Hennigsen for a copy as it was such a striking likeness.

DEDICATION.
TO LORD ELIOT[2].

My Lord,

      Your permission to inscribe to you these volumes affords me the highest gratification, as in the rough chapters they contain I have endeavoured to give a faithful description of some scenes of a civil war, in alleviating the horrors of which your Lordship played so conspicuous a part, and some passages from the life of an extraordinary man, whose character, even during the short intercourse that took place between you, your Lordship learned so justly to appreciate, and regard with the interest his genius and enthusiastic spirit were calculated to inspire.[3] These chapters I cannot more appropriately dedicate than to an Englishman, one of the very few who have in any way interfered in the civil strife now desolating Spain, whose name will not be a curse to her people, but on whose head the blessings of all ranks of Spaniards will be showered. I beg your Lordship to accept the tribute of my private feelings, and ray public expression of them, in thus assuring you of the deep sense I entertain of the manner in which you discharged one of the noblest offices of humanity, and of its effect in saving the lives of thousands.

      I have the honour to be, My Lord, Most sincerely,
Your Lordship's obedient Servant,
Charles Frederick Henningsen.
London, 21st. Feb., 1836.

---

[2] 1798-1877, Secretary of the British Legation at Madrid, later 3rd Earl St. Germans. Educated (like the present writer!) at Westminster School and Christ Church, Oxford. A Peelite Conservative, he was later Lord Lieutenant of Ireland.

[3] The Liberal government had Carlist prisoners executed, despite having the facilities to detain them. The Carlists, who had no such facilities, initially detained prisoners but, hardly surprisingly, retaliated when they saw the ill treatment of their brothers-in-arms. Hand-in-hand with the execution of prisoners was the practice on both sides of giving no quarter. The Liberal General Espartero asked Lord Eliot to lead a commission to broke an agreement. Lord Eliot approached Zumalacarregui first, who immediately signed the proposed accord without changes, rapidly enough to save the lives of 27 Liberal prisoners who were about to be shot. By contrast, the Liberals insisted on changes before he would sign, and the "Eliot Convention" had to be sent back to Zumalacarregui for re-signature.

EDITOR'S NOTE TO THIS EDITION

I have not updated placenames. It must be obvious to the reader what is meant by Pampeluna, Bilboa and Vittoria. I have in places added footnotes indicating the modern names for smaller places.

I have interfered little with the text in general, except generally to replace numerals for numbers over 10 written out in full, and sometimes (but not always) to modernise the punctuation.

PREFACE.

It is now two years since the insurrection of the Basque Provinces commenced, and the remnant of an expiring faction, as it was termed, hunted like a band of robbers amongst the mountains, repenting that it had ever embraced the cause of an outlawed Prince, has already swelled, as all sides admit, into an imposing party. The partisans of Don Carlos were represented as only the blind and bigoted[4] few, or an assemblage of those lawless characters who are wont (like the seabird which takes advantage of a wreck or havock, to appear on a clouded horizon) to profit, for purposes of plunder, or ambition, by the moment of incertitude which always follows the change of any ancient and established mode of government, marked and branded by public opinion, without friends or partisans. It was asserted that, aware how desperate was the cause they had embraced, they were rather endeavouring to escape from punishment than struggling with any hope of success.

Day after day it was announced, both in the French and English journals, that the last bands of Carlists had been dispersed, and that their leaders were about to cross the frontier. The French telegraph and the Queen's bulletins were their oracles, and the *Morning Herald*[5], whose correspondent gave all along consistent intelligence, was not for a long time credited by any party, and is not generally so to this day, on the affairs of the peninsula[6]. At last, however, they have been forced to admit, that whether the name and success of Don Carlos was a means or an end - his succession a pretext or an object - without foreign intervention it was

---

[4] At that time the word meant "intransigent."

[5] Founded 1780, by now edited by Stanley Lees Gifford

[6] It is to the correspondent of the Morning Herald, a Mr. Mitchel, that the public is indebted for the most impartial and correct narration of all that occurred during the civil war in the northern provinces of Spain, since the beginning of the contest. He spent some months in the Christino camp, and was afterwards repeatedly in our own. I do not mean to say that he has been always right; but on looking through the columns of the Morning Herald of the last year, I have been surprised at his general accuracy. (CFH)

impossible to quell the insurrection of the Basque Provinces; and this after announcing, for more than a year and a half, the successes of the Queen's troops during a war against a "faction" which, from its commencement had been announced as "at its last gasp," for the thousandth time.[7]

It is true that the game began against fearful odds, affording an addition to those examples which history reproduces at intervals under a varied form, of what the determined spirit of a people, and the talent of a leader, can effect a people without arms, without money, without any succours from abroad, boldly proclaiming the cause of a favourite Prince, in the face of large and disciplined armies, and of the treaties of two powerful nations, even when they had reason to believe that that Prince had abandoned his own cause. Rodil, in his famous proclamation on passing the Ebro, seemed not to draw an overcharged picture, when he described them as without means to resist[8], fortresses to screen, ally to lend them succour, or friend or arbiter to intercede for them. Now that Zumalacarregui's memory must descend, whatever be the issue of the contest, as an heirloom to all classes of his countrymen, as long as the Spanish language endures, and that his name must be mingled in the songs of the peasantry with that of the Cid, it would be superfluous to say that he was no ordinary man: but, although on the roll of those who have acquired a title to immortality, by the immense share he had in the early successes of the Royalist army, justice is scarcely done him. There is no doubt but that it required the iron frame and indomitable spirit of the mountaineers he commanded, to battle so long against man, want, and the elements. But now that it is an established fact, that he has left behind him a

---

[7] The fairness of Henningsen's point is corroborated by a letter which was published in the *Morning Post* on 12th. December 1834, which is all the more valuable for having been written by an officer of the Liberal Army. See the Appendix.

[8] Proclamation of Rodil at Mendavia on crossing the Ebro, July, 1834. (CFH). José Ramón Rodil y Campillo, 1st. Marquess of Rodil and 3rd. Viscount of Trobo (1789-1853) is one of the villains of this book, and deservedly so. Even his fellow Liberal general, Espartero, campaigned for him to be deprived of military honours. (HvB)

disciplined and warlike army, and has awakened such a spirit in the north of Spain, that the cause of King Charles would be difficult to lose, it would be gross ingratitude to deny that nothing less than his extraordinary genius could have overcome the apparently insurmountable difficulties which encompassed the Royalist party. When he placed himself at the head of the partisans of the exiled Prince, they had been defeated, dispersed, or disarmed in all the provinces. All that Zumalacarregui could then rally of his discouraged followers scarcely exceeded 800 undisciplined and badly-armed men; and with this force he bade defiance to the usurping government, which had then on foot in the Peninsula above 120,000 men, including the veteran army of the constitutional war. For months, reinforcement succeeded reinforcement, and one general followed another, even to the redoubted Mina[9], each with new plans and great projects, till their renown shrunk successively away before that of the Carlist leader, like waves that shiver against a rock. After destroying upwards of 50,000 men, and a number of officers which it is fearful to think of, after nearly clearing Navarre and the provinces, and taking or causing the enemy to evacuate 16 fortified places, he died in the hour when his fortune was taking those wide and rapid leaps, which we so often see in the career of a great character. He found, as I have said, 800 badly-armed peasants and 14 horses, and he left to the sovereign he had served so well, on the day of his death, 28,000 men[10] of well-organized and disciplined infantry, and 800 horse well mounted and appointed, 28 pieces of artillery, and 12,000 spare muskets, all won by his own good sword; for although the country offered him willing hands to wield them, it had been so completely disarmed, that every weapon he gave them he was obliged to take from a living foe, and his arsenal, as he expressed

---

[9] General Francisco Espoz y Mina (1781-1836)
[10] 39 battalions: 13 of Navarre, six of Alava, six of Guipuscoa, eight of Biscay, and six of Castillo; one regiment of four squadrons of Navarrese lancers; one squadron of lancers of Alava; one squadron of lancers of Biscay; one squadron of Castille; besides 500 horse and 1,000 foot between Merino and Villalobos, in Old and New Castille. (CFH)

it, "was in the ranks of the enemy." From thence almost all the Carlist equipments - muskets, horses, and cannon, with the exception of 1500 muskets (all that he ever received from abroad), and 200 horses, which would about supply the place of those lost in the campaign - had been taken. Whole battalions are armed with new muskets having the Tower proof[11] on them, or the marks of the French manufactories, supplied to the Queen in virtue of the quadruple alliance, by the ministers of France and England, who little imagined they were sending them eventually to arm the partisans of Don Carlos. As the man whose genius mainly contributed to produce such a result, and the people who maintained what everybody must admit to have been an extraordinary struggle, may not be entirely uninteresting; and as at a distance of 800 miles, and more than that, behind the barrier which the French government had hitherto established, it is difficult for people here to gather any information, except from sources whose intelligence, in a case of such party interest, is at least to be suspected, and who, like the two knights, always see the different faces of the black and white statue, I have drawn a few sketches from which the reader may form an incomplete, but, as far as it goes, a correct idea of this desolating civil war. I have interspersed them with some anecdotes of the man who disappeared from the theatre of his glory at the moment when he had attained the greatest eminence.

I served a year under his orders, having thrown myself with more enthusiasm than prudence into a party whose existence was then precarious, but which I left when it had grown under his guidance from the dwarf to struggle on full equality of stature with its opponent, whose efforts during its early growth his skill enabled it to baffle. The circumstance of my having followed him in every action and skirmish during that period, from the time when he was at the head of 6000 men till he left nearly 30,000, and polished off by a distant and random shot from the walls of Bilboa, when the

---

[11] The arrow-like mark used by the English royal armoury.

16

road to Madrid lay open to him, enabled me to see much of the nature of the civil war, and the character of its great leader, which I studied in storm and in sunshine, in hours of peril and disappointment, as well as of victory and success. Being, as the reader may naturally suppose, of Carlist opinions, and identified in sentiments with those in whose defence I have been engaged, and whose cause I still regard with attachment, I have, as much as possible, confined myself to the narration of facts, as these reason more powerfully than any arguments. The sketches here offered may be rough and unpolished, as they fell from the pen of a soldier, the greater part written during the moments snatched from the active life of this singular campaign; but if the reader should tire by the way, he can but raise the siege and close the unamusing chapter. I have merely drawn a rough sketch with charcoal on a guardhouse wall neither memoir, travels, nor history but which may have the merit, perhaps only the merit (but that is the province of the reader, not of the writer, to judge) of being a sketch from the life.

CONTENTS

18

20

21

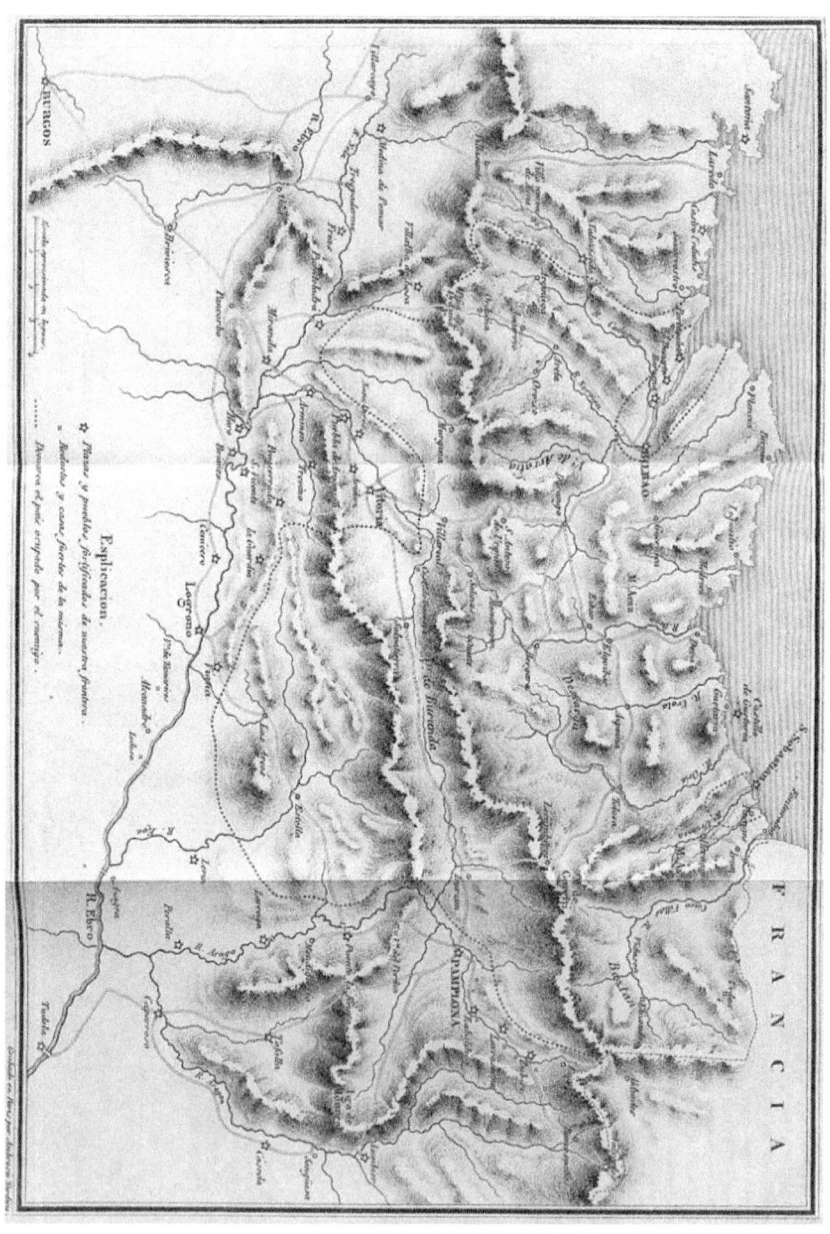

22

CHAPTER I.

State of Society in Spain - The Spanish Peasant - Parties - The Clergy - Monastic Orders - Royalist feelings of the Peasant - The Prince's chances of success.

Spain, whether on account of the character of its people, its political history, or the nature of the country, is infinitely farther from France than the distance in the post-book, or the Pyrenees that divide the two kingdoms, would seem to indicate. It is inhabited by a race of men, with ideas, feelings, and habits all different from those of their northern neighbours. They are a people apart, and cannot be weighed in the same balance with their neighbours: it requires a long and familiar knowledge to estimate them justly: they have exalted qualities and great defects; but to appreciate both, one must have become acquainted with them during those moving scenes which stir up the passions in men's bosoms to the surface. The stranger who has only viewed the inhabitants in their capital, their large towns, and along the Camino-real while travelling in his carriage, knows nothing of the Spanish nation. Scantily peopled, and little cultivated having, by the strange vicissitudes of her political history, retrograded while all the world advanced Spain is considerably behind the rest of Europe in civilization, and also in its vices as well as in its virtues. This backwardness may be in a great degree the effect of the American gold which poisoned her energies, and of the desolating wars of latter years; for war is like the bleeding of a patient, which leaves him either eventually strengthened, or long and fatally debilitated. With her, it is rather the ebb of a former civilization than the remnant of barbarism slowly dwindling away.

At the present, moment, society in Spain may be divided into two classes the agricultural and that which, in French, is so appropriately termed the "*industrielle*," which includes all those concerned in the artificial part of a nation's prosperity those who traffic, who manufacture, and who administer to the luxury of those classes which we are in England accustomed to look upon, if

23

not as exclusively respectable, at least as the most so in the nation, but which, producing nothing, in reality are living on the sweat of the labourers brow. These, instead of being classes of predominant weight, ought rather to be subservient, in every country, but more so in Spain, where, excepting the peasantry, and those who, living in the midst of the peasantry, far from cities, mingle aristocratic blood and pretensions with their simplicity, all orders are totally degenerated and demoralized selfish, treacherous, and effeminate. A Moorish ferocity is all that remains of their former high spirit and courage the national love of honour is dwindled to a self-sufficient vanity, and the national avarice now pierces through, without those redeeming traits of magnificence and generosity which were perceptible in the old Spanish character. Licentious in manners and in morals, cold-hearted, sordid, and dastardly, they have not the vices or the virtues of barbarians: universal corruption has destroyed their civilization. This seems a melancholy picture; but those who have mingled with their titled nobles, their statesmen, their higher orders of clergy, their commercial classes, their citizens generally, their military, and their rabble, will, I fear, not find it overcharged.

Sweeping as this judgment may seem, it is not, however, the character I must give to the Spanish nation in general, but to a portion of the community which, happily, only forms about one-tenth part of it, although including all that we are wont to term the "respectability," and possessing the wealth, the commerce, and the government of the state. By this fraction, as it comes immediately under the eye of the traveller, he is too apt to judge of all Spaniards. But there is a wide and striking difference between the classes I have mentioned and the immense majority of those who cultivate, on a larger or a lesser scale, the soil, consisting chiefly of a peasantry simple and untainted by the corruption which for the last century has enervated the inhabitants of her cities. Independent and high-spirited, the Spanish peasant, isolated from those congregated masses amongst which all revolutions of manners and ideas for the

24

better or the worse so speedily take place, has remained the same, or but little changed from what he was centuries ago. He has many defects, chiefly arising from his southern sky and his southern origin: he is indolent and cruel, but his faults are redeemed by many noble traits; and, on the whole, I have found in his character more to admire than to blame.

These observations are, from all I have heard, applicable also to Portugal, and readily explain why, during the war, both in that country and in Spain, the effeminacy and cowardice of the officers offered so remarkable a contrast to the behaviour of the men; why, in Spain, all those whom we are accustomed to see leading in a nation were the first to bow to the French, while the peasant untiringly resisted his oppressors; and why, although no country offers so many examples of self-devotion and heroism, none presents so many of treachery and pusillanimity the latter, I fear, all to be found in the classes I have first described.

The nobility of Spain, once the most warlike in Europe, has sunk into the most complete insignificance, as is always the case with an aristocracy when the sword has become too heavy for its grasp. The *industrielles*, who have already long thrown off the yoke of the clergy, seek to appropriate to themselves the power which has passed away from the nobles, and to rule with their gold the agriculturist, depriving the clergy of the authority the latter still retain over him. The former, as I have said, possess in their ranks the wealth of the kingdom, and the majority of the officers of the army; they also possess all the strong places and *matériel* of the country, which alone have enabled and enable them to sustain themselves as a party. They have adopted the cause of the usurping government from personal interest, some with a view of forwarding their own designs, others to retain their situations, or from fear of losing their property none, I may safely say, from attachment. A large portion are exaltados, ultras in liberal opinions, who aim either at anarchy or a republic. At the same time, there is a striking difference between republicanism in France and

25

England, and republicanism in Spain. In the latter country, perhaps, it would be the bitterest enemy to anything like Agrarian laws, democratic sentiments being chiefly confined to the rich (who wish for as perfect an independence as possible for their own cities, where they could establish an aristocracy of wealth) and a small portion of the lower classes in the large towns, who look forward eagerly towards times of anarchy and confusion, not only as a stepping-stone to their ambition, but to satisfy their brutal passions. To these are opposed the peasantry, who are all Carlists, and form the great mass of the population, who alone have retained the original stamp of the Spanish character, and who, when roused, still exhibit flashes of its former independence and energy. Proud, indolent, and attached to their ancient usages, they are all royalists and legitimatists. Accustomed, from their ancient mode of government, to a great degree of personal liberty under a despotic form, they look with suspicion on the modern innovations which the *liberals*, in their march of new ideas, wish to introduce. Experience has perhaps given them an exaggerated horror of that revolutionary fever which has for the last half century agitated Europe, and of which designing men have taken advantage to disturb nations, that, ever and anon returning to the same point, find they have only gone round a circle, and that the charlatans, who led the movement, alone rise uppermost by the changing of the wheel. The peasant, or rather the agriculturist, particularly in the northern provinces and of these principally I speak is not only devoted to his ancient mode of government and line of monarchs in consequence of his jealousy of all that comes from abroad, but also from his habits, feelings, and traditions. Having never suffered from the abuse of royalty, and, however it fared with the courtier and the citizen, having always enjoyed a great degree of personal independence in the most arbitrary times, he supports the rights of his sovereign with the same tenacity with which he would defend his own privileges if they were attacked. The sufferings of his country - and Spain, in the remembrance of the present generation, has been afflicted by many - are all associated with his recollection of the invasion of the French, who, although then slaves in fact, as undergoing the transition from a republic to despotism, came with the words of liberty and equality in their mouths.

Is it then altogether so strange and unaccountable, that a people should be so deluded and priest-ridden as not to see the advantages of progressing from a tyranny under which they are free, to a freedom rife with massacre and oppression? Are we to wonder if they remember that, under their kings and the ancient laws of Spain, they were prosperous and happy; that their fleets swept the ocean, and gold flowed in from the conquered Indies; that Austria, Belgium and Italy were under their dominion; that, since the march of liberal ideas, Spain has been a bankrupt in the scale of power, the jest of the stranger, overrun by his armies, ground down by his avarice, and deeply wounded in her national and proverbial pride?

Besides these evils, and the experience they have had of the dominion of their patriots under the government of the Cortes, the people are well aware that by the laws of Spain no female can wield the sceptre; and they feel it to be an insult to Spanish dignity to be governed by a woman. The Queen - Christina - so well knew how unpopular it would be to set aside the succession of the infant, Don Carlos, that when it was found that Ferdinand VII was to have no male issue, she was obliged to throw herself unreservedly into the arms of the liberal party. That party had indeed brought about her marriage, in the hope of legally excluding Don Carlos from the throne, whom, on account of his uncompromising character, they had every reason to fear. The army, which was in favour of the Infant, was officered anew, and placed entirely under the command either of the officers of the constitutional army, who had rebelled against him, or of men of known liberal opinions. The country was then divided into two parties, and so continues to this day. The majority of the inhabitants of the large towns, less than one-tenth of the population of Spain, are in favour of the Queen, either as a preliminary step towards a republic, or from interested motives. Wielding all the artificial resources of the country against the other nine-tenths, they have for a moment manacled the latter, who had no resource but the country, the mountains, their numbers, and their energetic and indomitable spirit. To these advantages were added, although not their main inducement, feelings of religious enthusiasm. The persecution of their monks and clergy, whom the liberals, still rankling with hatred at having been obliged to disgorge the church-lands bought in the time of the Constitution, had not only avowed their intention of attacking, but already proceeded to strip, produced an impression highly favourable to the cause of the Infant.

The period thus chosen for assailing the Spanish clergy was the worst that could have been selected. The many and terrible abuses which had crept, as is so often the case, into an unpersecuted church, where ambitious men make a stepping-stone to their evil purposes of the sacerdotal character, had disappeared and become things of the past. The abolition of the Inquisition, which Don Carlos is falsely charged with wishing to re-establish, and the difference the peasant found between the insensible rule of his clergy and that of his patriots in 1820, has confirmed him in his attachment not, only to his curates[12] and secular clergy, but also to the monastic orders, which it thus became highly impolitic openly to attack. The wealth of the convents and monasteries, when the peasant sees the life of mortification which is led within, (particularly in the north of Spain, where the orders are mostly very rigid) does not excite his cupidity: the poor have a right to profit by their endowments, and if he chooses tomorrow to abandon the world and enter their walls for shelter, it is at his option to share the cowl and cell, and the riches of the religious community. The people of Spain, not more sanctified than those in most other parts

---

[12] A mistranslation of the Spanish word *cura*, meaning a parish priest. Henningsen, despite his British background and polyglot abilities, had spent so long abroad that his writings are peppered foreignisms.

of the world, have a sincere faith in their religion and a deep and superstitious reverence both for its forms and its ministers; and when they witnessed the unprovoked ill treatment of men who usually led quiet and peaceful lives, it was not difficult to interest them in their behalf, and make them believe that the subversion of their religion itself was aimed at.

We are told that the northern provinces are struggling, not for Don Carlos, but for their own privileges. This is not the case: royalism in the Spanish peasant is that feeling not now easily conceived by the rest of Europe - that spirit which animated the French of a past century, when the last words on the lips of a dying Frenchman were *"Pour Dieu et le Roi!"* and the embers of which the republic that conquered Europe found it so difficult to quench in La Vendée[13]. It is natural that the Spaniard having seen his rights and privileges, which, from time immemorial, were respected by his monarchs, now trampled under foot by the liberals, should be strengthened in this feeling. The cause of Don Carlos, it will be seen, thus became identified with the laws, religion, and liberties of the peasant, not only in the northern provinces, but all over Spain. The modern and so called liberal innovations which have been attempted to be introduced, while they have left one class free and independent, have given it an ascendency over the other but little deserved, and which the latter will never brook, having so immense a numerical superiority. The peasant, whose recollection is still animated with the battles which his forefathers have fought so often for their independence against the spirit of liberalism a spirit that in Spain has attacked his happiness and his liberties with the mask fortunately from her visage, while in other lands she has veiled her hideousness till it became too late to struggle looks upon

---

[13] The massacres perpetrated by the Revolutionary government in 1793 against the royalists of the Vendée ceased only when the government convinced itself that the population had for practical purposes been wiped out. The aim was undoubtedly genocidal, regardless of whether the term is formally applicable. However, by 1815, the population had rebounded and was sufficiently unbowed that Bonaparte had to divert 10,000 soldiers from his Waterloo campaign to pacify them. To our own day, the Vendée remains a stronghold of French royalism as well as of adherence to traditional Catholicism.

29

these innovations with a natural hatred. He is indolent and ignorant, but not debased by servility. Time and tradition have attached him (and he is violent in all his feelings) to the royal authority which is but remotely felt, and to his clergy, who claim his respect, not for their merits as men, but as ministers of a superior power.

Ignorant as the peasant often is, he observes a nice distinction between the clergy in their sacerdotal and their individual character - at least in the northern provinces - such a distinction is at the present day infinitely better understood than I could possibly have believed; but this has diminished in no manner his attachment to the usages of the religion of his forefathers. I have seen a priest, while he was our prisoner for some political misdemeanor, and surrounded by the bayonets of the guards, joined by the soldiers in his devotions with the utmost fervour; but the instant after, had he made an attempt to escape, or had the order been given, the same soldiers would have shot him on the spot, and the bystanders would have made no further comment upon his death than if he had been a layman.

Whatever may be held out to the peasant as an inducement to change, he judges of the future by the past, with all the gravity and shrewdness of the Spanish character. He has found that all liberal improvements rendered him only subservient to the inhabitants of cities, and deprived him of his wild freedom and of institutions which age had hallowed in his estimation. Therefore he looks on all constitutional theories as a tyranny which would rob his princes of their heritage and himself of his independence, being satisfied as he is, even if he avoid the gloomier side of the picture, that they hold not out to him the prospect of benefit.

Having endeavoured to depict the feelings by which the people are animated, I shall now pass rapidly over the events that preceded and followed the death of Ferdinand. Such a summary may be the most satisfactory answer to the question of "Why Don Carlos has not already advanced upon Madrid?" a question which will naturally be asked, when I have stated that nine-tenths of the country are decidedly in his favour. The account of what occurred previous to Ferdinand's death shall be but brief, it being my intention principally to detail the enthusiastic devotion, the sacrifices of fortune, life, and family made by the followers of Don Carlos, in the northern provinces, even before he came to risk his person amidst a handful of followers in the mountains of his hereditary dominions, like Charles Stuart in the Highlands. Hitherto, it is true, his success has not been decisive; but of his eventual triumph those who are acquainted with the popularity of his cause in the Peninsula, protracted as the struggle may be, can have but little doubt. The northern provinces can only be subdued by the extermination of the male population, the transplanting of families, burning of harvests, and destroying every human habitation, as was attempted by the French Convention in La Vendée. But to effect all this in a country like the present seat of war, which baffled the genius of Napoleon with all his legions, and where every arbitrary act, instead of striking terror, arms fresh masses of its population, would require, I apprehend, a larger army than was ever marshalled under any man since the days of Xerxes. It would, moreover, be forced to feed upon itself, like a swarm of lemings, when its work was done. I am aware that the public at a distance has been accustomed to receive very different impressions; but people have so long been kept in ignorance of facts by the intrigues of the Stock Exchange and the confederate Jews, its rulers, the Rothschilds and Mendizabals, who, like the jackals and vultures, fatten their carrion carcasses where the fray has been, and, as Byron[14] so appropriately expresses it -

"Stand afresh,
To cut from nations' hearts their pound of flesh;"

---

[14] Henningsen was a fan of Byron, whose poetry and example inspired him to seek adventure with the Carlists.

that it is time they should be made acquainted with the real state of things. In the whole of the north of Spain, the country districts are, with trifling exceptions, favourable to Don Carlos; and the Queen, in all her usurped domains, has not by her intrigues been able to secure one town or village so entirely devoted to her, as the provinces now the seat of war are to the King. So intense is the interest they take in the war, that it exceeds belief: now, as in the case of Pizarro, when he had burned his navy, retreat is impossible; they have only to conquer, or die in the struggle. When we recollect that they are engaged against a purely artificial force, which diminishes day by day, while they are cheered on by the wishes of nine-tenths of Spain, who hail the royal army as saviours and liberators, the issue may be guessed. The death of Zumalacarregui, the modern Scanderbeg, no doubt has retarded for many months the triumph of the King; indeed, had that general died four months sooner, it would probably have proved fatal to the cause in that part of Spain; although I am convinced that the smouldering fire would, ere long, have broken out in another. But, in dying, he bequeathed to his party all the elements of success; he had, besides, destroyed that part of the opposing army which was composed of veterans of the Constitutional war, as well as the reputations of the best generals, who had been successively sent against him.

Although it is impossible to foresee the final issue of the contest, as this war has added another proof to the number already existing, that the race is not always to the swift, nor the battle to the strong - yet those who have really seen the spirit by which the people are animated, and the nature of the country, will judge, as well as myself, that even in case the royal army should meet with many and fatal reverses, it would be impossible to subdue the people otherwise than by extermination. Besides the sentiments by which they are animated, their families and fortunes are so entirely compromised, that they must risk the last chance. Their fathers, sons, and relations have either fallen, or are fighting in the Royalist

32

ranks. If the cause of Don Carlos triumph, they behold a prospect of happiness before them if it fail, of total ruin. For all they have already paid in contributions and rations they have his full receipt: with this they are content, knowing that, if he reach Madrid, indemnification will be granted for all their losses. At the present period of the war, one decisive victory in the plains of Vittoria, and the insurgents march on the capital; while such a battle, if won by the constitutionalists, would but little advance them, if lost, would be decidedly fatal.

Carlist infantry of the period. The beret or *boina* in any of several colours, strikingly distinguished the Carlists from the Liberals who mostly wore shakos. Later on, the Navarrese red *boina* became the distinguishing mark of Carlists everywhere, and remains so today.

CHAPTER II.

Events previous to Ferdinand's Death - Don Carlos in Portugal - Sarsfield and Rodil - Don Carlos and Don Miguel.

In the whole of Spain, the population is Royalist, with the exception of Estremadura, where the landed property is divided between a few nobles, the majority of whom belong to the liberal class, and exercise over a scattered population the same influence which in other parts is enjoyed by the clergy. The inhabitants of the coast of Andalusia and Catalonia, of the maritime towns and. the larger cities, which do not, as in other countries, form a large part of the population, in the midst of which they are placed at wide intervals, may also be considered as exceptions. I do not mean to say that the people in these districts are so intensely devoted to the Royalist cause as in the northern provinces at the present hour, where every suffering and sacrifice has added a fresh ink to their attachment, and, with that tenacity peculiar to the Spanish character, has bound them more firmly to their opinions. But there is fully as much royalism in the former provinces now, as there was in the latter at the commencement of their insurrection. The Andalusians and Catalans being less warlike, and their country less calculated for a struggle against an enemy who had taken all the precautions to crush the evil growing against him in the bud, and who had disciplined armies and all the resources of the kingdom in his power, were easily put down, although they rose more simultaneously and enthusiastically than their fellow subjects of the north. The party who wished to deprive Don Carlos of his rights, having secured the army, during the ministry of Zea Bermudez[15], by replacing all the officers of the Cortes, and expelling those who were known or suspected of entertaining opinions favourable to legitimacy; having also, by means of a numerous and highly paid police, laid hands on all who were

---

[15] Francisco Cea Bermudez 1779-1850, twice Prime Minister of Spain.

obnoxious to them, and armed their partisans under the name of Urbanos, or civic guard, were enabled, on the death of Ferdinand, to effect easily that, which, without these precautions, would have caused a rising en masse of three-fourths of Spain.

Although the Royalists foresaw the *coup d'etat* that was preparing, and Ferdinand was highly unpopular with them, they considered him as their lawful sovereign; and true to the tenor of their opinions, as it was contrary to their principles to rebel against him in favour of one who was still only *heir* to the crown, they allowed themselves, with their eyes open, to be shackled for a future day. Some few, indeed, and particularly the army, being well persuaded that the King was rendered imbecile by his malady, and indignant at his countenancing the attempt to deprive his brother of his heritage, were for rising immediately, and proclaiming the Infant Don Carlos regent, an event which, even by his strict and positive orders, he had great difficulty in preventing. The officers of the guard had many private interviews with him, but he constantly refused his consent; and these propositions being discovered, they were in consequence shortly afterwards dismissed by the ministry from the army. For the long series of intrigues by which the will of the deceased monarch was extorted from him, I refer the reader to the interesting work of the Baron de Los Valles[16]. By some it is affirmed that his last will was extorted from him when in a state of imbecility, and by others it is said to have been a complete forgery; although, from his unprincipled character, it is unnecessary to account for his having given away that which, although his, was never in his gift. It is certain that when speechless, and almost senseless, he was tortured by being driven, literally held upright, in his state-carriage, to quiet the royalist and ultra liberal party; and in the latter days of his life, the depriving his brother of his right - the fits of remorse to which he was subject, his retractation - and then his again doing that which

---

[16] Louis Xavier Auguet de Saint-Sylvain, Baron de Los Valles, 1796-1857

36

he evidently knew to be an injustice, affords the miserable picture of the second childhood of a weak and immoral character.

The friends and adherents of Don Carlos were already subjected to the persecution of the Liberals, particularly those who, from their known attachment to that prince, were most feared. The venerable Bishop of Leon, who had been long known as one of the most valuable and disinterested advisers of the crown, was dismissed from his office of councillor of state; and so far did the liberals proceed, that even the Duchess of Beira, a princess of the family of Portugal, and sister of the Infant's wife, who was hated on account of her firmness of character, and the attachment evinced to her by the Royalists, was banished. So beloved was this princess, that all those around her followed her in her exile. Don Carlos, finding that very soon no alternative would be left him but of remaining a captive, or authorising a civil war against his brother, accompanied his sister-in-law to Portugal, taking with him his wife and family. They left Madrid on the 16th. March 1833, and although every effort was made by the government to prevent it, all along the road the prince received the most flattering marks of esteem. Zea Bermudez then assembled the Cortes, for the ancient ceremony of the Jura, or taking the oath of fidelity to the King's daughter, Isabella, who was proclaimed Princess of the Asturias, and heiress to the throne. But though the ceremony of the Jura was rendered as magnificent and pompous as possible, the gloomy silence of the people, so unusual to a Spanish assembly, who evince their satisfaction in rather a noisy manner, clearly evinced that they did not acquiesce in what was going on. The absence of the highest prelate of the Spanish church, the Archbishop of Toledo, Don Pedro Inguanzo[17], to whom, according to an ancient custom observed for many centuries, the princes, bishops, and grandees of the kingdom were in the habit of taking the oath,

---

[17] Pedro Inguanzo Rivero (1784-1836) refused Liberal demands to swear in the Queen, died in 1836 and his see remained vacant till 1847.

appeared to render it invalid and incomplete. Cordoba[18] was sent to the Infant in Portugal, to demand, in the name of his brother, that he should publicly recognise his niece, Maria Isabella, as Princess of the Asturias, and heiress to the throne.

Don Carlos unites to a mild disposition a firmness of character which had long seemed lost in the family. When, by an act of unparalleled treachery on the part of Napoleon, in 1808, the prince was led prisoner to Bayonne with his family, and after a council held at the château of Marans (which has since been burned, and still stands in ruins in the midst of its vast garden), the Emperor proposed to the Infants to renounce their rights to the crown of Spain and accept in exchange that of Etruria frightened at his threats, Ferdinand and his advisers (excepting the Marquess of Labrador, one of the few Spanish grandees who have uniformly conducted themselves honourably[19]) acquiesced and signed the agreement. But Don Carlos, although there was little chance then of his ever coming to the throne, refused to abdicate his rights, saying, that "It would be a dishonourable concession, and that he would die first." It was, therefore, unlikely that, when in Portugal, out of the power of his enemies, he would commit the act of imbecility demanded of him. He published a declaration, which he sent to all the courts of Europe, and besides addressed the following epistle to his brother:-

"Dearest Brother, - This morning, at 10 o'clock, my secretary, Plazaola, came to inform me that Cordoba, your envoy, desired to know at what hour it would suit me to receive the communication of a royal order. I sent to say that twelve would be a convenient hour. He came a few minutes before one, and I immediately received him. He gave me the official document, which I read; after which I told him, that my dignity and character allowed me only to answer in a direct manner, that you were my king and lord, and moreover my brother a brother well beloved, whom I had attended in his adversity. You desire

---

[18] Luis Fernández de Córdova (or Córdoba) (1798 – 1840) general, diplomat and first Marquis of Mendigorria.
[19] Whig historians universally mock him as being slow witted and verbose at the Congress of Vienna.

to know whether I intend to take the oath of fidelity to your daughter, as Princess of the Asturias. I need not tell you how much I should wish to take that oath; you know me, and can judge that I speak from my heart. Nothing would be more agreeable to me than to be the first to recognise your daughter, and save you all the trouble and embarrassment my refusal must occasion; but my conscience and my honour forbid it. The rights I possess are so sacred, that I cannot put them aside - rights which I derived from God, when he caused me to be born in my present station, and of which he only can deprive me by giving you a son, an event I desire perhaps more than yourself. Besides, it is my duty to defend the rights of those who may come after me, and therefore I think myself bound to transmit the accompanying Declaration, which I address to you in the most solemn manner - to you, and to all the sovereigns, to whom I hope you will communicate it. Adieu, my dear brother; doubt not that I shall be ever devoted to you, and that your happiness shall ever be the object of your brother,

"Carlos.

"DECLARATION
"I, Carlos-Maria-Isidore de Borbon-y-Borbon, Infant of Spain, fully convinced of my legitimate rights to the crown of Spain, if I survive your majesty, you leaving no male issue, do declare that my conscience and my honour forbid my acknowledging any other rights but my own.
"To our King, from his affectionate brother and faithful vassal,

(*Signed*) "The Infant Don Carlos de Borbon-y-Borbon."
"*Palace of Ramalhao, April 29th. 1833.*"

Five months after, the death of the King took place. In the afternoon of the 29th. September he expired, his attendants still thinking him asleep. Don Carlos was then in Portugal, where he had been received by Don Miguel, who treated him in a way that soon evinced the indecision which eventually lost him his crown. The Infant had been followed to that country by a numerous suite, and was afterwards joined by many other Spaniards, although the greater part of those who attempted to reach him were cut off on the road. The Curate Merino[20] - the Mina of the plains - now more than 60 years of age, and already famous in two wars, proceeded

---

[20] Don Jeronimo Merino Cob (1769-1844) was a guerilla leader against the French and commanded 14 Carlist battalions.

to offer his services to Don Carlos; and Brigadier Cuevillas[21], ex-governor of Saragossa, endeavoured to join him with 500 horse, the greater part of which he was unfortunate enough to lose on the way. Cuevillas obtained in a singular manner the order of Charles III. On being introduced into the King's apartment, he said, "I have come to join your majesty, but not alone; 500 brave Castilians, armed and mounted, came with me to lay their services at their sovereign's feet." The King, delighted at such an unexpected reinforcement, and not yet knowing that the 500 had dwindled to a few horsemen on their long and perilous route, instantly threw the ribbon round his neck, as a reward for his fidelity. They both returned to Spain by order of the Infant, to be ready to raise partisans in his favour. Much might have been done by Don Carlos before his brother's death to counterbalance the energetic efforts of the Christinos, as the supporters of the infant princess and Queen Christina were termed; but unfortunately, although in a more honourable way, the Infant Don Carlos possessed the same weakness as Ferdinand. When every tie was broken between them, and common prudence required of him to counteract the intrigues of the Queen and prepare for the death of the King, by giving assurance to his numerous friends that it was his intention to join them, and thus encourage their efforts, he obstinately refused, saying, that it was a point of conscience with him not to stir while his brother lived. This was one of the first of those numerous errors against which the King's cause has so marvellously struggled; for if it has not been lost a hundred times, it is not the fault of those engaged in its support.

When the death of the King became known, the intrigues of the party who had usurped the government in the name of Isabella II were met by public indignation. Notwithstanding the precautionary measures which they had taken, all those provinces where the people had not yet been disarmed, or not kept down by

---

[21] Hilario Alonso Cuevillas Remon (1785-1853). His father and brother were also prominent Carlists

the Urbanos, (who, being composed of the wealthier classes, nearly all favoured the new government as a step towards the adoption of their liberal opinions) would have risen in favour of Don Carlos, and, if he had then presented himself, the Queen's party would have been overwhelmed. As it was, had it not been for the deplorable want of skill and activity on the part of the Royalists, and the absurd way in which they remained without organisation, communication, or intelligence, they might have retained possession of Castile, Leon, Navarre, and the Basque provinces, which were then all in their hands; but of this we shall speak hereafter at length. Don Carlos was prevented from joining them by the army of observation of Rodil, which, under the command of Sarsfield, was stationed on that frontier: thus the prince was necessarily subjected to the reproach of being a weak and pusillanimous character, afraid to draw that sword which he endeavoured to persuade his countrymen to use for him. This was the received opinion abroad; and before his arrival in Navarre, it was participated by many of his partisans.

Sarsfield, whose father was Irish and commanded one of the battalions of the Irish Legion, had always been known as a legitimist[22]. On the death of the King, he remained five days without sending in his adhesion to the Queen's government, evidently waiting for overtures from Don Carlos, who had now become Charles V, of the line of Bourbon. Whether the King's counsellors were actuated by jealousy of the general's foreign extraction[23], or that it was impossible to communicate with him, they committed the unpardonable blunder of sending in the first instance to Rodil. A more unfortunate error for the King's cause could not have been committed. Rodil was, in all his opinions, a staunch republican; and Sarsfield, stung at the idea of proposals

---

[22] Indeed, he came from a long line of legitimists beginning with the Jacobite General Patrick Sarsfield.
[23] Unlikely given that he was a third-generation Spaniard

having been made to one under his orders, instantly sent in his submission to the Queen.

In the midst of the wreck of Miguel's army, without protection, without money, often without provisions, and at last pursued by Rodil, who had orders to capture them, the King and his family suffered privations and humiliations which almost exceed belief. The Queen and Princess of Beira sold their jewels for £5000 for the relief of their followers, who were without horses or clothing; and when they embarked and were obliged to leave many faithful adherents behind, the princess parted with the last valuable article she possessed, a diamond comb, which, on account of its being a gift, she esteemed above all price. On this occasion Colonel Wylde[24] behaved very handsomely. To such a state were the royal family reduced, that when obliged to fly to Zamusca, from the pursuit of Rodil, having lost all their equipage, they found themselves without a change of clothes. On one occasion they were so badly lodged, that the rain, piercing through the roof, deluged their beds, and the Queen, already in ill health, was obliged to sit up all night wrapped in a mantle. On another occasion food was so scarce, that the royal children stole out and asked for bread from the gardes-du-corps, who, having eagerly devoured their own scanty pittance, had nothing to give them. The Queen, having discovered the circumstance, although a woman of great fortitude, could not help shedding tears. In the midst of all these sufferings, the King, however, preserved the greatest equanimity, and had always the usual smile on his lips which must have been far absent from his heart. When the disgraceful capitulation of Evora was about to be signed, he proposed a plan, too bold to have been expected from a man hitherto remarkable for his mild and unadventurous spirit. It was, that Don Miguel should shut himself up in Elvas with a strong garrison, while he should attempt, with

---

[24] William Wylde (1788-1877), later Lt. General. British Commissioner to the Christinist army. An expert artillery officer, he later played an important role in advising the Liberal artillery during the raising of the Siege of Bilbao.

13,000 men (still disposable), to effect the conquest of his dominions, and, if successful, then to return and liberate his ally. The plan was, however, more daring than feasible; for the Spanish army was too obedient to its officers, as the event proved, to have passed over to his standard; and he would have found himself between Rodil on the one side, and the Pedroites on the other. The venerable Bishop of Leon did all in his power to persuade Miguel, but in vain, saying, *"Your majesty may yet recover your crown; but, to find it, you must pass through Madrid with us."* "I would do as you wish," replied Miguel, "but I am convinced no one would follow me." And the capitulation was signed.

Carlist troops formed up for inspection. From the beginning, Zumalacarregui, who regarded guerrilla warfare as but a necessary evil, trained his men as regulars.

CHAPTER III.

Early Efforts of the Royalists - Zavala and his Daughters - Eraso - Description of Navarre - The Rivera - Habits of the Navarrese - Basques - Their Language - Nobility of Navarre and the Provinces - Fueros and Privileges - Guipuscoa and Biscay - National Costume.

It is a common error on this side of the Pyrenees to imagine that the partisans of Don Carlos are confined to the Basque provinces. On the death of Ferdinand, his cause was nowhere so warmly embraced as in Castile. The Royalist volunteers in that province and in Biscay, who had not then been disarmed, amounting to more than 38 battalions, proclaimed Don Carlos. Bands of armed men assembled - the peasant furbished up his musket which had lain idle at least since the days of the constitution - and retired officers and hidalgos of the class half peasant and half gentleman, of which Cervantes describes his hero as a member, took down their swords which had hung useless on their walls since the days when Spain was glorious. These weapons were the long straight, espadon of the heavy horse of France, the curved sword of the German trooper, or the broad-edged sabre of our own cavalry. Such were the leaders who, mounting their steeds, placed themselves at the head of knots of insurgents, which gradually swelled into imposing bands, but which, after all, were nothing more than armed crowds, a body without a soul, every one commanding and no one obeying, till they were dispersed by the government troops almost without an effort. Each one then returned to his home, and the faction was disarmed and punished in detail, for the want of some men of ability to take advantage of the disposition of the inhabitants. If Zumalacarregui had then been with them, they might perhaps have marched on Madrid without a shot being fired; for besides at least 30,000 men under the orders of Merino, Cuevillas, and Verastegui in Biscay, upwards of 20,000 men had been raised by Zavala[25], the

---

[25] Juan de Zavala y de la Puente, 1st Marquess of Sierra Bullones (1804-79) born in Peru, later Spanish Prime Minister

Marquis of Valdespina[26], Armencha[27], Eraso[28], and Simeon de la Torre[29], and held possession of Vittoria and Bilboa. Rodil was at that time occupied in watching the frontier of Portugal; guerrillas had been formed in Arragon and Catalonia, as the Carlists could not find arms sufficient to take the field there in any other way, and the whole of Spain was held on so uncertain a tenure by the Queen, that her army could nowhere spare detachments. With one-tenth of the sacrifices they have since made, the Royalists of Biscay alone might have procured an easy triumph; but as much apathy seemed to pervade the ranks of the Carlists as there was energy displayed by the Queen's party. The former were disarmed and dispersed throughout Castile, in a manner which to this day they have themselves difficulty in accounting for. The Curate Merino with 200 horse alone maintained himself, and has continued to do so down to the present hour, although so repeatedly killed by the French and English papers. A large body of Castilians also passed into the province of Alava; but on the entry of Sarsfield into Vittoria, which place General Uranga, who commanded the Royalists, was obliged to abandon in consequence of being unsupported, they shortly afterwards shared the same fate. Sarsfield had been made viceroy of Navarre, and had received orders to quell the insurrection in the northern provinces; but having embraced the Queen's cause more from pique than any other motive, he acted like a man fighting against his conscientious opinions. Sarsfield is descended from the celebrated general of James II of the same name, and has the reputation of being the best and bravest officer in Spain, but is said to be of a very hasty disposition, and to indulge in an excessive passion for drink, which often leads him to commit the maddest acts. It is related of him,

---

[26] José María de Orbe y Elío, 3rd. Marquess of Valde-Espina (1776-1850) was 58 when the war broke out.

[27] Brigadier Pedro José de Aranzamendía Armencha, executed by Liberals at Bilbao in 1834

[28] Francisco Benito Eraso y Azpilicueta (1793-1835) briefly (as he was himself dying of cancer) took command of the Carlist Northern Army after Zumalacarregui's death. In Basque, Eraso means "attack"

[29] Simón de la Torre y Ormaza (1804-86) later governor of Santiago de Cuba and Puerto Rico.

that on one occasion during the war of independence, having had some dispute with Minio, afterwards colonel of cuirassiers of the guard, he defied him to strike a nail in the gates of Barcelona (which was then garrisoned by the French) before him, and calling out to his staff that all who did not follow were cowards, he mounted his horse and proceeded full gallop with a hammer and nail in his hand, and it was only when half the officers around him had been swept down by the grape of the fortress that he could be persuaded to retire.

Notwithstanding the command of the Queen's troops had been confided to him, there was but little doubt that he repented already of having embraced the revolutionary cause; indeed, he did everything in his power to favour the insurgents as far as he could without compromising himself; and it is evident that it was his intention to have passed over with all his division, and proclaimed Charles V, had he seen a reasonable chance of success. Instead of marching on Bilboa, which he ought to have done in the first instance, he remained 20 days at Vittoria, thus giving the Carlist leaders all necessary time to make preparations for resistance. Everything was, however, lost by their mismanagement. The Brigadiers Zavala and Armencha, who was afterwards shot, and the Marquis of Valdespina, who already at an advanced age, and having lost an arm in the war of independence, had sacrificed a princely fortune to his opinions, advanced upon Oñate with upwards of 14,000 men to meet the Queen's army. But his followers having been left for several days without ammunition, without rations, and without organization, the greater part, tired and disgusted, retired to their own homes.

The Alavese dispersed in a similar manner, as well as the Castilians who had joined them; the Alavese reproaching the Castilians with having abandoned them, and the latter taunting the Alavese with their inaction. Sarsfield, finding that he would seriously compromise himself by further delay, at length advanced. When at Durango, about 18 miles from Bilboa, the authorities, who were suspected of attachment to Don Carlos, surrendered to him several hundred muskets; instead of taking possession of them, Sarsfield replied, "I have no time now to receive them keep them till tomorrow." This was reposing a dangerous confidence in them, which looked almost like the hope that they would carry them off during the night; but such was the discouragement that prevailed that it was not attempted; and the next day the Queen's army entered Bilboa without resistance. The general behaved with the greatest lenity, and was in consequence a very short time afterwards removed from the command, under the pretence that his health was too delicate. When, after the defeat of Valdes, as a last resource Sarsfield was begged to accept the command, he replied ironically, that "*His health would not permit him.*"

Armencha, Zavala, Eraso, all officers of high rank and influence in the country, and Simeon de la Torre, who had been a lieutenant of the guard, continued, however, at the head of the most determined of their partisans, to proclaim the cause of Charles V in the mountains of Biscay and Guipuscoa, where they maintained, with varying success, a guerrilla warfare, without exciting any serious alarm at Madrid. Petty skirmishes took place every day, but the Carlists were unable to keep their ground against the smallest corps of the regular troops. As Bilboa, like most commercial cities, contained a large population very favourable to liberal ideas, and as in a country like Spain, where opinions on both sides are carried to extremes, it is idle to look for anything like moderation, a degree of enmity was excited there against the Royalists beyond what party differences can warrant. Private as well as political feuds had, long before the death of Ferdinand, disturbed the city, and armed groups of either party used to go out, on the pretext of shooting game, but in reality to meet each other in the vineyards and woodlands around the town. The commencement of the civil war was therefore carried on (particularly in Biscay) with a degree of barbarity which is only witnessed in wars where family is armed against family. I will give an example of cruelty exercised against

48

Zavala, beyond what Europe would believe of the modern ages and of the party who profess to desire nothing but the improvement of Spain. Having, when pursued, sometimes obstinately defended himself, his two daughters, who had fallen into the hands of the Christines, were dragged about, and always carried forward with the tirailleurs in every encounter by the garrison of Bilboa, which had daily skirmishes with him. Zavala, fearful of injuring his own children, was obliged to prevent his partisans from returning the enemy's fire, and precipitately to retreat. At length, driven almost to desperation between the reproaches of his party and his paternal feelings, he sacrificed the latter to his duty; and having harangued his followers, placed them in ambush near a little village, of which I have forgotten the name, situated between Guernica and the sea. The enemy, being informed of the circumstance, advanced along the road, leading forward as usual his two daughters. Zavala, in a firm voice, but with tears in his eyes, ordered his men to open their fire; and, instantly rushing in with the bayonet, was fortunate enough to recover his children unhurt: they had, however, narrowly escaped, two of those who held them being killed by the first discharge. His devotion was rewarded with victory; the enemy was dispersed and routed, and the Regiment of Chinchilli left several hundred dead and wounded on the field.

Although this may appear more like a fiction, of the time of the Moslem dominion[30], or the dark ages, when chivalry was struggling with barbarism, than a reality, not only is it a story well known and accredited in the provinces, but attested by many credible witnesses whom I have seen and heard. In times of civil warfare, generally, men's virtues and vices are seen in extremes; and in Spain, whether from its climate, its limited civilization, or its remains of Moorish blood, its inhabitants seem always under

---

[30] A reference to Guzman the Good who, when threatened that his son would be put to death if he did not surrender the city of Tarifa, threw down his dagger to the besiegers for the purpose. A century after this was written, Colonel Moscardo repeated the exploit, and the recording has survived of the telephone conversation in which his son told him not to surrender the Alcazar of Toledo and he replied that he would not.

the influence of stronger passions which lead alike to crimes and virtues than those known to our northern regions.

Zavala was usually reproached with his timidity in exposing his men, although his personal bravery was incontestable. Simeon de la Torre had nothing in his favour but his valour. Eraso was, in reality, the man who organized the insurrection, and the only one capable of commanding with success. Of one of the richest families in the Roncal, he had distinguished himself in previous wars, having risen to the rank of colonel in the regular army, and commanded the frontier line of the western Pyrenees for several years. Attended only by a handful of men, he proclaimed Charles V. on the 12th. October 1833, at Roncesvallos, a spot already celebrated in history for the defeat of Charlemagne's army by the Basques, in 774, and immortalized as the place where Roland, one of the invaders, and the hero of ancient chronicle and legendary song, breathed his last. Eraso had, however, an enemy to struggle with far more merciless than the Queen's partisans; an illness which had long been undermining him, and by which at length he was so overcome, that he was obliged to be carried over the French frontier, where he took refuge in a *borde*, as the isolated cottages in the Pyrenees are called. Even these resorts of the smugglers, which in ordinary times the French police do not care to visit, were then strictly searched, so great was their vigilance, and he was taken and sent prisoner as far as Angouleme. In many other parts of Spain partial risings were effected; but although brave and full of hope, without plan or arrangement, or any chief worthy of notice to guide them, the insurgents were quickly crushed by the generals, who overran the provinces, proclaiming martial law, and executing it with severity by means of a force gained over by promised rewards and immediate largesses. Generally the Carlists were punished so effectually and so promptly, that the very names of those who raised the standard of legitimacy remained unknown to their fellow-partizans of other provinces. Andalusia, Grenada, Catalonia, and Arragon, where for a long time the bands of Carnicer (afterwards taken in Castille, where he was travelling in disguise, and shot) were never heard of, all had their martyrs to the popular opinion; but we know in reality of little more of what took place, than that some movements were made. On the death of Santos-Ladron[31], ex-governor of Pampeluna, who had proclaimed Don Carlos in Navarre, his party was at its lowest ebb; but as this circumstance forms a re- markable epoch in the sanguinary civil war of which it is my intention to detail a few passages, it may not be uninteresting to give a short account of that kingdom and its adjacent provinces, as well as of the character of the inhabitants.

Navarre is situated between the Pyrenees on the north, Arragon on the east, the Basque provinces on the west, and the Ebro and Castille on the south. Its population is computed at about 280,000 souls; but beyond the limits of his tiny kingdom, the Navarrese looks rather on the other Spaniards as his fellow-subjects than his fellow-countrymen. From the northernmost extremity to the large and fertile plains in the vicinity of the Ebro, called *La Rivera*, it is but one succession of mountains, where the stranger is lost and confused in the labyrinth of long and narrow valleys, deep glens, and wild and gigantic rocks. In the northern part, adjoining the Pyrenees, the hills are higher and bolder than in the southern districts; but there is no part where cavalry can march a whole day without dismounting. In some parts the mountains are girt at their base by forests of chestnut trees or the Spanish oak, called "*encina*" whose acorn roasted is as palatable as the chestnut; higher up they are clothed with brushwood, or mere heath or furze, and their summits exhibit in all its nakedness the grey or black stone of which lower down hucre and fantastic masses show themselves. Some of the heights are almost wholly barren, affording a scanty but aromatic herbage to herds of shagged mountain colts, or flocks of sheep and goats. The hut of a shepherd,

---

[31] General Santos Ladron de Cegama (1784-1833). Executed by firing squad on 13th. Oct 1833 after being taken prisoner by the Liberals

covered with large flakes of stone, or a lonely chapel to which a line of crosses points the way, is the only object which arrests the attention, with the exception here and there of a solitary tree which often either the wind or lightning has shivered, and whose trunk seems to have outlived the ambition of rising above its dwarf companions of the soil. Generally, the earth speaks more of the indolence of the inhabitants than of the avarice of nature; and there are thousands and thousands of acres on the mountains which, if planted, would produce a grape that would sparkle high in the glass of the epicure, and far surpass the heavy and luscious beverage grown in the fatness of the plains. In some parts the ever-green arbutus darkens the hills with its deep foliage, which is like that of the laurel, bearing in autumn a fruit, a perfect strawberry in appearance, but insipid to the taste and intoxicating in its effect. Occasionally in this wilderness stretches a deep valley abounding in corn and maize, and studded with villages; sometimes it is of considerable extent, like the plains of Pampeluna or those of Vittoria and Salvatierra, in which, from the heights of the Sierra, you look down on 40 or 50 villages stretched beneath your feet, between you and the blue ridge of hills which walls them in on the other side. In the southern part the vine and olive succeed to the Indian corn. From one valley to another lead many roads; and sometimes, on account of the natural obstacles, they deviate so much, that they are double the distance of the innumerable paths which cut straight across the mountain, but difficult for anything save a goat or a Navarrese to tread - rugged and steep, and at times so narrow, that, you may almost span the way with your extended fingers, with perhaps a ravine of some 100ft gaping or a torrent roaring below. From one cluster of villages to another, the distance is usually from 5-12 miles; but generally there are formidable defiles and deep precipices to encounter ere you reach them. In winter, the way which has been worn in the ascents of the solid rock, and into which the rain has beaten the soil, forming a succession of reservoirs of mud a foot or two in depth, considerably impedes the traveller's progress; and in summer presents a rugged and irregular flight of steps, where every instant the iron of the mules' or horses' shoes is slipping on the naked stone. Men who have to traverse such ground, particularly if they have to carry the baggage of regular troops, are exhausted by the shortest marches, while the people of the country go through wood and ravine, straight as the fox or wolf, and can always overtake, without the possibility of being overtaken. In some places the ground is so much covered, that an invading force has no idea of the proximity of the enemy. That enemy has his spies and guerrillas, and the invaders cannot detach men on expeditions of discovery, because when a few hundred yards from the main body they are always liable to be cut off. Go which road they will, still he has always time to take another - to leave them if pursuing, exhausted with the chase, in localities where to encamp or to quarter is equally incommodious or perilous.

The villages differ considerably in size and cleanliness; the church and steeple being a very prominent feature in the midst of the group of houses which are either built in reddish or greyish stone. Generally the *pueblos* or villages are in clusters, and it has a pleasing effect on the ear of the stranger when, at the termination of the hour, he hears it tolled forth in a wide valley from innumerable brazen tongues, as it were, echoing one another. In the north the villages are usually built in hollows; in the south, on the contrary, they seem to prefer a rising ground to the valley. The houses are of a middling size, and the shell solidly built, but incommodious. Perhaps the curate's house is partly painted white, and has, by way of luxury, a few panes of glass; but even this is rare in the mountain-villages. The ground floor is occupied by the stables: the kitchen, which, in the real Basque cottages, is only the base of an enormous chimney, being on the first or second story. One singular feature of every house, however mean, is the arms rudely sculptured over the doorway. Where the fire is not made in the middle of the kitchen, behind the dogs on which half the trunk of a tree is thrown, appears an enormous iron sheet, on which the arms of Navarre or the *fleurs-de-lis* are figured in relief. In their wars with an earlier dynasty, the kings of France little thought that the loyal emblem of the House of Bourbon would one day be banished to the cottages of Spain. The furniture is rude and simple; but in some houses a few chests, inlaid with ebony and ivory, and of antique workmanship, show that their forefathers were either wealthier or more luxurious than the present, generation.

Excepting in the *Rivera*, where many possess large properties, few of the inhabitants are rich: on the other hand, however, few are absolutely poor; and none need be so if moderately industrious. Wealth does not, however, seem to hold out sufficient temptation to induce them to continued exertion. It is true, that what they have of superfluous produce they can turn to gold; which, when they have it, lies idle in their coffers, without their seeking to multiply it, or procure those luxuries which render it desirable. In the. Rivera are many individuals, who, possessing many thousand dollars in specie, conceal them in time of war, and leave them unemployed in time of peace, and live and clothe themselves not a degree better than their neighbours. They have all the indolence common to the southron, which explains the fact of their having for so many years supported the contending armies of friend and foe; a fact which, without a knowledge of the people and their resources, it is difficult to understand. In time of peace, the peasant tills no more of his field than he requires, although his own exertions might suffice for producing three or four times more of bread and wine than he requires. In time of war, when he must furnish rations, he is obliged to work; and, therefore, excepting that he is forced to labour, remains much in the same condition as before the unquiet times, which ruin other lands, serving strangely enough to develop the natural resources of that country. In the war *of independence*, as it is called, that which was waged so long against the French under Napoleon, although his troops burned and destroyed whole villages in the mountains, a year or two after, to their surprise, they found others flourishing in their room. This fertility of the northern provinces is an element which facilitates the continuance of war, and may account for the memorable stand of the guerrilla chieftains of Napoleon's time, and the no less extraordinary struggle of the last two years.

On advancing to the south of Pampeluna - a city of about 20,000[32] inhabitants, situated at the farther extremity of a wide valley, and strongly fortified - the traveller finds the plains larger, and the towns and villages more populous and more considerable in size. The inhabitants, too, no longer speak the Basque, but genuine Castilian[33]. The richest part of the country, however, with the exception of a few plains which, like the Carrascal, may be barren and sandy, is the Rivera, as all the flat lands bordering on the Ebro and Arragona are called. Let the reader imagine a continued succession of vines and corn, excepting where the peach-tree and olive appear - a cool and rapid river winding amid green banks, and blue sandhills in the distance - the advanced guard as it were of the dim and distant mountains, where all is as wild and rugged as it is here beautiful and luxurious - a country abounding in everything; the bread the finest and the whitest in the world; the wine luscious and rich; and the fig, the melon and the peach in abundance. When there is snow knee-deep on the mountains of Navarre, the sun shines brightly on the Rivera; and if ever the snow fall there for half a day, it is such a curiosity, that the children run out and catch it in their hands.

In Navarre two-thirds of the labour is done by women. Whether this is partly caused by the present war having drained from the working class so many of its most useful members, I know not, but it is not at all uncommon to see females turning up a field with a sort of three-pronged spade, which, by the united efforts of two or three female labourers, throws up from the rich clay soil a

---

[32] Today the population has swollen tenfold
[33] This statement contradicts the claims of modern Basque nationalists who attribute the demise of Basque in Pamplona and more generally in Navarre to General Franco.

mass of earth eight times larger than the plough turns over. At other times they are seen driving their rude carts, which are so constructed that the axle turns with the wheels: the wheels are solid circles, in which the axle is fixed, and are drawn by a pair of oxen yoked together, governed by means of a stick which the driver wields, and which at one extremity is rendered pungent by a nail. According to the part on which the oxen are touched by this goad, they turn to the right or to the left. The peasant, as I have said, seldom tills more of his field than is necessary for his subsistence; excepting during the short period when it is indispensable for him to sow and reap, and attend to his vintage he is entirely idle. Whether rich or poor, there is little variation in his costume; if old or middle-aged, he wears a cap, breeches, and jacket, of the coarse brown cloth used by the Franciscan friars, having round the waist a red or blue sash; if young, he sports a beret, or blue round cap, woven all in one piece, and black velveteen trowsers. In the mountains, sandals, manufactured of hemp, are worn instead of shoes, and the peasantry wrap in winter a piece of cloth around the leg, which is tied by a horse-hair cord.

The mode of living of the Navarrese is sober in the extreme. If at all a substantial man, on rising he takes his cup of chocolate, as it is made in Spain one ounce dissolved in a small quantity of water, and boiled to the consistency of paste, which is served up in a cup the size of a very small coffee-cup with some thin pieces of toasted bread, which he dips in it; he then takes a large glass of water water being a luxury enjoyed alike by prince and peasant, and taken at all hours of the day. In the towns they offer with it *bolados*, a sort of very light puff made of highly-refined sugar, flavoured with lemon, and which instantly dissolves in the glass. At 12 o'clock the Navarrese dines, living much during the season upon tomata and pimento, which are introduced into every dish; and the remainder of the day until supper-time he lounges about the village, sitting in the sun in winter, and under the shade in summer, at his own door, under the piazzas of the "plaza," or the portico of the church, where the notables of the village love to assemble and hold their public *consejo*, the village council, or enjoy the "*dolce far niente.*" So long as he has got his paper cigar, and can lead this life of dreamy idleness, he lets the world wag as it will, and smokes away. Yet, when once awakened, it is certain that he seriously arouses. Does he adopt the precarious and uncertain trade of a smuggler, or even muleteer, he will traverse 30, 40, or 50 miles in the 24 hours, walking day and night without thinking it any hardship; sleeping on the bare ground, and supping on a piece of bread and pimento, with a draught of wine from his goat-skin. He is equally active in time of war, for which, from habit or natural taste, he has a decided inclination. The old and middle-aged are all men who have carried arms in the war of independence, which proved so fatal to the conquerors of Austerlitz and Marengo. Brave and disciplined as were the troops of the empire, then the finest in the world, and able to sweep their enemies like chaff before the wind on the field of battle, the number that fell, and fell unavenged, seems scarcely credible. There is not a pass or valley which is not pointed out as the spot where many of the French invaders lie buried. I have often watched the countenances of the elders of a village: although they have now sunk back to their natural expression of nonchalance and indifference which seems so congenial to their character, still they bear deep traces, like the old crater of a burnt-out volcano, of a more stormy period of their existence. Although they are not very communicative, still, on knowing their habits and entering into their feelings, I have drawn from them startling recitals of *la antigua guerra*, or "the old war," of which the campaigns of the British army formed only a brief, and comparatively a bloodless, episode. The war of the constitution which followed did not allow their natural taste for a half-brigand life to subside.

Although Ferdinand was universally disliked - and to this, not to the liberal sentiments that animated the population, may be attributed the success of the constitutionalists - Navarre remained faithful to him, and even raised five battalions of volunteers in his favour, called *l'ejercito de la fe*, "the army of the faith." Nearly all the Carlist officers and soldiers I have conversed with have told me that for Ferdinand they would never have taken arms, though wishing well to his cause. I have already said how averse the Navarrese is from all continued labour, and how in the patient endurance of hunger and fatigue he is unrivalled. From habit, tradition, and inclination, he is fitted for nothing better than that kind of guerilla warfare, which has always made his mountains, sooner or later, the graves of foreign invaders. The nature of the country and its people is too favourable to the inhabitants to render usurpation, domestic or foreign, like anything but an unhealthy plant, which, though fostered with all the care of power, must wither in the ungenial clime.

The courage of the Navarrese, and not only of the Navarrese, but of the Spaniards generally, is of a nature that requires some explanation. Of late years they have made the worst regular troops in Europe; but this springs from a total want of confidence in their own officers, who are drawn from those classes I have described as utterly demoralized, and who have often abandoned or betrayed their followers, or sacrificed them through ignorance. It is also true, that generally, in a fair, stand-up fight, the Spaniards will not behave with the determination of French or English soldiers, who like a few decisive actions, and then to have done. The reluctance of Napoleon's marshals and generals towards the close of his career to enter on fresh battles, in which, when once encouraged, they behaved with so much heroism, is a striking proof of this disposition; and the French veterans with whom I have conversed, as well as some French deserters serving in our ranks as brave men as ever wielded a musket bear me out in the assertion, that whenever the troops of that nation have reaped a harvest of glory they grow tired of fighting. This I believe to be the case with all the nations of the north. Their soldiers have cheerfully run the most imminent personal hazard in the actions in which they have been engaged; but, after a time, they like to sit under the shelter of the laurels they have gathered. The courage of the Spaniard, on the contrary, although it will not urge him with such deter- mined bravery in the face of danger, will lead him to run a greater risk by remaining for years, or a whole lifetime, in warfare, the continuance of which sweeps his race from the earth, with more certainty than the most bloody battles of a brief campaign or two.

In common with his neighbours of the Basque provinces, Biscay and Guipuscoa, the Navarrese forms part of the remnant of an ancient people, whose origin is lost in the obscurity of time; but as far back as anything is distinctly traced on the records of history, he has been unconquered and independent, and he retains to this day his own language a language that has no affinity to any other with which I am acquainted. Perhaps it may be that of the Gauls before they were overrun by the Latins and Franks. It is harsh in pronunciation, but rich and expressive; and, if I may judge, was never formed to flow from the soft lips of a southron. In Spanish it is termed *Basquense*, or *lengua Vascongada*. The following is the Lord's Prayer, which I have given to show the little analogy it has to our northern tongues:-

Gure aitan ceruetan çarena,
erabel bedi sainduqui çure icena;
Ethor bedi çure erresuma;
Eguin bedi çure borondatea, ceruan beçala lurrean ere:
Igucu egun gure eguneco oguia.
Eta barka dicteagutçu gure corrac,
gue gure gana cordun direna barkatean derauztegun beçala.
Eta es gaitçatçula utz tentamendutan erortcera.
Bainin beguira gaitçatçu gaitcetic. *Halabiz.*

From this stock the inhabitants of the northern provinces are descended, although so many have mingled with those who were for so many centuries under the dominion of the Saracen, that, except within sight of the Pyrenees, the Basque language is beginning to be forgotten. The farther you go from the mountains, (where, like their own mists which dwell there when they have cleared away from the valley, the old customs, traditions, and primitive races love to linger) the inhabitants present less of the distinctive character of an ancient people; they become gradually darker and of a different stature, till, on the banks of the Ebro, they are to all appearance a new race. The Basques are tall and thin, but firmly made and strong-boned, with grey eyes; they are generally less dark than the other Spaniards, and the Navarrese partake of the character of the one or the other according as they are nearer to or more remote from the Pyrenees or the Ebro. It is a common error in England to imagine that Don Carlos has been entirely supported by the Basques - at least the genuine Basques, who still retain the primitive tongue and distinguishing character of that people. These do not form one-third of the population of Navarre and of the three provinces of Guipuscoa, Alava, and Biscay; and do not, in fact, compose half the army now under the banners of the King.

How or when the Basques were converted to Christianity I am ignorant. But it is certain that, after the Gothic princes of Spain had been obliged by the followers of the Prophet, who overran nearly the whole country, to take refuge in the Asturias, where they shook off in its mountain-air the effeminacy which had undone their predecessors, and resisted for centuries all the efforts of the African conquerors - they found on descending into the plains, to repossess themselves of all that had been wrested from the weakness of their ancestors, that Navarre was already governed by a race of princes of its own who had expelled the Moors from their territory, of which these southern invaders had never been able to possess themselves entirely. When in the 15th century, all that part of Navarre which lies on the peninsular side of the Pyrenees was united to the crown of Spain by Ferdinand the Catholic, it was allowed to retain all its ancient laws, customs, and usages, on account of its having been for five centuries an independent kingdom. By reason moreover of the numerous adventurers who went forth to gather wealth and laurels under the kings of the

60

Asturias, Leon, and Castille, and who in consequence received knighthood and nobility, many of the inhabitants had become noble, and fueros, or particular privileges were granted to the people. Of a population of 280,000, there are now more than 15,000 who claim an aristocratic descent; and in every village it is a common thing to see a peasant labouring in his own field with a spade instead of a plough, though descended from the chivalrous knights who were at one time the admiration of Europe and the terror of the infidel. All that he retains of his nobility may be seen in his arms rudely sculptured over the doorway (generally they are Moorish emblems palm-trees, scimitars, and crescents), and in the pride which he shares with all the population of calling himself Navarro. The privileges enjoyed by this province, or rather kingdom, for such it is still termed, being governed by a viceroy, are exemption from all duties, as well as from all levies of men and money, excepting when demanded on extraordinary occasions - such as a threatened invasion of the kingdom, or some danger menacing the throne. There not being here, as there are in other parts of Spain, conscriptions, *quintos* are consequently not levied; and yet, in case of war, none of the provinces have furnished such numerous and willing troops. In everything the ancient mode of government is retained. Similar *fueros* are also enjoyed by the provinces of Guipuscoa, Biscay, and Alava, which recognise no monarch, the King of Spain being only lord of these provinces, which are merely seignories of the crown; and so tenacious are they in this particular, that even when the King reviewed the Carlist army, after the battalions of Navarre and Castille had been deafening the air with their shouts of *Viva Carlos Quinto! Viva Nuestro Rey!* those of the provinces, although much more clamorous, as he passed instantly changed the cry to "*Viva Nuestro Señor!*" "Long live our Lord!" or modifying it to *Viva el Rey, nuestro Señor!* "Long live the King our Lord!" Founding their ideas, most probably, on this and similar circumstances, the journalists have long gravely told the public that the insurgents fight with such determination and success, not for the cause of Charles V, or from any feeling approaching to royalism, but for their own rights and *fueros*. This certainly seems highly plausible and probable; yet, in fact, with the immense majority, this neither seems an additional incentive to their zeal, nor appears even to have struck them at all, although the provinces were certainly on the point of having these privileges curtailed. Of those now carrying arms, not one in twenty knows even the signification of the word *fueros*, although it may be familiar to his ear. When I was anxious to obtain some information on this subject, I interrogated the soldiers many times before I could obtain an answer in the least satisfactory; and on asking what they were fighting for, they invariably replied, "For Charles V," or, "For the King!" I do not mean to say that it is always either a reasoned opinion they hold in favour of the prince for whom they are fighting, or a reasoned affection towards him, any more than is to be met with amongst the masses of all parties. So popular was his name, even before his brother's death, on account of the persecution he had endured, and perhaps from the contrast of their characters, that in this feeling any wrongs they might have suffered were merged.

The provinces bear a considerable resemblance to Navarre with this difference, that in Guipuscoa and Biscay the mountains are nearer one to the other, and considerably lower, nearly all the valleys being so narrow, that a musket-shot sweeps across them. The town-houses are cleaner and neater, and the Basque language is more generally spoken. The inhabitants also bear much resemblance to the Navarrese; but, although something more civil and industrious, they are less firm and determined in character. Their costume differs in nothing - the blue cap, red sash, and *alpargatas*, or hemp-sandals, the material plaited into a flat, solid sole, and attached by blue or red ribbon to the foot, are common to both. To travel over the rugged mountain-roads nothing can be better than these sandals, excepting in wet weather, when they quickly unplait; but then the natives substitute for them (what, I believe, answers to the Scottish *brogue*) *espadillos*, a flat piece of hide, the ends of which are turned up and rudely sewn together, so as to form a sort of shoe, in which there is no want of apertures to let the water out as well as in. So accustomed are the mountaineers on long marches to their hemp sandals, that, among the Queen's troops, the regular army of Spain, distributions of sandals, as well as of shoes, are uniformly made. They are worth about a shilling the pair, and last a long while, except in wet weather; when, as I have just mentioned, they soon fall to pieces, and are far from economical. The muddy state of the roads when the movement was not of material importance, often caused the army of Zumalacarregui to delay a march, on account of the loss of sandals which would have been sustained. They are worn alike by both sexes.

CHAPTER IV.

General Santos Ladron proclaims Don Carlos in Navarre - Taken by Lorenzo - Suspicion of Treachery - Example of Ingratitude - Santos Ladron shot at Pampeluna - Desperate Condition of the Carlists - First Appearance of Colonel Zumalacarregui -Arrests Ituralde - Portrait of Zumalacarregui.

The Faction, as the Royalist party was once termed, with some appearance of reason - a name which, when the population had unanimously declared in favour of Don Carlos, and their bands had swelled into a considerable army, his partisans still seemed to take a pleasure in retaining - was at its lowest ebb on the death of General Santos Ladron. This man, a native of Lodosa, in the Rivera, of which he was one of the richest proprietors, had already much distinguished himself in previous wars; during that of the Constitution he commanded the Royalist volunteers, and afterwards became governor of Pampeluna. Being known as a firm and decided legitimist, he was placed under surveillance at Valladolid; thence, however, on the death of Ferdinand, he contrived to make his escape. As his influence in the country was very great, he, without much effort, persuaded the Navarrese to pass the Rubicon, and to declare in favour of their rightful sovereign. Unfortunately, he fixed on the Rivera as the rallying point, and first proclaimed Charles V at Estella, the second city of Navarre. In an instant from the surrounding towns Los Arcos, Viana, Lerin, Taffala, and Lodoso, more than 1,000 men flocked to his standard. Echeveria, beneficiary[34] of Los Arcos, and afterwards president of the Junta of Navarre, and Ituralde[35], a retired lt. colonel, were amongst the most remarkable of his partisans. 1,000 men formed already a brilliant commencement in Navarre; for one of the chief characteristics of its people is, to be as slow in adopting a resolution, as steadfast in adhering to it when

---

[34] i.e. Parish Priest. Don Juan Echeverria (1794-1844) was president of the Carlist Junta which normally consisted of four men plus a secretary and a lawyer. They kept constantly on the move to avoid capture and often hid in squalid conditions.
[35] Francisco de Iturralde. He was 46.

adopted. Every Navarrese who once takes arms may be depended on; he clings to his party through every peril and hardship, and is only rendered more obstinate and determined by ill success, or by being threatened with violence. The insurgents had hardly breathing time, however, before they were informed that Antonio de Sola, the viceroy of the kingdom, had set a price upon the head of Santos Ladron, and had despatched Lorenzo[36] with 1500 men to punish their temerity. Although it is impossible to judge of him from his short career during this war, in which he paid so dearly for his first fault, Santos Ladron enjoyed so undisputedly amongst the Navarrese the reputation of being a man of considerable ability, that it could not have been entirely usurped. With the enthusiastic but motley crowd around him, armed with the first weapons that came to hand, and void of all subordination or discipline, he marched to Los Arcos, a town which, although within sight of the mountains, is situated in the flat land on the road from Pampeluna to Logroño, on the banks of the Ebro. Having, in the first instance, committed the fault of sending half his force to Lodosa, he, with more courage than prudence, resolved to make a stand. It is averred, however, by the inhabitants and those who were with him, that on this occasion his head was troubled - a drug (probably opium) having, at Los Arcos, been given him by treachery in his wine, which had the effect of entirely suspending his intellectual faculties. It is certain that when the hour of danger approached, he took no advantage of the immense influence he possessed with the peasantry, of the nature of the ground and his acquaintance with it; but having once led his men to Los Arcos, unable to make any further dispositions, he remained stupidly awaiting the fatal hour, like the bird fascinated by the snake. The confusion and irresolution of such a crowd as he had about him, who all along confided in the talents of their leader, may be easily imagined, when they suddenly learned that the enemy was close upon them.

---

[36] General Manuel Lorenzo (1785-1847), later governor of Cuba

Santos Ladron, on being at last aroused from his lethargic state, mechanically placed himself with his drawn sword at the head of a few devoted followers; but the head to guide the hand was gone. As might have been expected, on the attack of the troops, after a few shots fired, instead of an engagement, it became a dispersion and a massacre. Santos Ladron, incapable of fighting or flying, was surrounded on a sandhill to the left of Los Arcos, on the road from the town to the mountains: those about him were either slain or compelled to share the same fate as himself. Lorenzo, with whom he had formerly been on terms of intimacy, although he had the power, was unwilling to shoot him on the spot, but led him to Pampeluna, to have him tried by court-martial; hoping, at the same time, that from his great popularity the government would not dare to take his life. It is said that the first observation the prisoner made, on recovering from his stupor, was on the mutability of earthly things – "Yesterday *la faja*" (the sash, alluding to the rank of Mariscal-de-Campo, which he held) "was mine - tomorrow it will be yours." The viceroy and his judges hesitated to put him to death, without an express order from Madrid, from fear of the effect it would produce on the people, and probably wishing also to gain time and a possibility of his pardon. An officer of Carabiniers, however, whose life Don Santos had on a former occasion saved, setting aside his gratitude, in the exaltation of his party-feelings, declared that it was their instructions to punish immediately with death all rebels taken with arms in their hands; and that if they delayed the execution of so notorious a ringleader, they would be rendered personally responsible, and he would be the first to accuse them of want of sincerity and zeal. As he was the organ of the exalted party, his representations had effect, and the prisoner was shot in the ditch of the citadel on the 15th. October, 1833. Many things unite to corroborate the circumstance of the draught having been administered; but his behaviour might perhaps have been caused by one of those diseases of the brain which sometimes overthrow the brightest intellects. He was sincerely and universally regretted in all Navarre, which has not been ungrateful to his memory; and such was the indignation his execution excited, that the following day 300 young men left Pampeluna to join the Carlists. This may give some idea of the spirit with which the population of this province was animated.

Ituralde contrived, after the dispersion, to save a part of his followers, rallying and conducting them to the mountains. Here, having effected a junction with the Alavese, he formed them into two battalions; but they were in the most destitute condition, badly armed, without clothes or money, and totally disheartened. Although the Carlists, being once compromised, did their utmost to spread the insurrection, and a number of persons best known in those localities were installed as a sort of governing assembly in the valley of the Bastan[37], under the name of the Junta of Navarre, of which Echeveria, the beneficiary of Los Arcos, was elected president, discouragement everywhere prevailed. The corps of *Peseteros,* or volunteers of the Queen, so called from the silver-piece *peseta*, about the value of a shilling, which they receive daily (four times the pay of the line), and composed of the very refuse of society, were daily augmented; and with the Carabiniers, the gendarmerie of Spain, and which were then very numerous, they scoured the country in every direction, arresting, plundering, and murdering those who were barely suspected of entertaining Carlist opinions. At this time the little force of the insurgents was menaced with speedy dissolution. Already obliged to fly by night-marches, the addition of any reinforcements to the Queen's army must then have been a death-blow to their cause. As usually happens in similar cases, to complete their misfortunes, jealousy and disunion reigned among the chiefs. In this state of things, nevertheless, the hopes of the party were revived; and, from so desperate a condition, it pursued, through perils and hardships, a course of gradual success,, till, from a guerilla band, it became an army

---

[37] This was also a kind of recruiting depôt and training ground for the Carlist army.

threatening the conquest of Spain. All this was effected by the arrival of a single individual, clothed in the usual garments of a peasant - the sandals and Basque cap - who, sallying from Pampeluna, joined the insurgents. That individual was Zumalacarregui.

The Val de Araquil, a long and picturesque valley through which winds the road from Pampeluna to Salvatierra, was, I believe, the place where he first presented himself to the discouraged Royalists, having effected his escape in disguise from the surveillance of the Christinos. It was less the reputation of being an officer of talent and a skilful tactician, which, as the colonel of various regiments, he had enjoyed in Navarre since the war of 1823, than the confidence with which he presented himself offering to command, when all were only anxious to get rid of a responsibility which it seemed could entail nothing but destruction and ruin, that made him to be looked up to by the partisans of Don Carlos as a man fit to guide them in their extremity.

Tomas Zumalacarregui[38], of a poor but noble family, was born on the 29th. December, 1788, in the little village[39] of Ormaistegui, in the province of Guipuscoa, on the high road from France to Vittoria, and about a league from the town of Villareal. At the age of 18 he quitted his home, during the war of independence, to enter the army as cadet; under Mina, he rapidly rose to the rank of captain. It is said, that in his earliest youth, he had entertained a strong inclination to republicanism; but, soon disgusted with what he saw of Spanish patriots, he became a partisan of monarchy and legitimacy, and boldly pronounced those opinions, from which he never afterwards swerved. As he was one of those men whose uncompromising manner and character could not flatter the minions of power, he was, on the conclusion of the war, laid upon the shelf, and we find him in 1822 with the same rank of captain; but shortly afterwards he commanded two

---

[38] Thomas Antonio Zumalacarregui Ymaz.
[39] Current population 1,300. His birthplace is now a museum.

battalions of Quesada's division in the Royalist army against that of the Constitution. In 1825 he had the command of the 1st. King's Volunteers, as lt. colonel; and subsequently that of the Prince's Regiment, the 3rd. of the line; he then became full colonel of the 3rd. Light Infantry; and lastly of the Regiment of Estremadura, the 14th. of the line. He had been thus often changed from corps to corps, on account of his singular talent, for organising and disciplining bodies of men. From this last regiment he was, however, removed by Lander, inspector of the infantry; who, aware of the incorruptibility of his stern principles, knew that when the King's death should take place the Queen's government would find in him a determined foe to her usurpation. He had him displaced and even arrested as an enemy to the state. On being liberated, the colonel sent in his resignation and retired to Pampeluna, where his wife[40] and children were residing. He had been there but a short time when the death of Ferdinand was announced. Refusing the offer of Sola, who promised him the rank of brig. general, if he would embrace the Queen's cause, although strictly watched, he managed, on the night of the 29th. October, to effect his escape from the city, and on the 30th. he joined the insurgents. He had always been considered a man of distinguished bravery, and after he had seen the French army under the Duke of Angoulême, had devoted himself to the study of tactics, in the knowledge of which he was allowed to excel. As colonel he kept an academy for the instruction of the officers of the garrisons of various towns in which he was quartered; but he was chiefly known as an excellent disciplinarian and administrator. The corps which he formed and commanded was always in the highest state of discipline; but, although his talent for organisation was universally

---

[40] Pancracia Ollo de la Mata (1798-1865), a native of Vitoria. She first met him in 1804, when she was six and he 16. They married in the Basilica of San Miguel, Vitoria, in September 1820. They had four daughters who moved to France for safety. When Pancracia joined them, she was placed under house arrest without charge at the Hôtel St Etienne in Bayonne by the French authorities. She wrote an eloquent letter to the press denouncing this abuse of her human rights. She is buried in the Cemetery of Santa Isabella (calle San Roque 102).

acknowledged, the last quality then attributed to him would have been that of a chief of mountain *guerilleros*. His renown, however, at that period, was one of those local reputations so frequently met with and often so little founded. Although he was received with open arms, and the other leaders gladly acquiesced in conferring the command upon him at such a moment, his *début* was not unattended with some difficulties, from which he extricated himself only by that boldness and decision of which he afterwards gave so many proofs. Ituralde, then the principal of the Carlist chiefs, not only refused obedience to him, alleging that he had earlier proclaimed the King and held office from him, but being of a rather violent disposition, sent two chosen companies to arrest the intruder. Zumalacarregui, who had already assumed that superiority over the soldier which men of great minds seem so easily to acquire, met the two companies as if he were coming to place himself at their head, and reversing the game, sternly commanded them to arrest Ituralde. He was obeyed; his rival was made prisoner in Estella; and immediately after was appointed by him second in command. Zumalacarregui then declared that, until the King's orders were received, he would cede the command to no one but Eraso, who had proclaimed Don Carlos before himself. Probably, at the time he made this declaration, the return of Eraso, then a prisoner in the hands of the French government, was not anticipated. When Eraso afterwards effected his escape, Zumalacarregui proved faithful to his word, and offered to cede the command. Divided as they had hitherto been, the dissensions and jealousies which had existed between the Carlist leaders, and till now had proved the bane of the party, all vanished before the ascendency of Zumalacarregui's superior genius.

It may not be amiss to add here the rough portraiture of a few lines to the engraving of the frontispiece, which faithfully represents the modern Cid, whose name has been rendered as imperishable as the mountains which witnessed his triumphs. He was a man at that period in the prime of life, being 45 years of age,

71

and of middle stature; but, on account of the great width of his shoulders, his bull-neck, and habitual stoop, the effect of which was much increased by the *zamarra*, or fur jacket, which he always wore, he appeared rather short than otherwise. His profile had something of the antique - the lower part of the face being formed like that of Napoleon, and the whole cast of his features bearing some resemblance to the ancient basso-relievos, which are given us as the likeness of Hannibal. His hair was dark, without being black; his moustaches joined his whiskers; and his dark grey eyes, overshadowed by strong eyebrows, had a singular rapidity and intensity in their gaze - generally they had a stern and thoughtful expression; but when he looked about him, his glance seemed in an instant to travel over the whole line of a battalion, making in that short interval the minutest remarks. He was always abrupt and brief in his conversation, and habitually stern and severe in his manners; but this might have been the effect of the hardships and perils through which he had passed in his arduous struggle, and the responsibility he had drawn upon himself. I have heard from those who were well acquainted with him before he became the leader of a party, as well as from his widow, whose testimony might be considered, however, too partial, that he had much changed in temper during the last two years of his life. He had always been serious, but without those sudden gusts of passion to which he was latterly subject; and also without that unbending severity of demeanour, which became afterwards a striking feature of his character. Those who have undergone the painful experience of a civil war, like that which for two years has desolated the north of Spain, will agree with me in thinking lhat the scenes of strife and massacre, the death of his partisans, and the imperious necessity of reprisals on fellow countrymen and often on friends, whom the virulence of party opinion armed in mortal contest; exposure to innumerable hardships and privations, the summer's sun, and winter's wind; the sufferings and peril in which his followers were constantly placed, and his serious responsibility, were enough to

72

change considerably, even in a brief space of time, Zumalacarregui's nature. It was seldom that he gave way to anything like mirth; he oftenest indulged in a smile when he led his staff where the shot were falling thick and fast around them, and he fancied he detected in the countenances of some of his followers that they thought the whistling of the bullets an unpleasant tune. To him fear seemed a thing unknown; and although in the commencement a bold and daring conduct was necessary to gain the affections and confidence of rude partisans, he outstripped the bounds of prudence, and committed such innumerable acts of rashness, that when he received his mortal wound, everybody said it was only by a miracle he had escaped so long. He has been known to charge at the head of a troop of horse, or spurring in a sudden burst of passion the white charger which he rode, to rally himself the skirmishers and lead them forward. His horse had become such a mark for the enemy, that all those of a similar colour, mounted by officers of his staff were shot in the course of three months, although his own always escaped. It is true, that on several occasions he chose his moment well, and decided more than one victory, and saved his little army in more than one retreat, by what seemed an act of hair-brained bravery. His costume was invariably the same - the *bouina*, the round national cap or berret of the provinces, of a bright scarlet colour, woven of wool to a texture resembling cloth, in the shape of that represented in the engraving, without a seam, and stretched out by a switch of willow inside, the *zamarra*, or fur jacket, of the black skin of the Merino lamb, lined with white fur, and an edging of red velvet with gilded clasps; grey, and latterly red, trowsers; and the flat heavy Spanish spur, with the treble horizontal rowels, originally used by the caballeros to ring on the pavement when they went lounging through the streets in their gay attire. The only ornament he ever wore was the silver tassel on his cap. As he rode or walked according to his wont, at the head of his column, his staff, about 40 or 50 officers, following behind - and then his battalions threading the mountain-roads as far as the eye could reach, with their bright muskets and grotesque accoutrements - the whole presented a scene novel and picturesque. The general's stern and uncommon features, his fur jacket, and cap, resembling at a distance a red turban, gave more the idea of an Eastern chief than a European general. One might have imagined Scanderbeg at the head of his Albanian army; and certes his semi-barbarous followers could have been no wilder in dress and appearance than the Carlists in the early part of the campaign. To me Zumalacarregui in character and feeling, as well as in costume and manner, seemed always like the hero of a bygone century. He was of a period remote from our own, when the virtues and vices of society were marked in a stronger mould partaking of all the stern enthusiasm of the middle ages; a something uncommon and energetic in his features seemed to indicate a man formed for great and difficult enterprises. You might have fancied him one of those chiefs who led the populations of Europe to war in the Holy Land; he possessed the same chivalrous courage, unflinching sternness, and disinterested fervour - disinterested so far as mere earthly things were concerned which animated those of the religious zealots who went thither because they found it easier to win heaven with their blood on a battlefield, than through penitence and prayer.

CHAPTER V.

Zumalacarregui - His Disinterestedness and Poverty - Anecdote - His Surname
- Difficulties he had to contend with - Force with which he began the War - His
Partisans -Their Equipment - Carlist Messengers and Spies - Blockade of the
Fortified Towns and *Partidas* - Carabineros and Peseteros - Bayonets made to
give incurable Wounds - Chapelgories of Biscay and Guipuscoa - Attack of
Vittoria by Zumalacarregui.

Tomas Zumalacarregui, like most men of an ardent temperament,
had the defect of being quick and hasty; and in his passion was
often guilty of acts which, although nothing after all but a severe
and unsparing justice, in cold blood he would have been incapable
of. More than one officer in the Carlist army owes his rank to
having been on some occasion reprimanded by him, in terms
which, when his anger was over, he knew to be too severe. I believe
him - as far as it is possible to judge of a man's character by a
year's observation and acquaintance - to have been as free from
any ambition of personal aggrandizement as he was from the love
of wealth. Wrapped entirely in the cause he had adopted, he
thought and dreamed but of that; and I believe that, from the hour
when he undertook to repair the broken fortunes of the Royalist
party, to that when he expired in the midst of his triumphs, his only
motive was to witness its success. The wish of augmenting his
military glory - the bubble reputation, which cheers the soldier on
his perilous career - perhaps added a fresh incentive. The contempt
of gold which he always evinced formed a striking feature of his
character. The following circumstance may serve to illustrate his
disinterestedness, and to show how slight is often the foundation
of calumnies directed against public men. I remember often seeing,
in the fragments of French papers which occasionally reached us,
accounts of the sums he had transmitted to France. The *Phare de
Bayonne*, in particular, on one occasion, as a proof of the desperate
state of Carlist affairs, stated that their chiefs, and in particular
Zumalacarregui, seemed determined to "make hay while the sun
shone" (*mettre du foin dans leur bottes*); that he was accumulating

75

all the money he could, and had transmitted 30,000 dollars to a certain bank across the frontier; and that the insurrection of the Basque provinces was evidently a scheme got up by him and others to rob and plunder the peasant, and then escape with the fruits of their rapine. All this was said of a man who, when he died, after paying the army for two years, and raising contributions in three provinces, left to be divided amongst his household all that he possessed in the world 14oz of gold, or about £48 sterling, and four or five horses. Even his barber, the waggish Robledo, was richer than the Carlist commander-in-chief. When Zumalacarregui sallied forth from Pampeluna, he had about £200 about him, which then constituted all the funds of his army. Having nothing, or next to nothing, to live on but his pay, which, if I am not mistaken, was not then even so high as during the last years of Ferdinand's reign, he was proverbial for generosity, and could so little trust himself with what he received, that he always gave it immediately into the hands of Mme Zumalacarregui. Any sum he possessed in the morning was sure by the evening to be dissipated; he gave it away, *sailor-fashion*, by handsful to his soldiers, or the first beggars who importuned him, and who, well aware of his foible, never failed to beset him. He used, quite out of temper, to exclaim, "Here – take - take! When you have got all I have, you will leave me in peace." Of an evening his subalterns were obliged to pay for him in the coffee-house; and on his wife's representing to him how unfit it was for a superior officer to permit such a thing, and inquiring what he had done with the money she had given him in the morning, he used to reply, that he was assailed by all the unfortunate, or those who pretended to be so. "But you give more," observed his lady, "than is reasonable, or than you can afford." "We are more like God when we give," was his answer, if in a good humour; "he can return us more than we can give away, and I feel that I shall be a millionnaire some day." His friends used to laugh, and say that he had taken the right way to amass a fortune as he was going on.

On passing through Libourne, and visiting Mme Zumalacarregui after his death, when inquiring into many particulars concerning the previous life of the deceased, I heard what I have just stated from her own lips. An officer, who had once lodged in the same house with him at Madrid, has told me that he was considered then a strange and eccentric character, conducting himself with much simplicity and bonhommie towards his inferiors, but stiff and starched towards those of a superior rank. My informant little dreamed that the poor provincial colonel would one day become the leader of the armies of the heir-apparent against a usurpation in favour of an infant yet unborn, and be the conqueror successively of the first generals in the Spanish army. It appears that he had always had some presentiment of one day rising to an exalted station; yet he uniformly refused meddling in any species of intrigue. The bluntness and frankness of his manner had, indeed, made him enemies amongst all parties. So long as Ferdinand lived, Zumalacarregui always declared, when tampered with by the partisans of Don Carlos, (who, against the wishes of that prince, were at one time projecting, and, indeed, effected a movement) that if anything of the kind were done, he would consider them, and serve against them, as rebels; but, at the same time, he added, that if the death of Ferdinand should take place, he would acknowledge no other right to the throne than that of the Infant.

I remember an instance of a lieutenant of the Battalion of Guides of Navarre, who, commanding a company *ad interim*, had gambled away the money given him to pay his men; a thing which, as it deserved, was severely punished in the army. Being, however, without any resource, he took the desperate resolution of throwing himself at Zumalacarregui's feet. "If you come to ask the money from me, take it, and *vaya usted con Dios* (God be with you); but if you come to confess your fault, I will hear nothing - it is one I never pardon." A French deserter, unable to march from indisposition, was maltreated by an officer, when the General passing, recognized him as having seen him behaving well during an action: throwing him a gold piece of ½. oz (36s.), he ordered the officer instantly to procure a mule for him, although, in common with all Spaniards, he had a deep and rooted prejudice against the French nation.

Stern and severe as Zumalacarregui was, and unsparing of fatigue for his men - leading them long marches with a rapidity which it seemed the human frame could scarcely have supported - he was the soldiers' idol. He obtained the sobriquet of *El Tio Tomas*, "Uncle Thomas," as the French called Napoleon *Le petit Caporal*; and he was better known under the appellation of *El Tio*, than by his Gothic name Zumalacarregui. His skill and valour, the peril from which he so often saved his soldiers, and the successes to which he led the way, seem scarcely sufficient to account for their wild attachment to the man they loved and feared above all others - an attachment which must be felt to be understood. Without garments, without pay, without provisions, his army would have followed him barefoot all over the world, or have perished by the way. The same degree of enthusiasm was entertained towards him as was displayed in the French army for l'Empereur, and this extended to the populations of the revolted provinces, excepting that it was difficult to say whether love or awe predominated - with the peasant, they were certainly strangely blended. He had thus become a host in himself. If a soldier were giving way in an action, or were fatigued or hungry on a march, the instant he caught a sight of El Tio's white charger, his fear and his discontent seemed to vanish. I was once inquiring of one of these volunteers what force was in Piedramillera, a village of the Beruesa, when the enemy were within a short distance, and, on being informed by him that there were two battalions, I could not help exclaiming, "Only two battalions!" "O, but the General is with them," said the Navarrese; and he looked as satisfied as if all the forces we could then muster were encamped upon the spot.

Some men, without seeming to covet them, appear endowed with the power of appropriating the affections of their fellow-men, by some unaccountable magnetism inherent in their genius. Until I myself shared the feeling, I could never comprehend that military love, of which Shakspeare, that admirable master of all human sympathies, and who has touched so exquisitely on all our passions, speaks but so imperfectly. I also believe that the love of the soldier, if we may judge from our own feelings of those of others, can be but a first love, which, once widowed, finds no other place in the affections.

I joined the Carlists and Zumalacarregui when he had nothing but the reputation of a guerilla chief, who had skilfully baffled the pursuit of the Queen's troops, and struck a few daring blows, but whom, from the description then given on the other side of the Pyrenees, I expected to find ferocious and ignorant. I remember at first my total inability to comprehend enthusiastic attachment, independent of private friendship, to any individual; but I ended by sharing entirely the feelings of the soldiers; and so long as he lived, in success or adversity, I would have followed him to the end, even if I had experienced no acts of kindness at his hands. It was of course for Don Carlos I had come to fight. I had been rather prejudiced against than in favour of his General: yet, in the brief space of a few months, if Don Carlos had abandoned his own cause, I should have remained to follow Zumalacarregui.

One striking proof of the superior talent of this extraordinary man was the ease with which he assumed, amongst a number of chiefs, of infinitely greater local consideration, that superiority which his successes enabled him so pre-eminently to maintain. The affairs of the Carlists were then in a deplorable position, and the courage of their leaders might well have failed them when they contemplated the lowering aspect of their horizon. The army of the Queen, exclusive of the garrisons of Ceuta and the Balearic Islands, consisting of 1500 foot, amounted to 116,000 men, besides irregular troops or volunteers to the number of 12,000 more, distributed under the name of Miquelets in Catalonia, Salvaguardias in Biscay, Chapelgorris in Guipuscoa, and Peseteros in Navarre. That this statement may not appear doubtful, I subjoin a list of the regular force the usurping government then had at its disposal, at least according to its own statements:

Lieutenant-Generals	73
Field-Marshals	132
Brigadier-Generals	323
Staff Officers	800
Officers	1300
Horse Body-Guards	750
Foot Body-Guards	150

FOOT GUARDS

Four Regiments	8,000
Four Provincial Regiments	6,400

HORSE GUARDS

Four regiments of cavalry	2.000
One squadron of artillery	250

VETERANS

Eleven companies	800
Cadres of three regiments of Swiss	300

INFANTRY OF THE LINE

Fourteen regiments, of three battalions each	29,500
Four regiments, of two battalions	5,600

LIGHT INFANTRY

Six regiments, of three battalions each	8,400

PROVINCIAL REGIMENTS

Forty-two regiments, of one battalion each	26,000

CAVALRY OF THE LINE

Five regiments	2,500

LIGHT CAVALRY

Eight regiments	4,000

HORSE AND FOOT ARTILLERY

Staff	470
Three regiments on foot	2,500
Two battalions	1,000
Two squadrons	450
Workmen miners	2,000

ENGINEERS

Staff	200
One Regiment	1000

GENDARMERIE

Carabineros, horse and foot	12,000
Escopetteros, &c	800

To contend with this force, Zumalacarregui found -

Infantry, armed with fowling-pieces or muskets	800
Cavalry	14
Artillery officers	1
Field-pieces	0
Battering train. Two old 18-pounders, buried in Biscay	
A treasury containing	£200

It is true, that although as yet totally disarmed and unable to assist him, he had the immense majority of the people, not only in the northern provinces, but in the whole of Spain, in favour of his enterprise; and by degrees, as he won from the enemy weapons, he placed them in their hands.

Had arms only been abundant, the struggle would have been but of short duration: but the Pyrenees and the Atlantic, closed by the vigilance of France and England, and the total want of money, left him no alternative but confining his exertions to a mountainous and inaccessible country; and to winning gradually and bv indefatigable exertions the means of extending the scale of his operations. It was the commencement that was the most arduous part of his task; for not only did he find the handful of partisans he had under his command without a shadow of order or subordination, and, like most mountaineers, wild, proud, and untractable, and totally averse from the discipline he introduced as his successes gave him more leisure and latitude; but he had against him men well acquainted with Mina's system of mountain warfare, and who knew the country inch by inch, *à palmas*, as the Spaniards express it, better than he did. His first care was to make himself feared and obeyed. He then began by organising and augmenting, day by day, his little army, leading them by mountain-roads through the most inaccessible territory of Navarre away from the enemy, and there training them, like the young hawks of a falconer, by bringing them into skirmishes, and exciting by surprises and ambuscades their thirst for plunder and victory - never at first attacking but where he could not compromise their safety. In the organisation of his army, he adopted the plan which has been proved decidedly the best for a mountainous country - distributing his force by battalions, each commanded by a colonel, instead of by regiments. Well aware that it could only be by the rapidity of his marches and the hardiness of his men that he could hope to struggle with the fearful odds against which he opened the campaign, he equipped them as lightly as possible. Instead of the cartridge-box and sword, which, dangling on a soldiers thigh, greatly fatigue him on a long day's march, he had leather belts made to buckle behind, holding in front 20 tin tubes, and two pockets containing each two packets more of cartridges all covered with a leather flap. This contrivance had the advantage of saving many cartridges, which are often let fall in the confusion of action, when the soldier has to take them from his cartouch-box. The belt, too, rather aids than incommodes him on his march, and allows him to fire much more rapidly. This cartridge-belt has hitherto been objected to in France and England, on the plea of the danger of the cartridges placed in front igniting from the fire of the musket, when the men fire in line. In a mountainous country, where men must be so much dispersed as skirmishers, this objection was overruled; and even otherwise, I am a staunch advocate for the adoption of this method, as the danger is little greater than that of the cartouch-box exploding from the fire of the second or third line, and the advantages are immense. Instead of the knapsack, he adopted little canvass bags, in which the soldier was allowed to carry only a shirt, a pair of sandals, and a day's provisions; although afterwards when our marches became less arduous, they were tacitly permitted to load themselves with anything they pleased, but then, of course, they had no right to complain. They had always a decided objection to the knapsack, which, with the shako, the stock, and the cartridge-box, were articles of the enemy's spoil they always left on the field as useless. The national beret he substituted for the heavy shako a gratuitous torment to the soldier, which does not even parry a sabre cut in a charge of cavalry, as it is vulgarly imagined, for no stroke is given perpendicularly downwards by a trooper; all are aimed diagonally, according to the rules of the sword exercise. With men who had thus nothing but their musket to carry, troops armed as heavily as those in regular armies usually are stood no chance of competing on a march.

One immense advantage the Carlist army possessed was the devotion of the inhabitants to their cause; everywhere the Carlist found a home and succour, and the Liberals bitter and determined enemies. Nor is this the case only in the insurgent provinces. I would undertake to go, representing myself as a Carlist, from cottage to cottage to within a day's march of Madrid, aided and assisted by the peasantry at the peril of their own lives. The intelligence and the orders which the Carlists wish to have conveyed to any part or to any distance, they can always depend on having carried more rapidly than the enemy could; their means are superior to what he can possess the sturdy limbs of a mountaineer. The speed of a horse, in a country like the greater part of the north of Spain, can be but very limited, as, on account of the shortest roads being always so rough and irregular, the animal can but walk, and often rather creep along. A man unaccustomed to the country can never rival the celerity with which the inhabitants traverse the ground; they seldom keep to any path, they go almost as the crow flies. The enemy never ventures, unless in a considerable body, across the open country. In the ordinary routine of things, a Carlist officer has but to give a paper into the hands of an alcalde, or even a verbal message to be forwarded in any direction; he immediately pitches upon the householder "*vecino*," who must either go or furnish the messenger each one of the inhabitants being liable in their turn. On reaching the next village, he may, if he finds himself fatigued, hand it over to another; but if the words "*Luego, luego, luego!*" despatch, three times repeated, should be upon it, when tired he may give it into the hands of the first individual he meets the herdsman must leave his flock, the labourer his plough, to carry it; and any man refusing or betraying such a trust would be denounced by his neighbours, his friends, or even his own family. Independent of the numerous regular spies kept up by Zumalacarregui, some extending to the environs of Saragossa and Burgos - whenever he entered into action the peasants might be seen on all sides running breathless over the mountains to give him gratuitously the news of all the movements which had taken place, often at the imminent risk of being shot by the opposite party. A *confidant* of the Royalists will carry a letter 20 miles, at the greatest peril to himself, and only receive half a douro, 2/6d., for his trouble, and is perfectly satisfied. The Christinos must pay several ounces for the same services. In the despatches which were intercepted, they constantly complained of the exorbitant prices at which they were obliged to obtain their information; and with such a singular fatality wore their spies always discovered by Zumalacarregui, that those who might have been tempted by gold to undertake that office were deterred from it by the certainty of detection. When a column of the Queenites was quartered in a town or village, not a peasant dared, on any pretext, unless before witnesses, enter the houses of the generals or any superior officers, lest he should be suspected by his neighbours of acting as a spy. Much of this was owing to the admirable manner in which Zumalacarregui had organised everything. Such was the ascendency he assumed over the population, that when they were placed in the alternative of being shot by the Christinos or of disobeying his orders, they have infinitely preferred the most imminent risk of the former.

The blockade of all the towns and cities occupied in Navarre and the provinces by the Christinos, which Zumalacarregui proclaimed when Rodil adopted the plan of fortifying all the towns and commanding positions, contributed greatly to his successes, and proved the boldness of his genius. At first it seemed a mere jest from the man who was obliged to fly before the smallest division of the Queen's army. But he had already formed a corps of Aduaneros, or douaniers from the smugglers of the Pyrenees. These men, who, from generation to generation, have followed the same mode of life, are of uncommon hardihood, and, like the wild Indian, seem aided almost by instinct in everything that regards their perilous profession. Zumalacarregui would place what was termed a *partida*, composed of some 50 or 60 of these men, with some of the boldest and most intelligent of the volunteers, who were acquainted with the locality round every garrison - proclaiming it at the same time death for any man, and the punishment of cutting off the hair and feathering every woman, who should be caught trying to enter. As the Spanish women have generally very fine hair, which they wear plaited into one long tail, sometimes reaching down to their ankles, this punishment, which is called *emplumar*, is considered of great severity by the female sex, as may be inferred from the circumstance that it was awarded for the misdemeanour for which the men forfeited their lives. By these means Zumalacarregui considerably straitened the garrisons for provisions, and prevented them from obtaining without great difficulty any information of his motions; moreover, unless they chose to sally out in numbers of 5-600, they were obliged to shut themselves up entirely within the gates. Not a cat could move from the walls without, its being known. When a column came out, messengers were instantly sent off, and Zumalacarregui, at any distance, in an incredibly short time, was informed of it, as well as of all their subsequent movements, by spies, or *confidantes*, despatched successively at short, intervals. The Aduaneros, for part of these *partidas* performed the service of custom-house men, also levied a tax on the muleteers that travelled along the royal road. When a division of the Queen's army came out from any of the garrisons, three or four, or a dozen, of these individuals would fire from a distance on the column, sometimes causing considerable damage; when a company was sent to dislodge them, they disappeared amongst the rocks like chamois - loading and firing as they fled. Sometimes a whole army has been delayed by the appearance of one or two of these hardy partisans, and the Queen's generals saw with vexation soldiers fall in the midst of armed thousands, who could neither protect nor avenge them. Members of one *partida* also would follow the column, hovering round and cutting off stragglers, till they were relieved by the *partida* of another station; and let the enemy take what direction he would, messengers, who, in the most favourable ground for the rapid march of the Queen's troops, would always gain two hours in six, preceded them like their shadows. These two hours, in a country where in most places only a half hour's start, on account of the nature of the roads, renders it impossible to overtake with any body of men those who choose to escape, left it entirely at the option of the Carlists to fight or fly, and to form their combinations accordingly.

So little, however, was the Carlist army yet able to await the arrival of any of the Queen's columns, that, excepting in the valley of the Bastan, they were at that time as if still in an enemy's country; for where the larger divisions of the Christino army did not penetrate, the Carabineros and Peseteros daily swept over the country, and, excepting near Zumalacarregui, there was no security from their inroads. The two corps I have mentioned have been since almost entirely destroyed, not one fourth of their number now remaining of 10-12,000 organised in the beginning of the war, although at its commencement they were the most redoubted opponents of the Carlists, and the most merciless persecutors of the inhabitants. The Carabineros were a chosen body of gendarmerie, as fine and as highly paid as any in Europe, consisting both of horse and foot. The cavalry were obliged to furnish their own horses and equipment; and no man could enter without having been at least a corporal in the line. Their pay, when on active service, added to their numerous perquisites, was equal almost to that of an officer of infantry: they were all excellently mounted; their uniform was black; their shakos low, something resembling those worn by the Russian infantry. Having always been employed as a military police - doing the same sort of service as the "Archers of the Holy Hermandad" we read of in *Gil Blas*[41] - the pursuit and detection of smugglers, robbers, and malefactors; they were already looked upon by the insurgent peasantry with terror and dislike. The Peseteros, although undisciplined, were still more formidable, on account of their cruelties and excesses - being natives of the provinces, and chiefly the vagabonds and outcasts of society - men escaped from, or condemned to the "*Presidio*" or the galleys, to

---

[41] Picaresque novel published in 1715 by Alain-René Lesage, translated into English by Tobias Smollett

87

whom their liberty was given, or who had made their peace with justice, on condition of entering the free corps or those of volunteers, to which they were attracted by their thirst for pillage and private vengeance. Besides their rations, and a shilling a day, they were allowed *carte-blanche* in the insurgent districts. Many also were deserters from the Carlists, who, as soon as they perceived the severe discipline Zumalacarregui was introducing, and the little latitude allowed them for plunder, immediately changed to a side where unbounded licence in that respect was allowed them. Many at the end of their muskets carried the same kind of bayonet as those vised by the Carabineros - long, four-edged, and about the thickness of a foil; about three inches from the point were several teeth like those of a saw; by means of these, the wound was rendered incurable. That such instruments should have been used by a set of miscreants who were loathed and despised by both parties is not surprising; but to give them to the regular and disciplined troops of an established government, which the Carabineros were, seems hardly credible, when we reflect that its only object was a gratuitous cruelty. The wound it inflicted did not so quickly disable a man as one from the ordinary bayonet; but he lingered on incurable, and died a miserable death. Zumalacarregui never allowed these bayonets to be used in the Royalist army. I remember seeing him in the action of Ormaistegui[42] cause several which the Guides of Navarre had taken and fixed at the end of their muskets to be broken. The Peseteros were chiefly clad in black or rifle-green; those on horse wore a yellow stripe down the trousers; but generally their habiliment was so dark, that they were called, as well as the Carabineros, *los negros*, the blacks, a term which was afterwards applied to all the Queen's partisans. The Chapelgorris, or the Biscayan Peseteros, wore red shakos; some red trousers; but many of those in Jauregui's division had no uniform whatever; they were dressed in the costume of the country. These men, like the

---

[42] Zumalacarregui's native village

88

Peseteros, on account of their ferocity and personal knowledge of the country and its inhabitants, at first inspired great terror: the establishment of *partidas* by Zumalacarregui, and the mortal enmity of the inhabitants, in the course of a few months deprived them of the means of doing further harm. In most cases they were renounced by their own families; and whatever had been the result, of the war, a man who had been a Pesetero, so strong was the feeling against this detested class, would have been pointed out as if the mark of Cain had been stamped upon his brow. After being several times surprised and routed by Zumalacarregui, their "*prestige*" was destroyed; but although they fought very desperately against the Carlists, the sentiment of hatred seemed to overcome that of fear. The latter always rushed with the greatest fury on these corps. In the ranks of the Queenites the Peseteros seemed to be considered as the Parias of the army. They fought certainly in many cases with desperation, knowing that there was not for them the remotest hope of quarter; but as to what I have read in a description contained in a Number of the *United Service Journal*, of their venturing to carry despatches for the sum of ½.oz from "Pampeluna or Bilboa to Elisondo," or anywhere in a similarly dangerous part of the country, I can unhesitatingly state it to be a "picturesque misstatement." The *partidas*, constantly on the watch, rendered it a thing totally impossible; and if it could have been managed in so off-hand a way by their own men, the Christino chiefs would not have paid the sums they did to corrupt the peasantry and gain over spies. On the whole, a great deal more has been said in England of these Chapelgorris than they deserve; they have non fallen into universal contempt both with their own party and the Carlists.

The following early exploit of Zumalacarregui, when his men, half armed, and wanting cartridges, could not be prevailed on to stand for ten minutes together, was characteristic of his enterprising temper. Learning that the Christinos had published in Vittoria that the Faction was exterminated, and that the Carlist bands only existed in the imaginations of the fearful, he made a sudden attack on the city, cut off a 120 Peseteros in the suburbs, and forced his way into the city itself, which would certainly have been taken, had it not been for one of those trifling incidents that so often occur in wartime, and create a panic which in irregular troops is irreparable. The garrison was completely surprised; the horses of the cavalry were unsaddled in the stables; but unfortunately it was impossible to keep the Royalists from entering the houses, when a little trumpeter, appearing at the further end of the square where they were advancing, sounded the charge. The foremost, crying out that the cavalry was charging, fled, and caused the rest to retire so precipitately, that 30 men were left behind and taken by the Urbanos, who shot them all. By way of reprisal Zumalacarregui shot his 120 prisoners. The effect of this expedition was, however, as he had calculated, not only to enlighten the population as to the falsehoods propagated by the government, but also to make them believe, from his hardihood in attacking, that the Royalists were more numerous than in fact they were, and thus to induce many Carlists to escape from the city and join his standard. He did the same by Pampeluna. The disposable force having sallied from the city in pursuit of him, he appeared under the very walls, where he cut off a convoy, taking a number of mules and prisoners. This not only carried terror into the place, but had a still more advantageous effect than at Vittoria. The death of Santos Ladron having considerably exasperated the population, several hundred young men escaped the next day, and joined his standard.

Zumalacarregui seldom tarried in the Bastan; on the contrary, he endeavoured always to entice the enemy to attack him elsewhere. As the men flocked to his standard, they were slightly drilled in the Bastan; they were then armed and equipped, and sent to join him. This plan, and the exaggerated notion the enemy entertained of the difficulty of the passage into the Bastan, was the cause of the repose the Junta enjoyed, which, until the arrival of

Rodil, who was the first that penetrated the valley, remained undisturbed. It was then peremptorily given out, "that he had swept the Bastan, the last hold of the Carlists, from one end to the other;" and thence it was concluded that he had triumphed entirely over the party; so erroneous are the ideas formed at a distance! In the same way Valdes[43] imagined, because the Amescoas[44] had been so long impenetrable, if he could force the passage into them, the Carlists would be undone. After marching through them, destroying the miserable huts of the shepherds and cottages of the inhabitants, he acquired the conviction, that this "den" of Zumalacarregui was but as a valley, like a thousand others in Navarre and the provinces; but the experience he acquired cost him his office and his party the most serious defeat in its consequences which they had yet experienced. It laid open the road to Madrid; but fortunately for the Queen's cause, the want of ammunition prevented the Carlists from following up their advantage.

---

[43] General Jeronimo Valdes (1784-1855) formerly commanded an army in Peru without much success, and was later governor of Cuba.
[44] A valley about halfway between Pamplona and Vitoria, off the main highway. It is still remarkably unspoiled

The Guides of Navarre, so called because they were supposed to be first in action. The skull-and-crossbones on their flag refers to heir own willingness to die. The flag used by both sides to indicate "no quarter" was plain red.

CHAPTER VI.

Departure from Bayonne - Crossing the Pyrenees - Basque Cottage - Smugglers -Vigilance of the French - Crossing the Nivelle - Frontier - Urdax - A Spanish Posada - Valley of Bastan - San Estehan - Carlists and Christinos - Levying Rations – Segastibelza - Carlist Troops - Elisondo - Cholera - Skirmish with Lorenzo.

Having left Bayonne on horseback towards evening, accompanied by a Basque guide, who went before me habited according to the costume of that people in a short jacket, black velveteen trousers, a broad red sash, sandals, and a blue bonnet, we proceeded by the road to the Pyrenees. As he trotted along on his mule, according to my instructions, I was only to keep in sight of him, and never to address him but when spoken to: so that in case of our being stopped he might not be compromised. This was necessary on account of the extreme vigilance of the French police, the posts of gendarmerie and douaniers, and the cordon of troops under General Harispe[45]; for the French government was then in earnest in its endeavours to prevent all succours from reaching the Carlists, and punished, with great severity, the Basques who were caught smuggling over the Pyrenees either men or supplies of any kind. From Bayonne to the frontiers of Spain, on the side of Zugaramurdi, the distance is only five leagues, but all the roads were so strongly guarded, that the smugglers were obliged to go a round which trebled the distance. My guide was a celebrated contrabandista; indeed, at that moment few would undertake to pass a traveller over, nor would they attempt it for less than 100 francs. It was now nearly dark, for he had chosen the period of the new moon for our expedition. As he rode along whistling, he was joined by an old woman, to whom probably he had been making a signal. She spoke a few words in Basque, which appeared so little satisfactory to him, that we struck off into another road when he

---

[45] Jean Isidore Harispe, 1st. Count Harispe (1768 – 1855). President Bonaparte made him a Marshal of France in 1851.

informed me that we must sleep in France that night, but it would be very near the frontier.

After crossing several rivulets, and mounting and descending, till past midnight, by paths where no animals, save the small horses bred in the mountains, or mules could keep their footing, we found ourselves on a height, stumbling every minute against the stumps of some huge chestnut trees. Having resolved on maintaining the strictest silence, we advanced, as well as we could in the darkness, until we reached a cluster of cottages, which it was difficult to distinguish in the darkness. We put up our two animals under a shed; my guide then knocked gently three or four times at a latticed window; a light was seen, and presently a young woman appeared at the window. Some whispering passed, after which the door was opened, and we found ourselves in a cow-house, where several oxen were reclining on the maize-straw. After providing for our cattle, the lady of the mansion introduced us into the kitchen of the cottage, where her mother was busily employed over her spinning-wheel. We appeared not only welcome, but expected guests, as was evident from our hosts being on foot at an hour when the peasant's family is generally plunged in deep sleep. After the first greetings were over, they talked to my guide for some time, very quickly and earnestly, in their incomprehensible language: the result, however, was, that a blazing fire of brushwood was made, and the younger female began to prepare our supper. We were treated with all the hospitality peculiar to the inhabitants of the Pyrenees. In this case we had, however, an additional right to expect a friendly reception. The girl, whose name I remember was Marineshi - the Basque corruption of Maria-Ignace - was the *fiancée* of the smuggler. After we had done justice to the supper, I was surprised at the appearance of coffee, very white sugar, and some orange marmalade; but on learning that the smugglers carry on a contraband trade in almost every article that comes from beyond the frontiers, the wonder ceased. The life these hardy borderers lead, although one of danger and adventure, is a money-making one; and if they have the good fortune to escape a prison or the galleys, at a certain age they retire with the property they have amassed, which, sometimes, for the country, is not inconsiderable. The greatest peril they run is from their reluctance to abandon the merchandise they are endeavouring to pass with. The number of custom-house men and soldiers who perish in the daily encounters they hold with them, is never known, as both government and the people of the country unite to hush it up. The contrabandistas generally choose a pitch-dark and rainy or stormy night for their expeditions. 50 or 60 men will sometimes pass along the very same road where the post either of douaniers or soldiers is stationed, each carrying a bale of considerable weight on his head, and, walking on tiptoe, in long file, imitate, by their tread, the pattering of the raindrops. If discovered, they roll their bales down the precipitous side of the mountain, and bounding after them like izards, are all out of sight in an instant. Sometimes, however, their long knives silence all opposition. These smugglers - and nearly all the Basques are so - seem to consider each other as brethren, and, as such, afford mutually every assistance. Although often very desperate characters are amongst them, either criminals condemned to death in France or in Spain, and who think but little of human life; nevertheless, if confided in, they never betray the confidence reposed in them, and you may trust yourself or your property fearlessly in the hands of individuals with whom it would not be at all pleasant for a traveller to make acquaintance on a lonely mountain-road, even if he had nothing to lose but his coat.

The French Basques, who are all in some way connected with the contraband trade, feel a deep interest in the cause of Don Carlos; partly on account of the thriving business which his struggle has enabled them to carry on, but more from a sympathetic feeling with their Spanish brethren. The courage which his partisans evinced in first proclaiming him, and the touch of romance and adventure in his afterwards crossing a hostile country, as France then was, to place himself at the head of his followers, gave an additional interest to that cause in the eyes of a people naturally fond of, and accustomed to, expeditions of a hazardous character. My guide was in the habit of carrying some little present to his *bonne amie*, after any successful enterprise. On my making some observation on a pair of earrings she wore, she took out of an old chest a massive chain and a very heavy cross of fine gold, that had cost 600 francs, which her lover had given her.

I learned that where we stopped we were within 200yds of a post of douaniers; and it was resolved that next morning I should cross into Spain in the disguise of a peasant. As it was Sunday it was easy to pass unobserved, for the inhabitants of the Spanish villages were in the habit of coming into France, and *vice versa*. It was, however, necessary to avoid one post, which was situated at the head of a bridge over the Nivelle. About midday we proceeded on our journey; and just as we were stopping to cross the little river, which is easily fordable, although very rapid, a sentinel cried out to us to halt. The guide shouted to me to cross as rapidly as possible. Having the advantage of a few minutes' start, although the post was alarmed and was hotly pursuing us, we managed to reach the mountain after half an hour's race. For my own part I was quite exhausted. Our pursuers, although they fired several times to intimidate us, were only just out of gunshot. Having once reached the mountain we were, however, safe amongst the brushwood. My guide mounted the rocky bed of a stream which had dried up in the summer's heat, and after crossing two or three more hills and ravines, we halted in a shepherd's cabin. Here, after exchanging a few words with its owner, and taking from a bag of goat-skin a draught of the strong wine of Spain, a most detestable mixture, on account of its tasting of the skin itself, as well as of the pitch with which it is lined, the shepherd conducted me right across the frontier, which was not a mile off. A row of white stone-boundaries, and a few stunted trees along the road, which winds in the middle of a bleak heath-covered mountain, is all that indicates the separation of the two kingdoms, for so may centuries rivals; yet on looking from this line of landmarks, there was a striking and discouraging difference in the picture which the country we were leaving and the one we were entering presented. In France many a white village and casarie peeped out from the midst of vines and gardens which covered the slope of the hills, and the scene gave everywhere the promise of plenty and fertility: on turning towards the Spanish side the mountains seemed barren and rugged, and towards the horizon, of that deep, gloomy blue which we only see in the pictures of the old masters, and which is peculiar to the landscape of the south. Bleak, dreary, and uninhabited, the bold and harsh features of the scene were only relieved from an aspect of total desolation by a village or two, built of a dark red stone, and occasional ruins which have remained through the long lapse of years as memorials of woes and feuds, of which the origin and history have long since been buried in oblivion.

It was now growing dusk, but we could still discern the sea, and the light of the Phare of Bayonne, and of innumerable villages sparkling beneath our feet. Amongst the high and barren hills covered with heath were quietly grazing a few flocks, apparently left entirely to themselves. At last the baying of a dog betrayed the presence of a herdsman; he gave us startling intelligence. We had reason to believe that the peseteros were then in Urdax[46], the village to which we intended going. They had been the day before at Zugaramurdi[47], a village a league from thence, where they had wantonly murdered the owner of the palacio, as the old decayed chateau is called, and had taken from the curate 25oz of gold. After a long deliberation, as it was now dark, my guide resolved to enter the village to reconnoitre, while I lay down in the heath. After the lapse of an hour he came and informed me that the coast was clear, as the peseteros had retired towards I run. In a dirty inn, or posada, worse than the most miserable French public-house, I took up my

---

[46] Or Urdazubi, known for caves and a disused monastery
[47] Zugarramurdi was the focus of witch-tials in the 17th century, which have now been exploited by the tourist industry.

abode for the night. The reader must not imagine that a Spanish posada is like an inn in any other part of the world, where the traveller generally gets civility at least for his money. The Spanish padrons, or innkeepers, evince an astonishing nonchalence. The traveller may enter the kitchen, every one seeing him and allowing him to remain all day, and unless he speaks no one will ask him his business. To the questions, "What have you got?" "What good things have you to give us?" *Que tiene Usted? Que tiene Usted de bueno? Lo que ustedes han traido?* "What you have brought with you?" is the common answer from the hostess. It is only by dint of teasing and coaxing that he at last obtains something, and then he must take it as it comes, and pay what is asked. If it be given at the hour which the padrona imagines not to be the right one for meals all over the world, because it is not so in her village, it is a very rare and signal favour. Supper was served; it was what I afterwards learned to consider a good supper stock-fish[48], ham, and eggs, all cooked with tomata and pimento, and soup, or rather a bread-paste[49].

I had scarcely sat down when four men entered; they were aduaneros, or custom-house men of the Carlists, who, being informed by their spies that a stranger had entered the village, immediately came from the mountains to inquire who the intruder was. They were dressed in the garb of peasants, being armed with carbines, and carrying cartridge-belts, or *cañanas*. One, who was called the captain of the custom-house, was distinguished by a red cap and a sort of uniform; he was also mounted. He demanded my papers, with which he was promptly satisfied; he then told me that I might sleep quiet, and gave me a guide for the morrow. It was impossible, however, when the morrow came to fix upon the way I should go; it would depend upon the intelligence which might be received in the course of the day, and it was already 4 p.m. before any news could be obtained. I was then dispatched by way of

---

[48] Bacalao, i.e. salted cod. It is still cooked in much the same way in these parts.
[49] So-called garlic soup, made with burnt bread.

Etchalar[50]. Having procured a mule with the real Spanish caparisons, made with abundance of badger-skin, brass, and red-morocco, an ancient saddle and huge stirrups, we proceeded on our journey through mountain-paths so steep and dangerous, that in ordinary times the inexperienced traveller would have done nothing but think on the natural horrors of the road. When a man has nothing else to fear, the reflection that one false step of his mule will make a glorious feast for the wolf and the raven - the more so as the boasted sure-footedness of this animal, if not apocryphal, seems much exaggerated - is not very pleasant. The sun was setting when the valley of the Bastan[51] opened before us. We had a long march over rugged mountains whose deep chasms were filled up with old and knotted chestnut trees laden with their prickly fruit. The hills above us were covered with goats and flocks of Spanish sheep, clothed in their long Merino wool, feeding on the scanty herbage which grew between the rocks. Bold and fantastic masses, high above the pathway, terminated sometimes in points and pinnacles; at others, seemed piled one above another, menacing the traveller below. The vulture or the sea-eagle, who sweeps inwards from the Bay of Biscay, stretching his wings for a flight of 50 or 100 miles, to fish in the Bidassoa or roost in his eyrie amid the craigs of the mountain, sailed overhead, or perched on points of the rocks to reconnoitre the stranger.

The road which runs along the river continues rude and romantic, till St. Esteban[52] appears in sight. This is the first village of the Bastan; the houses are mostly painted white, with roofs something in the style of the Swiss or Piedmontese dwellings. We passed by a stone bridge over the Bidassoa, which is here shallow, and rushes noisily over its rocky bed. Before the entrance into the village there is a promenade, shaded by old trees, to the right, where the bourgeoisie walk of an evening. San Esteban is inhabited

---

[50] Now spelled Etxalar, population 800.
[51] The valley of the Baztan has some 15 villages of which the principal is Elizondo. There is an abundance of fruit trees, besides oaks and chestnuts.
[52] Santesteban or Doneztebe

by many persons above the class of ordinary farmers; and there are many villas and country-houses in its vicinity, although now mostly shut up and abandoned, where the inhabitants of Bilbao and Pampeluna were wont to spend the months they could spare from commerce. The women may here be seen stealing to church in black mantillas, of the richest silk, and netted stockings of the same material, exhibiting an elegance far beyond that displayed in the ordinary villages. As in other parts, many of the houses have the arms of the proprietor carved in relief over the doorway. The principal house in which the junta was lodged I believe belonged to the Conde de Espeleta, who commanded for the Queen in Arragon[53], and afterwards succeeded to the unfortunate Canterac as captain-general. He appears to have been a considerable proprietor in Navarre, as his arms, represented by a divided shield, with twelve cannon and three palm-trees, are seen in most of the villages. I believe, however, that his family is of French origin; at least the title is so - "Espelette" being a little village not far over the boundary.

The alcalde, or mayor of the place, was holding a council of all the notables of the village, on the subject of a number of rations which had been demanded by the Carlists, and also by the Christinos. Each party, not content with receiving them, threatened punishment if any were delivered to its adversaries. The alcalde, although suspected of liberalism (for of the villages of the Bastan, two, St. Esteban and Yrurita, were against Don Carlos), was obliged to answer the Queen's troops, that the rations would be ready, but that they must come and fetch them. Some soldiers, tailors, and baggagemen were employed for the transport of the provisions. The place was so little secure, that Rodil, after having

---

[53] Jose Maria de Ezpeleta y Enrile, Count of Espeleta, 1787-1847. Formerly Governor of San Sebastian after the sack by the Allies, then Capt. General of Navarre, by now a Lt. General and Capt. General of Aragon. A brave veteran of the Napoleonic wars, he captured and shot a great many Carlist leaders.

expulsed the junta from Elisondo[54], left a garrison of 500 men in the hospital. Nevertheless, few ventured to sleep in the village.

Although St. Esteban and Yrurita had the reputation of being Christino villages, the reproach could not be applied to the peasantry in their neighbourhood. The King having passed through it shortly before, after being so long and so ardently wished for, had, on the one hand, raised their enthusiasm; but, on the other, the violent persecutions Rodil then carried on, made many despair when they saw thousands of well-dressed and well-armed troops, in the eyes of a villager an interminable multitude, opposed to him, while he had to depend on a mere handful of half-barefooted volunteers, who had marched with Zumalacarregui, and appeared in the most deplorable condition.

Several of the monks from the monastery of Bera[55], which on some trifling pretext had been burned to the ground by Rodil, were here. Even their library and manuscripts were destroyed by this General in his Gothic zeal. They were mostly old and venerable-looking men; but all the young monks had joined Don Carlos, and exchanged the breviary for the musket, which I must do them the justice to say they wielded well. Some few sunk under the fatigues of a life so different from that which they had been accustomed to lead; but, generally, they seemed to forget their monastic habits, and became, for the most part, perfect troopers. From what I have seen of the monastic orders in the northern provinces, I have been led to form a much higher opinion of them than of the secular clergy. They evinced a spirit of hospitality and toleration, and a degree of learning which it were vain to look for amongst those of their brethren, to whom the cure of souls is intrusted. The influence which the Spanish clergy exercise over the population is not so immediate as might be imagined. If, for instance, its members in the provinces could have been gained over

---

[54] Elizondo was the British headquarters during the 1813 Battle of the Pyrenees at which Soult was severely defeated. From July 1834 Don Carlos' court resided here.
[55] Bera de Bidasoa

to preach against Don Carlos, they would not for an instant have been listened to. While they chime in with the public voice all goes on well; but I question whether even the ban of the church would cause a single Navarrese to lay down his arms.

Early the next, morning, learning that the 5th. Carlist Battalion was within sight of Elisondo, in the villages of Lecaros and Yrurita, we started directly. St. Esteban is situated at the south-western end of the Bastan, and one of the largest valleys in the north of Navarre. It is bounded on every side by high mountains, at the foot of which lie scattered several villages, of which Elisondo is the capital. The fields are chiefly sown with Indian corn, which constitutes the main part of the food of the inhabitants and of their cattle. In Lecaros[56], a small and dirty village, we found the 5th. Battalion of the Carlist army, commanded by Segastibelza,[57] a good partisan leader. He is a man of about 50, rather corpulent, but with a quick, intelligent eye. The defence of the Bastan being intrusted to him, so ably did he execute his duties, that it was found impossible effectually to drive him out of the valley. When both Elisondo and San Esteban were fortified, and Lecaros occupied, he always kept the garrisons strictly blockaded. His men were all habited in grey greatcoats, blue caps, each with a *cañana* and musket. The officers being dressed in every variety of costume presented, at the first *coup d'oeil*, a singularly grotesque appearance. The army following Zumalacarregui, and that of the Bastan and the other divisions, offered striking differences. There was not one of Zumalacarregui's men who had not on his person some article of Christino uniform; by far the greater number were

---

[56] Lekaroz, present population 341. The Fire of Lekaroz was a notorious Liberal atrocity which took place on 12th. March 1835. The Carlists had succeeded in collecting sufficient bronze to cast a mortar, which they then hid. General Mina entered the village and rounded up the elderly males present. He then proceeded to shoot every fifth one, demanding each time that they reveal the location of the mortar. After having shot half a dozen or more and got no answer, he set fire to the village.

[57] José Miguel Sagastibeltza Barberia (1789-1836). Of gypsy extraction, he was a former apothecary. He was killed in the moment of victory over the British Auxiliary Legion commanded by George de Lacy Evans. Victor Hugo borrowed his name in his song *Gastibelza, l'Homme a Carabine.*

entirely clothed in what they had taken from their opponents. So motley an assemblage presented the idea of a troop of mountebanks; but the reflection that they were entirely habited in the spoils of an enemy banished the ridicule otherwise attached to their costume.

Segastibelza, having had few opportunities of obtaining clothes in this fashion, in comparison with Zumalacarregui, whose troops were engaged in skirmishes almost every day, was obliged to content himself with the cheap, coarse material manufactured in France. The men, however, went through their exercise, and his corps appeared well organized, every military distinction being as nicely observed as in the British army. The canvas bags on their shoulders, and their sandals, had a most ungainly appearance, but this was more than compensated by their lightness. There is more than one of the Navarrese who has never taken off his bag or morral for months together, excepting to put in or take out his provisions: hence it becomes like a part of his person - he marches with it, he lies down and sleeps with it; in case of an alarm, he has only to shake himself, and snatch up his musket, which is beside him, and he is ready at the word to march 50 miles. In short, he wears it when he walks, prays, eats, sleeps, and fights; and, if he dies, prowlers may, indeed, rifle the bag of its contents, take out the shirt, the broken pipe, and the sandals; but he dies without being parted from his unconscious friend.

As the Carlist outposts were within gunshot round Elisondo, we went thither to prevent the garrison of 500 men from coming out. On sallying from Lecaros we met four peasants who were carrying a Carlist, wounded in an action which had taken place a week before, from the mountain where he had been concealed. He had been for some days neglected, and his wounds thus began to fester; nevertheless, as he passed us he faintly shouted *Viva el Rey!*

We were for about ten minutes crossing a tract of rising ground covered with heather, whose sundried leaves rose almost half the height of a man. Numerous herds of semi-wild swine were feeding here, and sometimes galloped by in herds. Several orchards were on the other side of the acclivity, the boughs bending to the earth with loads of golden but tasteless apples. Elisondo is one of the largest villages of Navarre. I believe it is even a *villa*, or town. The Queen's troops had fortified an old solid building, formerly used as an hospital, which stands isolated at the extremity of the place. It was defended by a broad ditch, a palisade, and three pieces of cannon. They had also occupied and crenelled the adjacent houses. To an enemy not possessed of artillery it was impregnable, as the soil precludes the possibility of mining.

At that time the cholera prevailed in Elisondo. Amongst the Carlists, however, probably from the air and exercise they enjoyed, not a single case was ever known. As the Christinos were strictly blockaded, and crammed one upon another, they were embarrassed to know what to do with their dead, and were obliged to throw them out of the windows of one side of the building into the dry ditch, where they lay corrupting the air. A couple of huts had been constructed with boards, in which the Carlist soldiers on guard were lying down among the heather, or playing with old greasy cards. Six or eight men were stationed behind a bank opposite the different entrances, and amused themselves by firing when any one appeared in sight. The Queen's troops now and then replied, and intermitted firing to insult their besiegers with their low wit, extremely amusing, as they always said something new.

At Lecaros, while I was waiting to proceed farther, as soon as the roads were a little more secure, I was present at a trifling affair, to me remarkable, as it was the first time I had seen shots fired in anger, or heard the whistling of a bullet. I was then without any arms, except my pistols, assisting more as a spectator than as a combatant. Some hours before daybreak we were traversing the mountains in the direction of Pampeluna, when in one of the passes we suddenly stumbled on a number of troops. It was the 6th. battalion, which had been skirmishing with the column of Lorenzo, of 4,000 men, which was following at their heels. Our guide, a little before, had evinced a little hesitation as to the path we should take: if good fortune had not favoured us in his choice, we should have fallen right on the vanguard of the advancing column. We returned, therefore, to Lecaros with the battalion, who were bearing with them about 20 wounded men. Segastibelza, although only with two battalions, or about 1,200 men, resolved to make a stand in the strong position of Lecaros. Having joined the officers of a company posted to defend an eminence, one of whom spoke very good French, I looked on with thrilling anxiety to the issue of the contest. Lorenzo came up with his division so fatigued that no very serious attack was made to dislodge us, although the firing was continued till nightfall. Segastibelza's force, considering that he had the rawest troops in the army under his command, the 6th. Battalion having been the last formed, behaved with great gallantry. To pass undisturbed into Elisondo, it was necessary for the enemy previously to take possession of Lecaros, and during the whole affair I was struck with the hardihood of two or three companies lining the breastwork which they had erected round the hospital: they repulsed every endeavour of the garrison to sally. If we had given way unexpectedly they must have been all cut to pieces.

I observed on this occasion, for the first time, the nervous impulse which on the sudden whistling of a bullet over their heads caused many men to stoop. This, however, is no indication of cowardice: the great majority do it at first, and some men of distinguished bravery I have seen never omit it on first entering an action. The Queen's troops were all in grey greatcoats and pipe-clayed belts. The Carabineros wore dark pepper-and-salt coloured capotes. The Carlist soldiers were animated, at times, almost by fury, and, as far as I could judge, they seemed rather kept at their post by their excited feelings than by any steady bravery. Most of them being recruits, were firing hurriedly and quick, some closing their eyes, but never giving up an inch of ground. Amongst these a few veterans of Mina's school might be distinguished, aiming long and steadily, and scowling beneath their bushy eyebrows till an opportunity of taking a murderous aim was afforded them. Once or twice the clarion of the enemy, for clarions are used in the Spanish infantry, sounded "halto el fuego," or to cease firing; and then the loud and exulting *Vivas* of the Carlists rose over the din of the ceasing musketry with an inspiriting sound, that seemed to breathe a fresh enthusiasm into young and old.

The sun had just gone down, and the reddened glare it still imparted to the sky was giving way to the short twilight which precedes darkness, when we slowly retired from the village. At that time, solely occupied with what was going on immediately around me, and little accustomed to judge of the object of military manoeuvres, I was not aware that the Christinos had succeeded in turning our position. The loss of the enemy in this skirmish, from the circumstance of his being the assailant, was infinitely greater than that of the Carlists, who left about 20 dead, and carried off twice that number of wounded. One of the officers I was with was slightly injured in the head.

We only drew back about three quarters of a mile, the enemy having contented himself with taking possession of Lecaros. We lit our bivouac fires on the mountains opposite those of the enemy, and so short was the interval that divided us, that all night the shouts of the Christinos and Carlists, answering each other, were heard at intervals. Before daybreak, however, we retired on Lesaca.

CHAPTER VII.

Quesada first attacked and beaten by Zumalacarregui at Alsassua - O'Donnel, Count de Labispal, taken Prisoner - Shot by way of Reprisals - Death of his Father, on hearing the intelligence - Brief Account of his Political Career - Attack of Goulinas or Las dos Hermanas - Anecdote of a Soldier – Zumalacarregui's System in the early part of the Campaign - His Prudence - Why he did not quit the Provinces.

The first affair at all serious was that which took place on the 2nd. May at Alsassua[58], where Zumalacarregui attacked the commander-in-chief of the army of Navarre[59], at the head of a body of his chosen troops. Emboldened by the manner in which the Carlist leader, at that time the only one who gave him any uneasiness, had seemed to hang back, the commander-in-chief attempted to march, as he had often done before, by the Val de Araquil, through which winds the high road from Vittoria to Pampeluna. Having, if I am not misinformed, slept the night before at Olzagutia, he had reached Alsassua, the largest pueblo or village in Navarre; it stands on the left of the road, at some 100yds on the other side of the river, over which an old wooden bridge is thrown. The traveller may remember it, from an immense *venta* or rustic inn which touches the road: it is sufficiently large to lodge, with ease, a squadron and a half of cavalry. The village is on the acclivity, and behind it commence the woods, which extend towards Guipuscoa. Zumalacarregui, whose troops had been trained in a rough school, with three battalions of Alavese and three of Navarre, confidently attacked him. Quesada made the foolish bravado of sending a note to the "*Chief of the Brigands*" advising him to avoid the effusion of blood, by causing his followers to lay down their arms immediately. It was sent back with this reply "That, as it could not be addressed to anyone in the Carlist army,

---

[58] This battle in fact took place on April 22nd. 1834. The village was the scene, in 2016, of the Altsasu Incident

[59] General Vicente Generado de Quesada (1782-1836). He was eventually murdered by liberal extremists.

none had presumed to open it." Quesada thought proper, however, instead of assuming the offensive, to await the attack of the enemy, and occupy the rising ground. Zumalacarregui, although his volunteers were scarcely superior in numbers, by a skilful movement managed to turn his position: the defence was obstinate; the Carlist chief was everywhere in the fire animating his men, and at last forced the enemy back with considerable loss. In the first important trial the result was thus a victory, which was, however, rendered incomplete by the arrival of Jauregui, surnamed El Pastor[60], or the Shepherd, the bulky colleague of Mina in a former war, who, with a large column, came from Salvatierra to disengage Quesada from his *mauvais pas*. But for this timely aid, his division, entirely beaten and dispersed, must have been annihilated, and even without the exertions of Leopold O'Donnel[61], this succour might have arrived too late. Nearly 300 dead (as I was informed by the peasantry, who, having to bury them, are the best judges) were left upon the field; the wounded were of course much above that number. The baggage, the military chest, and 84 prisoners, besides a company of the guards, fell into the hands of the victor. Last, but not least, of the prisoners taken was the Colonel-Count of Labispal, Leopold O'Donnel, just mentioned, gallantly but vainly struggling to rally his men; he was surrounded by the Navarrese. Although the affair consisted of little more than skirmishes many hundreds were taken on both sides.

As hitherto the Carlist prisoners were shot as rebels, and the Christinos suffered death by way of reprisal, Zumalacarregui, anxious to put an end to this dreadful state of things, set at liberty

---

[60] Jauregui became a guerrilla chief at the age of only 19 and waged a persistent and demoralizing campaign on the French all over Guipuzcoa. For a while, Zumalacarregui was one of his men, and developed - ironically considering his later career - a dislike of irregular warfare. He left to join the regular Spanish army once it was reformed against the French, and served under General Espoz y Mina at that time.

[61] Leopold O'Donnel, second and last Count of La Bisbal. His father Henry, the first Count, was a distinguished general during the War of Independence. His brother Carlos, a Carlist, had three sons of whom three were Carlists and one, also called Leopold, a Liberal who lived to 1867 and was made Duke of Tetuan. His younger brothers Jose and Alexander were Liberals as were Alexander's sons Pepe and Emilio,

and caused to be escorted as far as Echauri[62], five miles from Pampeluna, two soldiers, who, unable from fatigue to follow the march, had been taken from Quesada's column. The next time the latter sallied from Pampeluna he requited the mercy of the Carlist general by shooting in Huarte d'Araquil[63] a wounded volunteer, and putting afterwards to death the alcalde of Atoun[64], who was suspected of Carlism, as well as several other individuals. Zumalacarregui now wrote to General Count Armilde de Toledo, from his headquarters at Etchari-Arenas, a little higher up in the Borunda, to state, "that since the chiefs appointed by the usurping government were unwilling to make any arrangement for the preservation of the lives of their respective followers, although he, willing to bury in oblivion the murder of General Santos Ladron, had several times set them the example of clemency, the blood of those that perished must be now on their own heads." It was his intention, he declared, to shoot, by way of reprisals for the alcalde of Atoun, Colonel O'Donnel (Conde de Labispal), two officers of the guards, and one of carabineros; for a corporal shot at Pampeluna, six carabineros (who hold the same rank in the line); and for each of two volunteers shot at Tolosa, six soldiers of the guard; together with six others, for a Carlist bayoneted at Calhahora.

He kept his word. Of all the prisoners who were executed, perhaps the fate of Leopold O'Donnel was the most melancholy. Although a colonel in the service he was then merely accompanying Quesada, to profit by the escort to Pampeluna, whither he was going to celebrate his nuptials with a young and wealthy heiress. He perished through that valour which seems an heirloom in his family, and sacrificed himself with a company of the guards to save Quesada and his staff. He offered that, if Zumalacarregui would spare his life, he would pay a ransom that

---

[62] Etxauri, population today 650. A great many of its villagers joined the guerillas during the War of Liberation.
[63] Araciel, a practically deserted village.
[64] Ataun

109

would equip all the battalions of Navarre; but, knowing the necessity for making an example, the chief remained inexorable. He died, with his brother-officers of the guards, in a manner which added another example to the many, that often those who have most enjoyed a life of luxury and pleasure, and to whom it still holds forth bright prospects, can relinquish it with the least regret. His father, the Count of Labispal, celebrated both during the triumphs of Wellington and the revolution of 1823, callous and heartless as he had been throughout his political career, was doomed to prove, on hearing of the death of his son, that there was still one point where his sensibility was vulnerable. He died of a broken heart on learning the tidings in the south of France (I believe at Montpellier[65]), where he had been long residing. In his changes of principle Labispal had been the Talleyrand of Spain. Descended from a family of Irish extraction, and which had long figured in the military annals of its adopted country, he distinguished himself in the war of independence. He was first known as General O'Donnel; and when Gerona was besieged by Augereau, he cut his way through the ranks of the French with several hundred mules laden with provisions to relieve the city on the side of the Bispal, and afterwards forced a passage through them to retire again when he had thrown in succours. For this gallant action he was created Conde de la Bispal. He also afterwards raised in Andalusia the army which entered France with the English. A little before the revolution of 1820, which for a time dethroned Ferdinand VII, although holding an important charge under government, he became very intimate with many of the revolutionary party, to whom he offered his services. He actually joined in a conspiracy with some of its leaders. When all was prepared, as a servant worthy of such a monarch, he caused them all to be arrested, and then went and informed the king of everything. Ferdinand threw the grand cordon of Charles III round his neck, allowed him a handsome pension from his private purse,

---

[65] Indeed. He was en route back to Spain following a long exile.

and named him, if I mistake not, Governor of Madrid, granting him his entire confidence. Labispal, who was an intriguing character and *au fait* to all that was going on, soon saw, however, that all the public functionaries were gained over, and that a revolution was inevitable; he then passed over to the Constitutionalists, who, not forgetting his former treachery, looked on him with all the suspicion which his conduct naturally inspired. At last, on the entrance of the Duke d'Angoulthne and the rapid advance of the French army, the Constitutionalists, aware of his superior talent, and considering him as the only man capable of serving the Constitution in its agony, placed the direction of everything in his hands, and he became *de facto* dictator of Madrid. He levied troops and money; issued proclamations; and for a moment revived the cause: but finding it must eventually sink, he one night fled to the Duke d'Angoulême with the treasure he had amassed. It does not appear, however, that his ill-gotten wealth prospered with him. Before he died, he had sojourned some years in France in retirement, and in rather reduced circumstances.

In another battle, that of Las dos Hermanas[66], the loss of the Carlists was comparatively insignificant, while that of the Liberals was so great, that although they took the position's from the enemy, they were obliged to retire to Pampeluna, leaving the King the range of the country. The wounded they carried with them made a great impression on the inhabitants of the capital of Navarre, and directly contradicted the government bulletins, which duly set forth that the Carlist faction had ceased to exist. This affair took place in that end of the valley of Goulinas, which touches the highway, and opposite the village of that name[67] which is built upon a rock within gunshot of the road from Pampeluna to France. The valley leads through high and steep mountains; two gigantic rocks, which seem as if riven asunder by the river, overhang, brow against brow, the narrow pathway, and defend the entrance into the

---

[66] 18th June 1834
[67] Gulina, population today 53

111

Borunda, through which the road from Pampeluna to Vittoria runs by the village of Irurzun. These two rocks, which are called the Two Sisters, have given their name to the place. The Queen's army, under Quesada and Lorenzo, attempting this passage into the Borunda, where only they expected to meet the Carlists, were surprised to find it occupied by them under the orders of Zumalacarregui, of whom they were principally in quest, and who gratified them by what became rather an unpleasant interview. He had occupied all the heights with his battalions, and taken advantage of the irregularity of the ground and the woods of evergreen oak. This was necessary, on account of the inexperience of his troops, and the superiority of the enemy's numbers. Rock by rock and tree by tree were defended; and when, after having been much annoyed and galled by the fire from any particular point, the enemy made a desperate effort to take possession of it, it was abandoned, and the next thicket afforded another fortalice. After using as many of his little stock of cartridges as was prudent, Zumalacarregui retired, leaving the field of battle to the enemy; but they were so well convinced that it was no victory, that they never attempted pursuit. Counting the dead and wounded, 600 of their men were put *hors de combat*, while the loss of the Carlists did not exceed 250. This action took place some time before I joined the Carlist army, but I am well acquainted with the localities, and have heard it related over and over again by our officers and the peasantry.

I must mention one trait of a Carlist soldier, which deserves to be recorded. Four or five of the volunteers had taken up their position in some holly bushes, whence they kept up a galling fire on a company of the Christinos stationed near them. The latter at last made a movement to clear the spot, when they all, excepting one, retired, the patch of brushwood being isolated. This man vowed to bring back the epaulette of a lieutenant who was with two soldiers in advance of the company. Imagining the thicket to be entirely abandoned, they had reached it, when he sprung forward, and was instantly fired at, apparently without being touched. A few yards farther on he shot one of the soldiers through the head, stabbed the officer to the heart with his bayonet, tore off his epaulette, and, waving it in triumph, escaped from the company that was coming up, and just gained a rock where the Carlists were making a stand, before he expired. He had received two shots of the enemy, slower in effect, but no less deadly than his own.

This engagement requires, perhaps, some explanation; and as Zumalacarregui so often sought affairs of this kind, it may be interesting to state the object he had in view. Throughout it was the policy of this great leader - for such he undoubtedly was - on finding himself with infinitely inferior numbers, and inferior troops, not only to carry on a war of surprise and destruction, in detail, as Mina had done, and which is the natural mode of fighting all undisciplined armies, where the nature of the country presents great obstacles, but to accustom them to operations of greater magnitude. The mountaineers in their mountains - the Tartars and Bedouins in their deserts, are difficult to be subdued, and will often succeed in wearing out a foreign invasion. But in a civil war the case varies considerably. His object was not to maintain himself only, and watch the progress of events (the plan Mina adopted during the war against the French), but to conquer and destroy the armies of the government by some more rapid process, and lead the monarch - whose cause he was defending - to Madrid. Unless the tide of events were turned by his own efforts, there was little likelihood of its setting in his favour. Under a foreign yoke, a people become more restive and impatient every day; but a native, though usurped, government, strikes only deeper root the longer it remains. It therefore became necessary that the insurrection should make its existence and extent everywhere known, and, by destroying the government troops as quickly as possible, strike terror into one party, and animate the other in the rest of Spain with the hopes of speedy assistance. Besides carrying on a war of surprises, Zumalacarregui's system was, therefore, always to fight where he could not lose by it, and in every favourable spot to give battle with sometimes only a handful of men. Generally he chose positions which it was difficult to turn; he defended them obstinately till the enemy were near taking him in flank, which nightfall almost always prevented. If the positions were forced, it cost a great sacrifice, and then a retreat took place, more resembling, from its rapidity, a flight, excepting that the companies and battalions fled all together, and in good order, their officers in their respective places, and without ever losing a musket. The General was usually the last of his little army on such occasions. If the enemy attempted to pursue, he was stopped by a few companies, who swept the narrow roads, and covered the retreat. These were only to be driven back by other tirailleurs, who were obliged to proceed with much caution, each man of the Carlists being hidden by a rock, the trunk of a tree, or the evergreen bushes which abound in that country: while, remaining still, the Carlists, not being seen, take a deadly aim at those who are advancing. When at last the game became too hot, and they were too closely pressed by their adversaries, these companies, whose number it was impossible to ascertain, easily effected their escape. Each man, like a fox or wolf, traversed hill and dale, rock and ravine, and at night joined his comrades, who, by that time, had rapidly retired so far, that, it would have been impossible to overtake them. If any were adventurous enough to follow them, they found the rear guard in good order waiting for them; and where anything like a plain or a piece of table-land intervened, the Carlist cavalry was so disposed as to charge them before they could form on the open space.

All night the Carlist army occupied always nearly four times as many villages as their adversaries, as they had no fear of extending their line, being "*a l'abri d'une surprise*" on account of their intelligence, kept up through the country by their spies and *partidas*. Everything went on with them as usual - the soldier receiving his full rations - while their adversaries, who perhaps had flattered themselves with a victory, were often obliged to bivouac in the mountain, or to occupy some miserable village which could not even shelter their officers; the men perishing with cold, and always either bread or meat, or wine, and sometimes the whole of their rations being deficient. By night they durst not stir, even to retreat, and the next day, if they advanced, they found the indefatigable chief occupying a similar position a mile or two farther on - if they retired, he followed on their rear. There was thus no proportion between the loss of the Carlists and Christinos; the latter, therefore, in case of success, only obtained the empty honour of having purchased, at an immense loss of life, the power of occupying an unimportant spot. Zumalacarregui was too well aware of the advantageous game he was playing, not to enter into action whenever the opportunity was offered him. In this manner he destroyed, in a few months, the veteran armies of Spain, to an extent of which no idea appears to have been formed in this country. The loss which his force sustained was comparatively trifling, and the more so, as even if the number of his followers killed had been equal to those who fell on the side of the enemy, a man could always be afforded, if his musket were saved. He found ten peasants eager to wield it in the place of the one who had fallen.

The enemy raised his recruits with difficulty; the veterans that fell were not to be replaced by men dragged unwillingly from their homes, like the quintos or conscripts. At the same time, little by little his own soldiers were formed. At first, like Washington, he could only get his recruits to stand fire for a few minutes or half an hour; by degrees, however, they not only obstinately defended positions against superior numbers for the whole day, but dispersed the enemy by the bayonet. His favourite battalions of Guides always went into action singing. It must be understood that I do not assert having seen them cross bayonets, excepting very partially - a thing in which I think I shall be borne out by old and experienced officers, in saying seldom happens in any engagement. I believe it was only rarely witnessed during the whole of the Peninsular war and the campaigns of the French against the Russians. I merely testify to their having rushed on with fixed bayonets, and taken in this way a position from the enemy or driven in his line.

It was after the battle of the 27th. and 28th. October in the plains of Salvatierra and Vittoria, that the losses of the Liberal army augmented so much in consequence of this circumstance. Having on that occasion formed in line of battle, which was instantly broken through from the impetuosity of the Navarrese, and the entire destruction of the divisions having in both instances followed, the Queen's generals ever after moved their men in heavy masses and in order of column, which it was found the Royalists were shy of charging, although they rushed upon a line with the most desperate determination. Zumalacarregui, well aware of their failing, and knowing that the result would have been very problematic, never attempted it; but generally placed half his battalions in reserve, dispersing the rest *en tirailleurs*. In this mode of fighting they always displayed great intrepidity, and every shot told when fired on the broad expanse of a column; whereas its front could do little harm against isolated men, neither could they send tirailleurs against those of the Royalists, excepting at great disadvantage, as they were always liable to be cut off under the eyes of their own masses the instant they separated from them. While they were slowly advancing, backed by the column, and skirmishing to clear the ground for it, which is after all but child's play for the skirmishers, their masses were suffering horribly from the incessant fire of their adversaries. As far as a musket will carry which, by the by, is no trifle theirs were almost certain to do some mischief.

There is a Spanish proverb (for Spain is the land of proverbs, and, in the character of Sancho Panza, Cervantes in this respect did not much caricature some of his countrymen) which says, *Una ves à la guerra nos engañamos* - "Once in war we are mistaken." This with Zumalacarregui was a favourite saying, and is characteristic of his excessive caution and prudence. I do not

116

mean in a personal point of view, for his temerity unfortunately lost the Royalists the soul of their party; but as far as regarded the safety of his army, he piqued himself on risking as little as possible, and on striking all his blows with certainty. Never did he give a battle which, if not won, left him any the worse for his failure. There is one remarkable circumstance in his career: from the day he assumed the command till the day of his death, although circumstances were ever varying, it is impossible to take any month in which, when compared with the month preceding, he had not considerably increased his army, and advanced the Royal cause. How necessary this prudence proved to have been, those who have seen the unsteadiness of volunteers who fight only for their opinions can appreciate. Even the inhabitants of La Vendée were, we read, also subject, to this fickleness, although their astonishing resistance was the admiration of the world, and to this day fill a page which is unequalled in the history of devoted heroism. The men who one day took the cannon of the Republicans with loaded sticks, the next, were seized with an unaccountable panic, and fled before the slightest danger without firing a shot. The impetuosity of their chief was evidently a principal cause of their perdition. If they had not made their rash attempt on Nantes, or crossed the Loire, till they had become completely organized and disciplined, they might have met with signal victories, and have chosen their moment to march on Paris - a capital which, to France, is like the sacred banner of the Peruvians captured by Cortes - that, once taken, all is lost.

Zumalacarregui was blamed for not pushing on into Castille, particularly after the battle of Vittoria. But if the affair of the 12th. December, 1834, at Mendavia, had taken place in the plains of Castille, where would have been the Royal army? Whereas, just before death closed his glorious career, his march on Madrid, if he had followed his own judgment, and gone thither, instead of to Bilboa, would have been probably unopposed. He had said and he never made an idle boast that the next time he crossed the Ebro, he would not repass it without having seen Madrid, and once showing it to his wild followers, as Hannibal showed his soldiers Italy from the Alps, and Peter the Hermit pointed out to the Crusaders the walls of Jerusalem. With the prospect of vengeance and plunder before them, it is scarcely doubtful that the Carlists would have entered Madrid, even supposing a defence to have been made.

CHAPTER VIII.

The Curate Merino - Merino and Zumalacarregui - The old Castilians - Rodil -
His proclamation to the Insurgents on crossing the Ebro - Anecdote of Rodil
during his defence of the Castle of Callao - His pursuit of the King - Straits to
which he was reduced - Fatigues the Carlists had to undergo - Party spirit of the
women and children - A village on the passage of the Carlist army - On that of
the Queen's troops - The Spanish barber -The Carlist Brig. General Armencha
taken prisoner and shot at Bilboa - Description of his death by a French veteran.

In the meanwhile Merino, the soldier-priest, who had visited the
king in Portugal to assure him of his devotion, returned to Castille
to raise in his favour the old and new kingdoms, which had been
the scene of his exploits in the war against the French. Although as
the head of a few *Guerrilleros* he is perhaps unequalled, his
capacity extends no farther; and as he had to do with people well
acquainted with the country, he met with no greater success than
that which attended all the Carlist chiefs who were not under the
direction of Zumalacarregui. His force was generally the same,
consisting of from three to 400 horse. Occasionally his followers
were much more numerous; but his talent for command seemed to
be limited to about that number; and a few weeks always brought
them back to nearly the same as before. The enthusiastic Castilians
constantly made movements in his favour, and he was joined more
than once by large bodies of insurgents, but being always
immediately attacked by the Queen's troops, they were dispersed
after a short period of partial successes. With his cavalry, however,
he kept his ground, and became the terror of Old and New Castille,
intercepting couriers, surprising the garrisons of towns, and cutting
off detachments, sometimes in the very vicinity of Madrid. Several
regiments of the guards suffered in particular, his followers being
nearly all mounted and equipped from the spoils they made. On
one occasion, 20 cuirassiers with their lieutenant passed over to his
ranks. So well has he maintained himself, that unless when he
attempts to gather infantry around him, the enemy has given up all
hope of surprising him.

Merino, now 62 years of age, was born at Villaviado, and spent his early years in the humble capacity of a goatherd. He had, however, picked up, in the religious establishment of a neighbouring town, the rudiments of an ordinary education, when an old clergyman, discovering in the young herdsman indications of ability, undertook to bring him up for the church. In six months the youth made such rapid progress under his tuition, that he was enabled to take orders, and was appointed curate of his native village. It seems difficult to associate the idea of a talent for any species of literature with those requisite for a leader of partisans like Merino, whose career, excepting that his conduct showed him to have been moved only by patriotic motives, resembled that of a daring and reckless brigand, encouraging and committing every sort of excess against the enemy, but never touching the least portion of the rich booty his followers often obtained. He conducted himself in a similar manner in the war waged against Napoleon, when he might have possessed himself of immense treasures. The moment the war was concluded, he retired to his home, the rank of Brig. General having been conferred upon him in consideration of his eminent services. There are, indeed, innumerable instances of this disinterestedness amongst the Spaniards, and often too exhibited by men who seemed in other respects influenced by the most brutal passions. Whatever may have been the case during the invasion of South America, venality is the last of their sins at the present day. They can, perhaps, less than any nation, be accused of being actuated by any mercenary spirit, the commercial classes only excepted. Nothing, perhaps, more clearly shows the popularity of Don Carlos' cause, than the circumstance that, on the side of the Queen, none fight but those who are desirous of following up a military career, or who are in some way interested. Whereas, if the Carlist army were to reach Madrid tomorrow, I am convinced that above half its officers would give in their absolute resignation, and retire to their native mountains. Yet many of them were peasants who have risen by their valour from a homely station to one of ease and consideration, which rank in the army affords in Spain. They are fighting really from no ambitions motives, or from any inclination for a military life.

A glance at the leading characters of either side, and the contrast they offer, would be the strongest proof of my assertion as to the conscientious motives of their respective partisans. Mina, who had refused to accept the command of the Queen's army till he had received all his arrears of pay, occupied himself chiefly in levying contributions and getting in convoys from France, and retired after a few months a rich man. Cordova[68], who had formerly been saved by Don Carlos, when Infant of Spain, by hiding him at his own imminent peril from the fury of the mob under his bed, and who had always avowed himself devoted to that prince, has risen from the subaltern situation of secretary of legation to that of commander in chief. Mendizabal[69], who has ascended from being a Jew boy, under the name of Mendez, selling old clothes at Cadiz, or wandering about the country as a pedlar, or receiving from his customers, on account of his Hebrew origin, many a kick and cuff which he was obliged to pocket with their copper monies, first became a millionnaire, and, lastly, prime minister of Spain, through his enlightened patriotism and affection for that country from which, in common with all his caste, he had received usage which might have turned the blood to gall, if the blood and spirit of his race had been like that of the rest of the sons of Adam. Zumalacarregui, after having had every opportunity of amassing wealth, died the possessor of 14 oz. The Marquess of Valdespina, at an advanced age, abandoned £20,000 per annum to lead a wandering life in the mountains. Eraso, although supporting his

---

[68] Luis Fernández de Córdova (or Córdoba) (1798-1840) first Marquis of Mendigorria. A diehard supporter of Queen Christina, he was replaced by Espartero and then in 1838 led a failed Christinist uprising against Espartero's ultra-left government.

[69] Juan Alvarez Mendizaval 1790-1853. Illegitimate son of Rafael Alvarez Montañes, a cloth merchant, and Margarita Mendez, who was of Marrano (Jewish convert) origin. He was first and foremost a businessman, next an anti-clerical freemason and Liberal. He was Prime Minister for under eight months from September 25th. 1835

family by his pay of Colonel, placed himself at the head of a handful of insurgents, evidently without the ambition of leading, as, when the cause was in a much more flourishing condition, he refused to accept the command at Zumalacarregui's hands. Eguia[70] was a lieut. general, but threw up his commission and retired to France.

It is worthy of remark that all the classes which have espoused the interests of the King are precisely the same as those who, during the war of independence, resisted so energetically the French usurpation. The others made but feeble efforts till the tide had set full against their Gallic conquerors. Merino is the true type of the Guerrilla chief. Of small stature, but iron frame, he can resist the greatest fatigues, and is wonderfully skilled in all martial exercises. His dress is rather ecclesiastical than military, and reminds one more of the curate than of the Brig. General. He wears a long, black frock coat, round hat, and a cavalry sword. The only luxury in which he seems to indulge is in having a good horse beneath him. He has two magnificent black steeds, which are not only renowned for their excessive speed, but are said to climb among the rocks and mountains like goats. These are both saddled and bridled, and have been trained always to keep abreast, so that at whatever pace the mounted one may go, the other is always by its side. Merino, when he sees that one is tired, leaps from one saddle into the other, even when they are going full gallop. He always carries, slung by his side, an enormous blunderbuss or trombone, the discharge of which, loaded with a handful of powder and a number of slugs, is said to be like that of a piece of artillery, and would fracture his shoulder if fired in the ordinary manner. But he places the stock under his arm, and holds the barrel tight with the other hand. The last effort the Christinos made to take him was by sending against, him a Colonel named Moyos, who had also been a chief of partisans much in Merino's style. This man, of gigantic frame and stature, was well acquainted with the country,

---

70 Nazario Eguía y Sáez de Buruaga, conde de Casa-Eguía (1777-1865)

and of undaunted energy. Merino favoured him with an early interview, and in the first skirmish he met his death from the discharge of a trombone, whether from that of the curate I could never learn. The curate has seen sufficient of the fidelity of partisans, it appears, to trust only an old servant, who has been with him for the last 40 years. Every evening, when he has disposed of his men, he rides away for the night, no one, excepting his faithful servitor, knowing whither he has gone. This has given rise to a report that he never sleeps above a few minutes in the 24 hours, a story in which the Castilians place implicit faith, and, indeed, they may well believe anything of a countryman who neither smokes nor drinks wine. He is simple, and even patriarchal, in all his habits; but the successes he has obtained have always been tarnished with cruelty. An indefatigable and faithful adherent to the cause he has adopted, he has ever been found a bitter and merciless enemy; and his stern and inevitable decree against his prisoners is death. In his disinterestedness and bravery he resembles Zumalacarregui; but beyond that, their characters bear no comparison. The latter only put his enemies to death after long forbearance, and by way of reprisal, which had become almost an act of justice to his own army; constant and repeated instances of mercy and generosity illumine the darkness of this sanguinary page of his history, contrasting with deeds to which he was forced by the obstinacy of his opponents.

Merino, as I have said, is a mere Guerrilla chief, and as ill calculated to command any large bodies of men, as the genius of Zumalacarregui was well suited for their organization. The curate of Villaviado is no doubt one of those uncommon characters who take the lead in the walk of life where chance has thrown them; but Zumalacarregui was a great man, and formed to play a conspicuous part in those scenes of higher interest and importance, where thrones and empires are disputed. His early death - early in reference to his brief but glorious career - was alone able to snatch away the triumph he had earned so well.

Merino, having heard of the success of the royal army in the north, signified to the commander-in-chief his intention of endeavouring to effect a junction with him, as he was no longer able to hold out in Castille. The truth was, that most probably he was tired of leading a vagrant kind of life, constantly pursued by the enemy. Zumalacarregui, aware, however, of the utility of Merino's remaining where he could keep up communication for the Carlists when they should march on the capital, informed him that his post was in Castille; and that if he ventured to cross the Ebro he would have him shot. The soldier-priest, contented with this menace, never felt inclined to try whether the general was a man of his word. Zumalacarregui rendered justice to Merino as an enterprising and daring leader; he once observed, however, after the actions of Vittoria, that "if we had all the men the curate has lost we could march upon Madrid when we chose." It must be, however, admitted that the champagne country is by no means so favourable as the northern provinces as the nursery of an insurrection an infant army being always liable to a dispersion in the outset.

The country is flat, with the exception of a Sierra, which runs at right angles from the sources of the Ebro, wilder but not so lofty as the chain which there forms a continuation of the Pyrenees. It may be termed the Apennines of Spain. Traversing Old Castille in a south-easterly direction, on the southern frontier of Arragon it separates into two branches, one crossing Cuença and Murcia, the other the western side of New Castille, passing within a few miles of Madrid, and losing itself in the plains of Estremadura. Although the soil is fertile, immense wastes lie uncultivated, and the towns and villages are "few and far between." The former, having been garrisoned previous to the death of Ferdinand with troops or urbanos, were checks, instead of being of any assistance, to an insurgent army; and the mountains, which are much more desert than the northern provinces, afford no resources to maintain a considerable force.

124

Castille, too, having been so completely disarmed, became, although containing the best disposed population in Spain, one of the worst possible theatres for an insurrection. There is no doubt, however, that were a respectable armed and disciplined force to advance upon it, the inhabitants would rise to a man. Though greatly changed from the time when the *Vieilles Bandes de Castille* were renowned throughout the Old and New World, and it was a saying that the Castilian was cast steel, there is still much that is estimable in his character. His chief bane is indolence and pride; but there is more morality in his opinions than in those of any other portion of the Spanish people. He acts neither from interest nor feeling, but according to what he believes to be right or wrong, and remains faithfully attached to a cause he once adopts. Perhaps one third of what is termed the army of Navarre is composed, both officers and men, of Castilians, who at every risk left their homes to serve in a strange province a cause to which they have proved themselves sincerely and devotedly attached. As to what I have seen of the soldiers, I must do them the justice to say, that I ever found them the last to retire from their post on the field of battle, and the last to murmur on a march or brag in a guard-room. They are naturally grave and serious; but faithful, conscientious, and of an honesty *à toute epreuve*. It is true, that if they have distinguished themselves in other provinces, they certainly have not earned much glory during this war, in their own. The readiness with which they armed, but suffered themselves to be disarmed, seemed to prove as well the loyalty of their intentions, as their incapacity to carry those intentions into execution. The latter circumstance should be rather ascribed, however, to the nature of the country and the Castilian pride, which, although much less obvious than formerly, only lies dormant. Having been unhappily awakened, it caused those divisions and jealousies which proved fatal to them. The old and pompous mottos still preserved beneath coats of arms over the doors of houses sometimes of the meanest appearance, in which, at the present day, there is little more to be seen than the bare walls,

125

and windows closed by an old oak shutter, containing a small aperture, sometimes covered by a sheet of oiled paper, may give some idea of what must have been the pride of their forefathers. I remember one motto in particular, of the family of the Bellascos, which is blasphemously ridiculous:

"Antes que Dios fuesse Dios,
O que el sol illuminaba los peñascos,
Ya era noble la Casa de los Bellascos."

"Before God was God,
Or the sun shone upon the rocks,
Already was the House of the Bellascos noble."

These feelings of pride had, however, one good effect - they encouraged notions of chivalry and a sense of honour, before Cervantes did his best to put them to the rout. The Castilian gentleman was the mirror of truth, high bearing, and generosity, which tempered the cruelty that seems always to tinge the blood of those born beneath the sun of a southern sky. Similar traits may still be traced in the character of the Castilian. Nevertheless, in those instances in which his ancient spirit of chivalry has abandoned the Castilian gentleman, he quickly dwindles in the country to a level with the peasant, and in the town becomes that venal thing of selfishness and numbers, with which, when the absolute reign of steam and railroads is arrived, and the world becomes one large smoky city, Hume would people his Utopia.

When Rodil arrived in Navarre, to take the command of the army, he had with him a force of 10,000 men, which, with the late reinforcements, augmented the army under his orders to about 40,000 men, mostly picked troops, perfectly armed and appointed, and including a large portion of veterans who had fought in the war of the Constitution. His own division had, moreover, returned fresh from a bloodless but successful campaign. So manifest a superiority inspired his party with the most sanguine anticipations; and it seemed almost a folly to doubt of their success. Universal gloom and terror spread through the country, damping the hopes which the presence of the King had excited. When it is considered that Rodil's army had only to contend with from 5-6,000 men, all the force which Zumalacarregui then had under his command, and from whom succour and supplies (excepting a little saltpetre that was smuggled over the frontier) were cut off by Harispe's division on one side, and by the English and French fleets on the other, there was nothing overstrained or bombastic in the proclamation which their Commander issued on crossing the Ebro, from his headquarters at Mendavia; although, when he recrossed that river in disgrace, dismissed from the command of the miserable remains of his once fine army, it would have been a bitter sarcasm to have placed the same document under his eye. In this address to the Navarrese, Biscayans, Alavese, and Guipuscoans, he offered pardon to all those who would immediately lay down their arms, and give up the ringleaders and comrades, as some proof of the sincerity of their repentance.

"He would not" he added, "have condescended to offer them peace and pardon, unless he had been confident in his own strength and immense resources. They had seen the enthusiasm and martial bearing of the troops under his command. Lest they might take his clemency for a sign of weakness, he assured them, however, that while he extended one hand towards them in mercy, he upheld in the other the sword of vengeance, which should fall inexorably on the heads of the obstinate." After showing them their hopeless condition, he menaced them with annihilation, if they did not choose the alternative of submission. Rodil had a wide and easily-earned reputation, from having terminated the war in Portugal, by his mere appearance in that country. By his campaign in South America, he had acquired the character of being energetic and unsparing of human blood in the pursuance of his designs.

Amongst several stories of the same nature, I remember often hearing from officers in our army who had served with him, the following anecdote. During his defence of the castle of Callao, in Peru, in which he held out most gallantly, till everything was knocked to pieces, and the garrison had eaten every cat and rat in the fortress, he was informed that some of his men, worn out by famine and fatigue, had entered into a conspiracy to surrender the place to the enemy, and thus end their misery. Rodil assembled the whole garrison next morning, and harangued them to this effect – "That, having resolved to defend the castle to the last extremity, he had determined to dismiss all those who were either unwilling or unable to support the privations of a siege; and that those who felt inclined to surrender to the enemy had only to step out of the ranks." More than a third of the men eagerly pressed forward: they were commanded to lay down their arms and accoutrements, and to form in line opposite to those who remained firm. Rodil then ordered the latter to level and fire! He was obeyed - the recreants were butchered without remorse by their comrades on the spot; and Rodil retired, with the assurance that he had now a faithful garrison.

After burning the monasteries of Beira, Ronscevallos, and many others, under the pretence that the monks who lived in those edifices had favoured the Carlists - although, in truth, they had done no such thing, until these injuries proved that their neutrality availed them nothing - he swept the Bastan, and fortified the hospital at Elisondo. Then dividing his army into numerous columns, he pursued both Zumalacarregui and the King, who had been advised to separate from his General, and continue with a small force, flying from the enemy under the direction of Eraso, who, with singular skill and activity, always managed to elude pursuit. While Zumalacarregui was preparing to give the enemy such occupation as would make them leave his royal master in comparative quiet, the army of Rodil being then all fresh and enthusiastic, and meeting with scarcely any opposition, followed with the utmost vigour; and the King's life was saved more than once by a hair-breadth escape - sometimes pursued day and night by several columns, the insignificant numbers he had with him, alone enabled him to elude his persecutors, his route being thereby more easily concealed. It is not easy to conceive all the unfortunate monarch suffered at this time, aroused at all hours to undertake long arduous marches during every inclemency of the weather, through snow and rain, and by roads where half the time it was impossible to proceed otherwise than on foot. Although several times in imminent danger, and advised to enter France, he always evinced the same firm determination of conquering back his crown, or of dying in the contest for it on the soil of Spain.

On one occasion Rodil had tracked him to a mountain which he surrounded with 9000 men. So actively had the pursuit and search been carried on, that a young officer of artillery, Don Tomas Reyna, who had been endeavouring to manufacture a few pieces of artillery in the mountains, was also obliged to fly with his artisans and artillerymen. The night fortunately was dark and stormy; the King on one side with about 100 followers, and Reyna on the other, were wandering about benumbed by the small piercing rain, and obliged to retrace their steps many times on account of having met with the bivouac fires of the Christinos. At last the two fugitive parties approached each other. Reyna, exhausted from fatigue and finding himself close upon what he imagined to be a patrol of the enemy's horse, was just about ordering his men to fire, when fortunately a mutual recognition took place. The fidelity of the peasantry, who knew that the King was in such a strait, saved him by leading him out of danger during the night.

All effort to overtake the King having proved useless, and his majesty having been ultimately extricated from further peril by Zumalacarregui, who was rapidly destroying the Christino divisions in detail, Rodil, as the readiest means of concluding the war, directed all his attention to attacking and crushing that chief. He carried his resolution into execution with so much perseverance and vigour, that it required all the determination of the Carlist leader and the Navarrese to baffle his efforts. Frequently the royal

129

army had to march for 16, 18, and 23 hours successively. On one occasion Zumalacarregui being with the King, I remember that the march continued 20 hours, no halt for above 25 minutes being made during this time, and the soldiers scarcely quitting their arms. At daybreak, after this harassing march, we found ourselves in the very village from which we had started the preceding morning, two of the enemy's divisions having in the meanwhile passed through it! Another time we were also with the King, and halted at nightfall, after a long day of fatigue, on a mountain where there was nothing but a shepherd's hut. The King slept in the only room, if such it could be called, which the hut contained. His ministers retired to the stable, and Zumalacarregui, like the rest of his army, stretched himself on his cloak beneath a tree.

Rodil marked his way with fire and blood. Quesada had indeed shot the sick and wounded Carlists who had fallen into his hands; but the former commenced that persecution of the inhabitants which the Christino generals who succeeded him afterwards continued. The houses that had afforded a shelter to the fugitive monarch, which it was not in the power of their occupiers to refuse, were burned to the ground. The alcaldes were shot for not delivering up rations which had been anticipated by the Carlists, or for not acquainting the Christinos with the movements of the insurgents, from whom they would have met the same fate for acting as spies. The injustice and cruelty of the Queen's troops had, however, the effect of rousing such as had hitherto been lukewarm; and from infancy to age all became partisans of the King. Women, children, and old men, all took an active part in the insurrection watching, carrying information, and assisting by every means in their power. In a mountain warfare they became powerful auxiliaries.

On passing through a village in the Rivera, I was once much amused at the surprise of an officer. Being on half-pay at Madrid, he was forced to join a corps which was marching to the army of the north; but his opinions being decidedly Carlist, he took the first opportunity of passing over to the King before he had been obliged to draw his sword against him. On seeing the absolute frenzy of the inhabitants, and hearing all the bells ringing, and beholding the women in their best attire, coming out to meet us at a distance from the village, stunning us with their questions for brothers, lovers, and relations, and almost dragging us from our horses to partake of wine, chocolate, or some refreshment, while handkerchiefs, shawls, and curtains were waving from the windows, and flowers were showering down upon us as we rode along, his astonishment knew no bounds; he could not help contrasting our reception with, that which the Christino troops experienced the last time they had passed through the same place. "Then," said he, "a dead silence reigned in the village, broken only by the tramp of our horses' feet; it seemed like a deserted spot; the doors were all closed; a few old crones only looking on with their blear eyes, and some children hovering about the corners of the street. Here and there a head might be popped out of a window above, but was as quickly withdrawn again. If our soldiers asked for wine, no one knew where any was to be obtained; and they veiled their antipathy to us under an appearance of intractable stupidity. The very children, who are now chattering so fast, when we inquired where the *Factiosos* had last been in the village, did not know what we meant, or had never seen them. The soldiers and officers, uttering' an oath against the ill-licked cubs, would pass on." In all probability, immediately after the column had gone through, the *partida*, which had left in the morning, on returning would be surrounded by 20 urchins, who had made observations concerning the *Negros* of a precocious shrewdness and gravity, acquired during the unquiet times in which they lived. They communicated everything eagerly to the *Carlistas*, as they vulgarly mispronounce the word.

I must here mention an anecdote among innumerable others of the same kind. The Christinos being informed that a wounded Carlist was concealed by an old man at Sumbillo, Rodil had him

131

arrested and led out to be shot. After making his confession, his eyes were bound, and he was placed on his knees. When he felt the cold iron of the muskets on his breast, he was promised his life if he would give up the concealed rebel; but he still protested his entire ignorance as to the place where he was to be found. The officer at last, persuaded by his earnest assurances, released him, saying, "If he does not know, he cannot tell." The column having next day marched on, the wounded soldier was seen sitting at the old man's door as usual.

Although not playing so conspicuous a part as formerly, the Spanish barber holds still a marked and distinct place in society; he is not precisely what Cervantes or Le Sage has painted him, nor yet the bustling Figaro; he may be best described as a mixture of all these characters. Unfortunately the march of intellect has made too many of the inhabitants of the towns practitioners on their own chins so that within the walls of cities he has lost much of his importance and all the means which the monopoly of that part of the male toilet formerly afforded him for penetrating everywhere and into everything, and carrying on those intrigues which rendered him a personage of so much consideration. In the country, however, he has preserved more of his ancient character; there he is still the wit, the orator, the man of physic, and the confidant of the youth of both sexes. He has advice and hope for the young, scandal for ladies of a maturer age, and a choice collection of local anecdotes, strange news, and witty sayings, too often, unfortunately, sharper than his razors, for the travelling patient who may be under his hands, as well as for his staid and sober customers. The gravity, becoming a disciple of Aesculapius, seems mingled with a certain degree of facetiousness; and, after the curate, he is generally treated with vast respect by the community.

There are, however, various grades, shades, and distinctions of *barberos*; and though in a very inferior capacity, the army-barber is not the least diverting. One is allowed for each company or troop: sometimes he is a soldier and sometimes only follows with the canteen women; but he is always easily recognised by his iron basin and, generally, his guitar. The barber is a privileged person, and therefore allowed to carry all his shoulders would bear. Even when the regulation, limiting the contents of the soldier's morrals to a shirt and a pair of sandals, was most strictly enforced, I have seen some who, besides one of the enemy's knapsacks, their own canvas bag, and a loaf of bread fastened to it by means of a hole bored in the centre, through which the strap was passed, had their basin and guitar, and yet marched along as merrily as the rest. Many a time, I recollect, when we were formed and awaiting the enemy, the day being whiled away by the guitars which these disciples of the strop and the muses seldom failed to strike, to kill the heavy hours we spent in patient expectation of the enemy's uncertain movements.

After the affair of *Alsassua*, when a number of prisoners had been shot, and the remainder were passing before Zumalacarregui, scarcely anticipating a better fate, he rather sternly questioned several as to "Why they had taken arms against their lawful sovereign?" One of them, with a very pitiful countenance, replied, "That when his comrades had been drafted into the guards, he had only been induced to follow them from professional motives, and for a similar reason found himself on the field, being barber to the company." The General put his hand to his chin, and finding that it afforded a fair opportunity for the exercise of the artist's talent, with the confidence he usually displayed, immediately trusted his throat to the razor of the prisoner, who performed so much to his satisfaction, that he was appointed to the especial honour of shaving him, preserving the rank of serjeant which he had held. This barber's name was Robledo: he was a little, pale, thin man, and a most notorious coward, always escaping, when any action came on, from the company of Guides to which he belonged. The General having been informed of this, one day when the barber was shaving him (and, seeing his master in a good humour, was diverting him with

133

his usual drollery) said, "So, Robledo, I hear you distinguished yourself in the last action?" "General," quoth the barber, "I am a living instance of what a circumstantial thing is valour. I certainly did run away, but it was because my eye caught at that moment a stone, and I thought how much better it was to have it said, '*Aqui Robledo se escappo*' - Here Robledo ran away, than that they should write upon it, '*Aqui Robledo murio,*' - Here Robledo died."

The success which at first attended Zumalacarregui was confined to his own army; afterwards it extended only to the divisions immediately under his command. Carnicer, a chief, something in Merino's style, but still perfectly independent of Zumalacarregui, and who had made some progress in Arragon and Catalonia, was defeated and taken afterwards in Castille, where he suffered death. Zavala and the brigadier Armencha were also defeated by Espartero, near Bermeo: on that occasion Armencha was taken. He had dismounted to rally his troops, and his servant escaped during the confusion with his horse. His aide-de-camp was killed by his side. Armencha, who was a great friend of Valdespina, was a rich proprietor of Lequieto[71], and perhaps the most influential person in Biscay and Guipuscoa. He was shot at Bilboa on the 14th. April, and suffered with the courage of a soldier. The following is the account of him given me by an old French soldier now become an artisan in the suburbs of that town, who was shut out while we were besieging it in June, 1835, and who had been present at the execution.

"The condemned was led out between a monk and a curate, escorted by a detachment of the line, which was in waiting at the gates of the prison: - excepting for the *fanfaronnade* of this ceremony, and a crucifix he held in his hands, which, however, is the custom for all criminals in Spain, he behaved as manfully as one of the *Grande Armée* could have done. His attitude was calm, and sometimes his countenance assumed even a contemptuous expression, although a man may be excused for looking a little

---

[71] Lekeitio, population today 7,250

134

serious when his *feuille de route* is given him for such a long journey, and he is going where no furlough is to be expected. He marched, Sir, with as firm and assured a step as one of the *grenadiers de la garde*, and had a countenance as unclouded as if he had been invited to a wedding; although two drums and a fife, playing a dead march all the way to the Campo Valentino, would have been ugly music for a bride to have danced to. A lady very fashionably dressed stepped out from the crowd, and, waving her little white hand in his face, applied several insulting epithets to him. *Passez pour la Dame*; but several Urbanos were unmanly enough to utter some jokes on his situation[72]. In France, would the guard have allowed a *pekin* to do so, even if they had been escorting Sir Hudson Lowe? Armencha bore it like a *militaire*, smiled, and passed on. On his arriving at the Campo Valentino, he coolly inquired of the officer where he must place himself, and received the volley without the approach of death having discomposed one muscle of his face." The Frenchman's picture of the scene was so characteristic that I noted it down nearly word for word. It was a few days after this that Leopold O'Donnel, Comte de Labisbal, suffered death at the hands of the Carlists.

---

[72] However, the English liberal sympathiser John Francis Bacon wrote that he was present and that the woman in question had borne a child to Brigadier Armencha and was asking if he had made arrangements for the child's benefit. His reply was that she was not to worry, he had arranged everything.

The action at Alsasua, April 22nd. 1834

CHAPTER IX.

Carandolet - Surprise at San Faustus - Count Via Manuel - A Spanish Grandee taken - Shot - Attempt to surprise Echari-Arenas - Failure - Punishment of two Companies for cowardice - Attack on Viana - Interview with Zumalacarregui - Punishment of his Quartermaster - Punishment of a Deserter - Mutiny suppressed - Maicasco disgraced - Curate of Allio.

While Rodil was thus making war on the peasantry and monks, the Carlist leader was not idle, and struck a blow which caused the Queen's general some uneasiness. It was the surprise of Carandolet[73] and his total defeat. This general, I believe a Frenchman by birth, was throughout so unfortunate in all his encounters with Zumalacarregui, that his name became proverbial in the royal army for awkwardness or misfortune. To give an example of this, a soldier of the Battalion of Guides - who, on account of his remarkable hideousness and deformity, might have represented the Quasimodo of Notre Dame de Paris, but being, notwithstanding, of a very amorous disposition, generally bore the marks of a pair of nails, which he had received in endeavouring to ravish a kiss from the country damsels - was called, on account of his little success, General Carandolet. I remember, also, that an old misshapen gun dug up in Biscay, which could never be brought to bear where it was required, on account of the shot varying sometimes in one direction, at others in another, was christened by the volunteers by the name of this hapless general, the Carandolet. Not dreaming of any surprise or encounter with the enemy, when it was reported that the insurgent army was so closely pressed by Rodil, that he could scarcely hope to be in with his division for the death, if even the Carlists and their celebrated leader were not already long brought to bay, Carandolet had no hesitation in traversing a part of the country which had been so completely swept by the Queen's army, that it was fancied no danger could possibly exist. His escort consisted of about 700 men: with him

---

[73] Baron Luis Angel de Carandolet

137

were a number of officers of distinction, sent to join the army of the North, and amongst others the Count of Via Manuel, a Spanish grandee of the first class, who was coming to serve from inclination, with the rank of Colonel. Zumalacarrcgui, acquainted with their movements, by a long and secret march placed himself in ambuscade near the rocks of San Faustus, within a short distance of Abarzuza, where they were necessarily obliged to pass, intending to penetrate by the Val de Olio into the plain of Pampeluna and Huarte.

The rocks of San Faustus[74] rise in one of those wild districts where dense patches of wood fringing the very edge of the road, and gigantic masses of stone, detached from the parent rock, and fixed by their own weight in the soil, afford a position highly favourable for an ambuscade. So well had Zumalacarreomi concealed his march, and the force he had in ambush, that the horsemen of the vanguard had already passed unsuspectingly without perceiving anything - the rest followed singing the song of *Muera Don Carlos - Viva la Reyna!* At this moment a peasant on the lookout appeared on the mountain just before them, as if watching the movement of the advancing column. The foremost horsemen, probably without much hope that he would obey their injunctions, called out to him, as they were wont to most of the peasantry of the provinces, *"Baja-te! Queres bajar, Falso! Factioso"* - Come down - down directly, traitor! rebel! The peasant disappeared; but at that moment, right and left of the column, the rocks rung to the volley of musketry, and the discharge fatally announced to them that they had fallen into the jaws of the lion.

In an instant Zumalacarregui, and the four battalions which had been lying in ambuscade, rushed upon them at the bayonet. Taken by surprise, surrounded on all sides, it became nothing but a massacre. Nearly all his staff, and the officers with Carandolet, were either killed or taken, although he himself effected his escape, owing to the fleetness of his charger, through volleys of musketry;

---

[74] Las Peñas de San Fausto. The Ambush of San Fausto took place on 19th. August 1834.

138

a few isolated individuals also got away during the confusion, from the slaughter, and afterwards joined him; but, excepting these, the destruction of his little column was complete. The Conde de Via Manuel, whose horse had been killed at the first discharge, had mounted successively two others, led by his domestics, and had endeavoured to follow Carandolet, but they were both shot under him, and he was taken with 15 other officers. Amongst the dead were several Colonels and the Brig. General Haranoz, then commanding the provincial regiment of Valladolid. Thus, either from the first onset, or unable to escape from the pursuit of the Carlists, nearly all the little column perished; a considerable sum of money, important papers, and many mule loads of military equipment fell into the hands of the former.

Of all the prisoners Via Manuel behaved with most frankness and firmness, when led before the Royalist General. He stated "that he always had and would entertain liberal opinions, which he considered it his duty to defend and diffuse, and for which he had come voluntarily to fight; that he was aware that those who served the government had no right to expect mercy from the Carlists; but if mercy were shown him, he would give his word to take no further part against them, and consider his political life as concluded."

Zumalacarregui was so well pleased with the openness of his character, that, although he followed as a prisoner, he was invited to his table, and treated with every distinction; and he wrote to Rodil, offering to exchange Via Manuel and others for an officer and some volunteers taken a few days before, giving man for man, and waiving the difference of Via Manuel's rank. This he never doubted a moment of Rodil's accepting. They were at dinner, at Lecumberri[75] when his answer was brought in to Zumalacarregui that note contained only the following sentence: "The rebels taken have suffered death already." This was clearly the sentence of the prisoner. Zumalacarregui handed it over to him with the same

---

[75] Population 1500 today

139

sang-froid with which he would probably have received it had it been the message of his own fate. Via Manuel changed colour. His host politely, but firmly, expressed his regret at being obliged to perform so unpleasant a duty, but informed him that he might be with his confessor till sunrise. His life had been spared so long, that this intelligence came like a thunderstroke on the unhappy grandee. At his request Zumalacarregui consented to delay his execution while he sent a message to the King intreating his clemency. He returned with the answer, that when soldiers and officers of inferior rank taken with arms in their hands had suffered death, it was impossible to pardon a Spanish grandee. Via Manuel was shot at Lecumberri but did not die so well as his deportment at first announced - probably it was the shock of the sudden disappointment, after he had so long entertained hopes of life, which had unnerved him.

I must not omit to mention a singular instance of fidelity. Shortly after his death a serjeant, as he stated himself to be, and as his galons indicated, deserted to us, and was placed in a company of Guides; he afterwards surprised and stabbed a sentinel and disappeared. We were informed by other deserters, some months afterwards, that this very individual was a servant of Via Manuel's, who took this mode of communicating with his master, but arrived a day too late, and having acquired the certainty of his execution, on the first opportunity carried back the news of it, and some relics of his lord, which he had bought from the soldiers who shot him.

After the defeats of Quesada, what Zumalacarregui chiefly wanted was artillery, particularly when Rodil adopted the system of fortifying every important town and village; and for the want of even a single field-piece, the Carlists were obliged to turn away from mere crenelled houses, and found themselves absolutely in the situation of those primitive warriors who, unacquainted with the composition and effect of gunpowder, found the stone walls of any building or castle an almost insurmountable barrier. Not only were the Carlists without cannon, but devoid even of the means which the ingenuity of our forefathers had in some measure substituted for it. To obtain this necessary sinew of modern warfare, Zumalacarregui applied all his attention; and the old spy Ximenes, of Villafranca, whom I shall afterwards have occasion to mention, was despatched to see if none of the Christino officers could be bought over to betray some place containing what was so indispensable to his army.

At Echari-Arenas, one of the central points of the Borunda, where almost every village had been garrisoned, he had at last succeeded in inducing two brothers, named Mansano, lieutenants of the regiment of provincials of Valladolid, who had always been adverse to the cause they were fighting for, to agree to deliver up the place. When their turn came to be on guard, they were to sally with a few soldiers on whom they could depend, and having opened the gates, on a given signal, admit the Carlists. The place, which was garrisoned by about 500 men, contained 4,000 muskets, six guns, and numerous military stores, the benefit, of which would, at that period of the war, have been immense to the Carlists. Echari-Arenas[76] is a large village divided by a wide street running at right angles from the Royal Road, which is masked from it by a *posada* or inn, and a group of six or seven houses. These had been all crenelled, tambours built round them, and the whole, surrounded by a deep ditch, was still further secured by a strong double palisade; each side was swept by a four or 8-pounder. A pitch-dark night, when the confederates were on guard, was chosen. Several battalions were roused without beat of drum, and marching across the heath which extends from Arbissu to Echari-Arenas, were formed in silence in the village. Two companies of Guides, and two of the 3rd. Battalion of Navarre were picked out to enter with fixed bayonets and take possession of the place the instant the gates should be opened. The signal agreed on was the mewing of a cat. A long silence ensued, but on its being repeated, it was answered by the confederates. By some means, in the two

---

[76] Etxarri-Aranatz, today a bascophone village of some 2,500 inhabitants

companies of Guides whispers of treachery on the part of the Christinos had got afloat, just before they were ordered to advance, and the ditch having been forgotten, upwards of 20 stumbled into it. The gate was already opened, and the two lieutenants and several soldiers, with a covered lantern, had already sallied, when some one, on hearing the noise of those falling into the ditch, shouted out "treachery!" of which the men had already some vague apprehensions; on this those behind, seized with a sudden panic, made a discharge on the gate, and killed one of the lieutenants, who thus received the reward of the dishonourable action he was committing; they then took to a precipitate flight from before the works. The sentinel, finding that he was so ill received, suspected, probably, that the Carlists intended to pay one kind of treachery by another, or that some of the garrison, not in the plot, had already reached the gate; it was, in consequence, immediately closed. The surviving lieutenant, and the soldiers that were excluded, cried cut, "It is all a mistake! - we are shut out:" it was, after a little while, reopened.

As the Royalists had given back in so cowardly a manner, they could not take advantage of it; the opportunity was lost, and as the garrison was awakened by the report of the shots, they rushed to their guns, and in the darkness opened fire in every direction. Mansano, however, and the soldiers with him, effected their escape. The fury of Zumalacarregui knew no bounds at the disgraceful conduct of the two companies. In the first moment of his anger he was going to shoot all the commissioned and non-commissioned officers; but, on inquiry, it was found that they had fled the last, if that was an extenuation. They were, however, publicly degraded, and reproached in the most bitter terms, for their cowardice before the whole army. The companies were forced to draw lots for one man in each to suffer death, as an example to the army. Of the two on whom the lot fell, unfortunately one individual perhaps least deserved it of any in the company: they were both shot. This may seem a gratuitous piece of cruelty; but it was only by acts of such ruthless severity that it was possible to struggle against the difficulties that surrounded the early Carlist leaders, and check the insubordination and unsteadiness of the men. The disgraced captains of the two companies, a little while after, sent in from their retreat to the General a most humble petition, praying that they might be permitted to enter the ranks as the last soldiers of the army. On reading the petition, Zumalacarregui took up his pen, and dashed across it - "*Que no hai lugar por cobardes.*" - There is no room for cowards. Some time after, however, they enlisted privately, and, step by step, worked their way up of course favoured by the colonels and officers who recommended them, and were well acquainted with their story.

Zumalacarregui, after eluding the pursuit of Rodil, till the latter was glad to take breathing time, his army being in a dreadfully exhausted condition, reached the small town of Santa Cruz de Campezzu[77], the 3rd. September; thus getting entirely to the south of the army of operations of his opponent, and on the verge of the flat lands of the Ribera. Here, being informed that Carandolet was, with 800 foot, and the Regiment of Caçadores[78] of the Royal Guard, unsuspectingly in Viana, a town on this side of the Ebro, but on the extreme frontier of Castille and Alava, he resolved on attempting another surprise. Zumalacarregui and his disposable force were supposed to be then so closely pursued by Rodil, that his appearance was never dreamed of, particularly as he had, before reaching Viana, to descend into the plains 13 or 14 miles away from the mountains, where he was exposed to certain destruction, if any division of Rodil's came on his rear, as it could cut him off with the greatest facility. Well knowing, however, the state of his opponent's force, and that before Rodil could discover his track or obtain any intelligence of his movement, so skilfully

---

[77] Santa Cruz de Campezo, in Alava, current population just under 1,200.

[78] Literally, huntsmen. As in France and Germany the term is used to refer to light infantry or light horse. These were the latter.

and rapidly had he concealed his march, he would be in safety, he moved on the 4th. November[79] from Santa Cruz, with his five battalions and all his cavalry, consisting then of only 200 lancers, to Viana. The distance, about 16 miles, was traversed in an incredibly short space of time; his vanguard stopping all the peasants they met. Viana covers a rising ground in the centre of a large plain; the streets, as in all old Spanish towns, are narrow, and a few trenches had been dug, and barricades thrown up in the streets, for the protection of a handful of men who were sometimes left to crarrison it; so that if Carandolet had properly disposed his men, they might easily have baffled the attempt of between three and 4,000 Carlists to enter, at least for the few hours they could have tarried in the plain. So great was their security, that the possibility of its being a hostile force, even when the glitter of the muskets of the advancing column was seen in the distance, does not appear for a moment to have struck the enemy: gradually, however, it drew so near, that there was no mistaking the reality, and the garrison was hastily turned out, and formed in front of the town. The good order in which the Carlists were led on, their enthusiasm, and the superiority of their numbers, did not long render the struggle doubtful; the infantry directly gave way. The Caçadores, attempting to charge, in order to protect their retreat, and to take advantage of an instant confusion in the ranks of the pursuers, were resolutely charged by the small body of Carlist lancers; and, their colonel being killed, were driven back with loss. This was the first affair in which the Navarrese lancers distinguished themselves; at that time, perfect cossacks in appearance, some were without coats, some with handkerchiefs round their heads, many with only one boot or sandal, and some with their spurs lashed on a naked heel. The enormous size and ponderous weight of their lances, which, however, only rendered them more unwieldy, added to their wild and singular aspect, and having triumphed in their first encounter, their appearance became

---

[79] Seems to be a mistake for 4th. September

144

rather terrible than grotesque in the eyes of the Queen's troops, and they were ever after a subject of infinite terror; although most undeservedly so; for, until the arrival of O'Donnel, they were almost as undisciplined and ignorant of all military evolutions as a horde of Bedouins, and owed to the terror they had so unaccountably inspired, and the blind confidence with which they charged, the success they invariably met with. The Lancers of Navarre when O'Donnel died was, however, well mounted, perfectly clothed, equipped and disciplined, and able to go through all the manoeuvres as well as the best regiment of the Queen's army. A wonderful improvement had also taken place in all the cavalry.

The vanquished entered Viana pell-mell - the Carlists at their heels, forcing their way through the streets, which were still feebly defended. The commandant of the 3rd. Battalion had fallen back on reaching a small church on the right of the first plaza that presents itself on entering the town, I believe, called St. Magdalen[80], as the fire was rather galling from the houses. Zumalacarregui, however, coming up, broke him on the spot, and himself led the way: the captain of the grenadier company who followed along side of him had his sword struck out of his hand; but the presence of the General had the desired effect; and the greater part of the houses being taken possession of, the town became one scene of massacre. Some of the cavalry of the enemy who had rallied, got entrapped by the trenches dug in the streets, and, as the Carlist cavalry wisely had been kept out, were picked off one by one by the infantry. Several houses filled by the enemy refused to surrender; these were set fire to by Barrez, the second of three brothers of that name I shall have hereafter occasion to mention. The remnant of the fugitives reached the convent, a large and strongly-built edifice on a plaza at the further end of the town: here they barricaded themselves; and every preparation was made to burn them out, when intelligence having reached

---

[80] Cesare Borgia is buried there

Zumalacarregui that a reinforcement of several thousand men was marching from Logrono, which was but at a short distance, he quickly retired. He left upwards of 400 of the enemy dead in the streets and before the place, and carried off above 100 prisoners and 200 horses; had there been time to collect those that were running loose, he might have taken many more. The division that came to the relief of Carandolet saw him retire in such good order, that they did not venture to pursue, and he was allowed, unmolested, to take the road to the mountains with his prisoners.

I first saw Zumalacarregui, after this affair, in some village of the Beruesa. It was almost dark when I dismounted before the door of the house where he was lodged. The serjeant of the guard attempted to disarm me before I was admitted, by taking a pair of pistols I carried in my red sash for I had adopted the Basque costume. Not immediately understanding his motive, I resisted; some altercation ensued, when the voice of a person in the balcony above us authoritatively ordered him to let me pass. I was ushered into a room which was unoccupied, excepting by the person who came in from the balcony; in a small adjoining chamber two secretaries were writing. I was asked by this person, whose features I could not then distinguish, but whom, if I could have seen, from his broad shoulders and the habitual stoop, I should instantly have recognized even in the darkness, as Zumalacarregui, whom I wanted, in a manner rather stern and abrupt. I replied, that I wished to see the Carlist General. He then asked me what I came for; I answered, that it was my intention to go on to the King's quarters, but as I was well mounted and armed, until Zumalacarregui joined the wandering court, I would follow his army, on receiving his permission, as volunteer. I spoke to him at some length, making several complaints of different functionaries, of whom I spoke rather freely, which seemed to please him. I perceived that he immediately grew impatient at everything that did not come directly to the point as during our conversation, I kept inquiring if I could not see Zumalacarregui: at last he said, "I am

146

Zumalacarregui," and dismissed rather more graciously than he had received me. I afterwards learned that I had made a favourable impression on him; the manner in which I spoke to him, and the circumstance of my following as a volunteer for some time after, were the surest roads to his favour. He used to say that he always "loved best the man who trusted to his sword as a letter of recommendation;" and officers who brought introductions from his friends, from the ministers, or from his wife, always saw the letters thrown aside, and were often so themselves.

The manner in which Zumalacarregui punished his quartermaster-general was highly characteristic of that prompt and half-barbarian justice he so summarily administered, and which rendered him so popular with the soldier. We were stationed in the village of Decastillo, when a fresh battalion which had come a great distance, marched in at beat of drum. Zumalacarregui, who was dictating to his secretary, therefore knew of their arrival. It was already raining; and after the soldiers had waited an unreasonable time for the purpose of being quartered, as it now begun to pour down in torrents, the men made a rush towards the doors of the adjacent houses. At the sudden noise the secretary started on his chair; and the general comes to the window, and seeing that the battalion was not yet disposed of, he called up all the officers, and inquired, in a voice of thunder, why their men were not yet lodged. The colonel represented that he was as wet as those under his orders; but that the "*bolletas*" (billets), which had been retarded because the aposentador was at dinner when they arrived, would be ready immediately. "Oh! he was at dinner," said the General, "while the troops were getting wet through in the street: fetch me that rascally quartermaster instantly!" He then ordered the llamada or appeal to be beat. The poor aposentador came pale and trembling; and when he saw that the troops were formed, and heard the order given to lead him out, he firmly believed that his last hour was come, and uttered more than one pious ejaculation, expecting every moment to be turned over to his confessor. In the middle of

147

the square is a large basin and fountain: before this, having, from his balcony degraded him from his office, he ordered him to kneel, and then caused two enormous buckets of water to be poured upon him, to the infinite merriment of the soldiers. After witnessing this ceremony, he retired as gravely as if he had been assisting at a christening.

Zumalacarregrui had taken the command of the Carlists in the autumn. He had none but volunteers. While the weather was fine - and that season is in Spain perhaps the most delightful of the year - things went on well enough; but when the winter came, with its cold winds - its storms of snow and rain, and the comparative scarcity of everything, he found himself abandoned by half his followers, who deserted home. At that moment, to enact any regulation to punish desertion, might entirely have alienated the affections of the mountaineers; he therefore managed for a time with the handful of men which the caprice of his followers had left him. The fine weather returning, and a few blows having been struck successfully against the enemy, the peasantry again flocked to his standard in increased numbers: he then published an order, that every man returning home without furlough, a deserter in time of war, as such should be punished with death. This had the desired effect. I do not mean to deny that occasional instances of irregularity did occur: when the men were passing near their own village, they would skulk home, and after spending a day or two, would join us by a march of sometimes 50 or 60 miles, but this was winked at by their captains, at whose mercy they were. On one occasion, when we were in Alegria, an example was to have been made. It was of a corporal, a very brave fellow, but who had aggravated his offence by enticing two men of his *escuadre* away with him; he was sentenced by the court-martial to death, and all the troops in and about Alegria were drawn out to witness the execution. The grave was dug on the plaza, before the mairie, in which he was confined. At the hour appointed, he was led out between two ecclesiastics, with whom he had spent the night

148

preparing for eternity. When on the ground, according to custom, his sentence was read by the adjutant, and to the surprise of every one, mitigated to 500 *palos* or strokes with a stick, which were immediately administered. This perhaps was not a more severe punishment than 20 lashes would have been as inflicted in the English army; and a man very seldom faints under this number, although no intermission takes place between the blows.

Perhaps the most serious difficulty in which Zumalacarregui ever found himself was, however, on one occasion when money was so scarce that the pay of the men was a month in arrear, and at that moment by some mischance they were two days without rations of wine. Two battalions were quartered in the same village as the general - one was the third of Navarre; but I do not precisely remember whether the other was the battalion of Guides. On going to the factors at the distribution of provisions, and finding that a second day they were without wine, and had no money to buy any, they no longer concealed their discontent, but went, under the general's window murmuring, and by degrees shouting, *La paja! la paja!* - the pay! the pay! and threatening to disband; in short, the two battalions were in a complete state of mutiny. The officers, by giving them assurances that on the morrow they would be paid, contrived to disperse them at a late hour of the night. The general sent then to the royal quarters, to say that a little money must be sent at any sacrifice. Early the next morning groups of soldiers were lounging about, and their cries recommenced under his window. The drum immediate beat to order, and while it was read Zumalacarregui placed himself at the balcony. This order was as follows: first, that each and every one who publicly expressed his discontent, or cried out for pay, which only the Navarrese had hitherto ever received, should immediately be arrested and shot; secondly, as a punishment for their insubordinate behaviour, although it had been the intention of the Commander in Chief to have paid them that day when the other battalions of the army received their arrears, these two should receive nothing for a

149

fortnight, during which term their pay should be forfeited. The crowd was instantly silenced, and retired somewhat silly and abashed; the troops in the surrounding villages received both their pay and wine, these two their half rations of wine only. Not a syllable further was uttered by the malcontents, for Zumalacarregui was known to be a man of his word by all his army. This was the first and last time that anything resembling a mutiny occurred, and although on a long march the soldiers would sometimes grumble, their complaints were always uttered in a very subdued tone when within hearing of *Uncle Thomas*. Everything he could do for the soldier he did, and he was accordingly beloved; but he always held them in with the same rigid hand. Justice he promptly administered.

After the battle of Vittoria a soldier stepped out of the ranks, and complained that 40oz of gold, about £120, which he had taken from a dead officer of the Christinos, had been seized by one of the staff under pretext that all arms, horses, and money taken belonged to the king. The officer charged with this act was chiefly known in the army under his soubriquet of Malcasco or the headstrong; he was one of those characters who, in the ferment of unquiet times, are often borne upwards; he had long been celebrated as the most notoriously quarrelsome and desperate character in the country, and was accused of having, among other misdeeds, shot an alcalde who had once fined him, for which he was condemned, *par contumace*, to the galleys. His present spouse was the widow of an officer in the constitutional army, whom he had killed in the Carascal; it was said, however, in fair fight. During the early part of the insurrection he had rendered the Carlists such services, that his former rank of captain was given him. His countenance, dark and scarred with the marks of innumerable frays, was of most forbidding aspect, and bore the trace of all the brutal passions by which he was swayed. Zumalacarregui immediately inquired what he had done with the soldier's money. He stoutly denied ever having seen the man, and threatened him with the bastonade for his impudence. Another witness now stepped out of the ranks, and corroborated the complainant's statement. Malcasco very coolly said that they were both liars. The sword of Zumalacarregui, who was now convinced of the glaring injustice of the case, in an instant flashed over the head of the criminal, and he swore he would cleave him down to the belt if he did not instantly produce the money. Malcasco, who perhaps dreaded nothing, either in this world or the next, more than the general, instantly flung the purse to the ground, and after this public exposure skulked off muttering between his teeth, like a surly dog deprived of a bone. The soldier was ordered to pick it up, count it, and re-enter the ranks. Malcasco was disgraced, and only in some degree restored to favour on having had his arm broken some time after between Cirauki and Mañeru. Where all men's passions, good and evil, are in the extremes, as in Spain,

"A land
Where law secures not life;"

and they are to a great degree unbridled by the ordinary restraints of society, such characters are unfortunately too often met with. They are less numerous, however, in the ranks of the Carlists than on the other side, as the former were, excepting, in the very first moment, particular not to receive any notoriously bad characters, intending thereby to throw back the slur of brigandage, which the liberals had cast upon them, on themselves. A striking instance of this was their refusing twice the services of the notorious curate of Allio, who was in the habit of making so many excursions from Vittoria, sweeping the plains at the head of 50 or 100 horsemen, and levying rations and carrying away the obnoxious authorities of the villages prisoners; in short, he was quite the Merino of the Christinos. In the commencement of the war he offered to join the Carlists, where a much wider field for his talents would have been opened, as they held possession of the

151

country, but on account, of his infamous and debauched character he was rejected, and immediately joined the Christinos. In truth, he did us most serious mischief. All around Vittoria and Salvatierra *"el cura de Allio"* was the terror of the Carlists. At all times and seasons any stragglers who loitered in the plain were liable to a visitation from him. He was twice, however, very nearly taken, and I had both times the honour of being one of his pursuers. In one instance, we had suddenly come from Alegria, and had nearly cut him off; we saw him with his horsemen in their white cloaks (his detachment being mostly composed of hussars of the princess) scampering across the country, and clearing hedges and ditches like fox-hunters, but to cut him off we must have been exposed to a very warm fire of grape from Vittoria, and we were consequently recalled by the general, much to our regret.

After the death of Zumalacarregui, the warlike curate again made overtures to Brig. General Belingero, who, after O'Donnel's death, commanded the cavalry, and I may say, *en passant,* was acknowledged, by both parties, to be one of the most brilliant cavalry officers in Spain. Don Carlos refused his proffered services again, in which perhaps, as usual, he displayed more integrity than judgment.

CHAPTER X.

Zumalacarregui recrosses the Ebro - Battle on the Plains of Vittoria 27th. October, and defeat of the Queen's Troops - General O'Doyle taken prisoner and shot - Battle of the 28th. and defeat of Osma.

I have now come to what may be termed, in every sense of the word, a regular and glorious battle - no longer the defence of a strong position, or a cunning retreat equally ruinous to the enemy, and where often greater numbers perished in detail, but a fair fight on an open field the numbers, it is true, limited, but the slaughter terrible in proportion. Zumalacarregui might be said to have conquered Rodil by his Fabian tactics, and had reduced to a jest the terror his name at first inspired in the revolted populations. He had met him but seldom, and when he did, always retired with advantage, and by rapid and unexpected marches, even when pursued by several columns, had fallen on and defeated the division that least expected him. From his knowledge of the country, and the extraordinary spirit he had excited or awakened in his hardy mountaineers, possessing the faculty of attacking when and where he chose, and defying all pursuit and the most skilful combinations to surround his little army, he had, by degrees, augmented his force, which was entirely equipped and armed from the spoils of that of Rodil, which had wasted to a shadow - having already lost by fatigue, disease, and the constant skirmishes from which they could never derive any advantage, above one-third of their number. Worse than this, they were morally as well as physically beaten; his troops found that in their pursuit of the King, neither plunder was to be obtained, nor laurels gathered, and that nothing but hard blows could be expected from Zumalacarregui, who seemed to thin their ranks with an arm that was beyond their reach, and whose capture they now began to look on as a mere chimera. Under these circumstances the recall of Rodil became necessary. Whilst he was still, however, in the province, Zumalacarregui had crossed the Ebro, and obtained great success at Cenicero and Fuenmayor, where, besides making prisoners of a company of foot, he had surprised a convoy containing, amongst other things valuable to his army, 2,000 muskets. Hearing that General Osma[81] was about to recommence operations and had sallied from Vittoria, by a sudden march he recrossed the Ebro, although Cordova, Lorenzo and Lopez[82], after endeavouring to prevent his leaving Navarre, were now attempting to prevent his return to it, for which purpose they were posted along the banks of the river which divides it from Castille with infinitely superior forces.

He slept at Zuñiga[83], and there learned that Osma was with a strong column in the village of Alegria, which is at about a league and a half from the city of Vittoria, and is distinctly seen on the further end of an immense plain, in the midst of innumerable villages: this plain, narrowing as it takes a north-easterly direction, leads to the town of Salvatierra, at five leagues from the former city, and on the high road to Pampeluna, which, a little farther on, winds through the Borunda. As he knew the intelligence of his arrival at Zuñiga had not probably reached them, he ordered the march to be beat before daybreak: by a rapid movement, leaving the fort of Maëstu considerably on our left, we reached the plain of Salvatierra. Three squadrons of cavalry, three battalions of Navarre, and one of Guides with a division of three more, the 6th. Navarrese, the 3rd. Alavan, and 2nd. Guipuscoan, were sent, considerably on our left, Ituralde having orders to place himself between Vittoria and the enemy's column, which Zumalacarregui had counted on drawing out from Alegria, by skirmishing with the garrison of Salvatierra. The latter was too feeble in reality to sally from the walls against anything but a *partida*; and as they believed that the Carlist army was beyond the Ebro, it was not improbable that they would detach some force to cut the *partida* off, as they

[81] Field-Marshal Joaquin de Osma y Tricio (1772-1835)
[82] Narciso Lopez (1797-1851). Born in Venezuela, he later led an attempt to overthrow Spanish rule in Cuba, whose present-day flag he designed. He was captured and garroted.
[83] 26th. October 1834

would suppose our troops to be. The governor of Salvatierra, who had just sallied forth to conduct a number of political prisoners to Vittoria, as Zumalacarregui's army descended into the plains, was forced precipitately to retrograde; but fearful that the fire of the tirailleurs, although the day was clear, might not perhaps be heard, after driving in the governor, they were sent in the direction of Alegria, still keeping up a discharge, as if skirmishing with an enemy. Zumalacarregui was soon informed that the bait had taken. Not doubting but that it was the governor of Salvatierra, who was either harassed on his route, or driving a few troublesome *partidas* before him, Osma detached the Brig. General O'Doyle with six battalions, some companies of peseteros, and horse and foot carabineers, in all 3,000 picked men, and two mountain-pieces, either to disengage the governor, or to cut off the Carlists, as the case should demand. Zumalacarregui having formed his four battalions in line of battle, supported by his cavalry, in the plain at about two miles from Salvatierra, we boldly but slowly advanced. O'Doyle, who perceived the Carlists so confidently advancing upon him in the plain, although without artillery and scarcely equal in numbers, and already surprised at having fallen in so suddenly with Zumalacarregui, began to suspect that some trap was laid, and therefore resolved to wait the attack of the Royalists in a favourable position. As they did not seem at all inclined to escape, but, on the contrary, were marching straight upon him, he could not be blamed for taking advantage of the ground, and acting on the defensive.

On a little eminence to the left of the high road, going from Salvatierra[84] to Vittoria, and between the former place and a little village which almost touches the highway, called, I believe, Arieta, he took up his position, covering the hill; his left flank being protected by a small wood, his two mountain-pieces from the eminence played into the ranks of the Royalists as they advanced. Zumalacarregui, as soon as he was assured that Ituralde was ready

[84] The twin battles of La Alegria and Venta de Echavarri, which the author calls collectively the Battle of Vittoria, took place on 27th and 28th. October 1834

to fall upon the rear, passed along his line, and finding that the men were all in excellent disposition, gave them a few words of encouragement; the attack had only a short time been commenced by the Guerrillas, when the whole line advanced simultaneously, the Guides demanding with loud cries to be led on at the point of the bayonet. It was a magnificent theatre for a battle-scene for - large as is the plain, every object being thrown out by the surrounding mountains, the eye can discern at a great distance the innumerable objects over which it sweeps - steeples, villages, and convents are scattered on every side, even to the gates of Vittoria. On the left hand, from a hill which only appears dwarfish from its contrast with the Sierra behind it, the old Moorish castle of Ladrones of Guevara, with its picturesque and ruined towers, overlooks the plain; in the background, the town of Salvatierra, with its ancient walls, stretches itself up to the road. It was at the further end of this wide valley that the celebrated battle was fought, and the victory won by the Duke of Wellington, in 1813, and it was now destined to become the scene of a signal overthrow of a division of the regular army of Spain by a handful of enthusiastic mountaineers. At Zuñiga, accounts of the last devastations of Rodil, the burning of villages and cottages, and the massacre of the wounded Carlists, had reached the Carlist army and had, therefore, worked them up to a degree of excitement which accounts for their impetuosity. The great difficulty was to keep them in something like order. Their loud cries of *A ellos! Muera la Reina!* were vigorously answered by the enemy, as well as their fires; but as they advanced, in spite of the volleys of musketry which the whole line of the Liberal army was pouring in, their replies grew fainter although the fire was redoubled. The order which the Carlists preserved, with their impetuosity, their martial bearing, their wild shouts, and the black flags with a death's head and cross bones, seemed to have had an appalling effect on O'Doyle's troops. The Guides, notwithstanding the steady volley kept up, charged in upon and broke a battalion of the 6th. Regiment of the line; the whole of

156

the column gave way as the other Carlist battalions advanced to the charge; and at the same moment Ituralde appeared in sight upon their rear. The General's escort of lancers and the first squadron of Navarre now charging in amongst them, a terrible massacre ensued. The two pieces of artillery were taken, the artillerymen being bayoneted on their guns: and General O'Doyle himself, endeavouring to rally his men, so as to effect some sort of retreat, had his horse shot under him, and was taken prisoner as well as his brother.

The slaughter continued till nightfall, the enraged Royalists giving no quarter, and the night coming on, alone saved the miserable remains of O'Doyle's army. About 400 made their way to the village of Arieta, where they shut themselves up in the houses. About 1,000 were killed, the field for two miles being covered with their dead bodies - the miserable wretches being dragged from the woods and thickets in which they attempted to conceal themselves, and slaughtered by their angry opponents. I remember seeing twelve dead bodies lying together at a ford of the rivulet, between the field and the road. I judge the killed to have been 1,000, or thereabouts; because, after the following day's battle, the different parishes buried 1,740 men; and I do not certainly think that more than 600 were killed on the 28th. If I say that on the first day 50, and on the second 100 Carlists were killed, I am overshooting the mark, as they only had to suffer from the first volleys, having broken the line of the enemy at the bayonet, and the great loss in an action is always when the dispersion of either side takes place. The darkness of the night enabled the wounded, who had dragged themselves into places of concealment, and the remainder of the fugitives, to reach Vittoria; but only one by one, or two by two, so entire had been the defeat, the 400 who had taken refuge in the village being the only group that hung together.

The pursuit had continued so late, that the greater part of the Carlist army was obliged to sleep on the field, and we bivouacked amongst the dead. In the meanwhile, part of the 3rd. battalion of Navarre was detached to attack those who were in the village, where they had barricaded the houses. After firing all night, the Christinos, not choosing to surrender, a quantity of combustibles were collected, and placed against the houses. In the morning, the Christinos sent a parlementary to the captain, who was charged with his company to set fire to the piles; and stated that they had got amongst them the curate, the regidor, and a number of the principal inhabitants, with their wives and children; and that if the Carlists attempted to burn them out, they would commence by putting all these persons to death. The captain, who was a Frenchman, named Sabatier[85], now lt. colonel, and who has often since distinguished himself, sent to Zumalacarregui to know how to proceed. The Carlist General determined to blockade them next day; as they were entirely without provisions, he knew that hunger would force them to surrender. 84 prisoners were brought in, whom the soldiers had made when tired of killing; for, excepting in these few cases, no quarter was given. Even two chaplains of the Queen's army had been slain upon the field, as hitherto all the prisoners taken had been shot by the Christinos, not sparing even the sick and wounded, often as Zumalacarregui had set them the example of pardon. It was supposed that, according to the existing regulation, they would all suffer death; they were, however, remanded, and next day pardoned. O'Doyle, the general of tbe division, his brother, a captain, and several officers, were however shot. Zumalacarregui was inclined to have pardoned him, but amongst the despatches intercepted a few days previous were the minutes of a court-martial held at Vittoria, in which O'Doyle had given his vote for shooting the wounded prisoners. These papers had not yet been destroyed, and the part O'Doyle had taken in this transaction was mentioned to Zumalacarregui by his secretary, who brought them forward; this sealed his fate. O'Doyle, a middle-aged man, was said to be a Swiss; but his extraction, from

---

[85] Alexis Sabatier (1809-1854)

his name, I should imagine to be Irish. He behaved like a brave man on the field, but with less firmness afterwards. When he was led up as a prisoner, a Carlist officer was mean enough to make some insulting observation. O'Doyle replied, "You are bearing arms, but you have never been a soldier, or you would know that a real soldier obeys his orders, if they came from hell itself." The officer was more severely reprimanded by the murmurs of the bystanders. O'Doyle the next morning begged to see the General; and when admitted to on interview, stated that he was a soldier who fought for those who paid him, that the fate of war had thrown him into the hands of the Royalists - and that he would serve them, if admitted to that honour, as faithfully as he had served the Queen. Zumalacarregui answered him briefly, that it was out of his power to spare his life. He then began to implore, with clasped hands, "*La vida, por Dios! por Dios!*" Zumalacarregui turned his head in disgust, and said, "*Un confesor luego*" - to confession; and the wretched man was led out, and, after being half an hour with his confessor, shot; as well as his brother and the other officers. His execution took place on the very field where he had been defeated. Poor O'Doyle's was a melancholy fate, but it is impossible to deny the singular retribution of his punishment. Even a quiet grave was denied him; although he was buried - or rather a little earth and a pile of stones were placed over him, by way of distinction, through the deference which the soldier bears to the rank even of his dead enemies. I remember, on passing three months after near the spot, witnessing the disgusting scene of bodies disinterred, and in most cases cleaned to the bone by the birds and beasts of prey. The dogs, as is often the case near a battlefield, sallied from the adjacent villages at night to feast upon the slain. The pile raised over O'Doyle and his brother had been thrown down, and the two bodies, dragged amongst the stones, were half devoured. What made, the scene of action more appalling was, that the bodies were always stripped of everything excepting the *corbatin,* or leather stock this and the shako being the only part of the equipment the

159

Carlists could never be induced to wear - they would take everything excepting these articles from the dead. I remember seeing in that very plain many skeletons, the flesh having been picked from the bones, but the leather collar still remaining round the neck.

Being either a Sunday or a fête day, Mass had been said in a little hermitage which is upon the field, when Zumalacarregui was informed that all the disposable force was sallying from Vittoria. This was the morning of the 28th. October. Osma, informed of the defeat of his division, but imagining that the number shut up in Arieta was much more considerable, made a desperate push to relieve them. Having still under his orders 4,000 men, he added to this all the disposable force he could collect in Vittoria - peseteros, carabineros, and Urbanos, or national guard, who very unwillingly were forced to march, to the number of about 1,000 more, supported by four pieces of artillery. His best troops had, however, perished the previous day, and many of those that remained were recruits, which he had to lead, under the discouraging circumstances of knowing that their companions in arms had been beaten, and that they were marching against an enemy flushed with victory. Zumalacarregui, having informed his troops that Osma was advancing, inquired whether they would abandon a field yet covered with trophies of their victory; he was answered by cries of *"A ellos! a ellos!"* - meaning, to lead them to the enemy. If, instead of marching to attack them, we had remained in our position, the victory would have been much more complete; but that brought the scene of action much nearer to Vittoria, and rendered their escape easier. Osma bad scarcely time to form in line of battle, when his left and right wing were attacked with an inconceivable impetuosity; on that day I believe our volunteers would have charged anything. The recruits and the national guard gave way directly, and carried confusion into the whole division. Zumalacarregui vigorously pursuing his advantage, in a short time the rout became as general as on the preceding day. The cavalry being ordered to charge, got into a mauvais pas, and arrived too late to take the artillery, which was saved. Osma and his staff only owed their safety to the fleetness of their horses.

The slaughter became very great, when Zumalacarregui spurred into the midst of the pursuers, and cried out loudly, "To give quarter, and not to hurt another Christino," ordering the cry to run from man to man. The rapidity with which he was obeyed, in the midst of a scene of such confusion, has always been a matter of surprise to me, and showed more strongly than anything the empire he had over the minds of his followers. I do not think that 100 men were killed alter he had given the order, although 600 prisoners were taken. One company piled their arms, and surrendered. A part of the Christinos had retired to a small piece of wood, where they endeavoured to make a stand, but were either slaughtered or made prisoners. I must not omit to state that the Christino cavalry behaved well. One squadron retreated in admirable order, facing about every now and then, and their tirailleurs executing a retreat *en échiquier*, thereby keeping a troop of our lancers, which had come up, entirely at bay.

On both days I must mention the personal bravery of Ituralde. Zavala and the Marquis de Valdespina also, who were then in disgrace, both rode forward with the tirailleurs, and were ever in the thickest of the *melée*. The latter is a shrivelled old man, with only one arm, wearing a round white hat, blue dress coat, a lion and a V embroidered on the corner of the *chabraque*, and a little court sword. The Christinos were pursued to the very gates of Vittoria by the Carlists; and if the latter had had an hour of daylight more, so great was the confusion, they might have entered Vittoria with the fugitives. The event of the day's action was 600 killed, and 600 prisoners. The only standard the Christinos had brought out was that of the 6th. Regiment of the line, which was taken the preceding day by a Serjeant of cavalry, who was made officer in consequence. They ever after adopted the wise resolution of leaving them in the fortresses when they took the field; which has

161

left them room to boast that, excepting that one, up to this day, they have never lost a standard. This defeat must have been so much the more mortifying to Osma, as he had, it is reported, much criticised the proceedings of all the other generals, and had spoken very confidently in his communications with government, of what he would do when the opportunity was afforded him.

The night of the 28th. when after the victory we were retiring in two divisions, one of those occurrences took place which it is difficult to prevent in the fury of a civil war, but which, nevertheless, makes the blood run cold at the mere recital. Zumalacarregui, as I have said, had ordered quarter to be given during the day, and the march had already been beat, when those who had been foremost in the pursuit returned, bringing back, after the other 600 had been despatched to the rear, between 80 and 100 fresh prisoners whom they had captured under the walls of Vittoria. These were sent, under escort across the mountains. As night was coming on, the captain of the company who had charge of them, and who had only been able to assemble 30 men of his company, found himself seriously embarrassed in the narrow and rocky roads, bordered on each side by a thick brushwood. Two of his prisoners had already made their escape, when he sent to Zumalacarregui to inform him of it, and that, as he had only 30 men to guard them, he could not answer for his prisoners. "Get cords," said the General. He was answered, that the villages had been abandoned, and that they had searched in vain for some. "Then put them to death - *passar los por armas*." With this reply the messenger returned; but immediately an aide-de-camp spurred after him to say, that care must be taken that Ituralde's division was not alarmed by the firing. The captain, who was an old Navarrese of Mina's school, on receiving this order, sent for a serjeant and 15 lancers, and causing his men to fix bayonets, commanded them to charge into the midst of the unfortunate wretches, who were all miserably slaughtered on the spot. The scene is said to have baffled all description; the unfortunate victims were shrieking for mercy,

162

and clasping the knees of their destroyers and their horses several young officers were amongst the slain. We passed the spot where the massacre had been, but I did not hear until the next day all its horrors recited. I have always wished that this page, which tarnishes the glory of that victory, could be blotted from the history of the war; but in sketching its prominent features, while I feel as the partisan, I have resolved not to swerve from the impartiality of the historian.

**Carlist lancers attacking the Liberal Light Horse Guards at Viana
on Sept. 4ᵗʰ. 1834**

CHAPTER XI.

Skirmish at Sesma - Story of a Vendean Officer - Stratagem - Capture of Spies - Ximenes - The Urbanos - Attack on a fortified Church - Conflagration of the Steeple - Surrender of the besieged - Martial Schoolmaster.

After the battle of Vittoria we were some time without seeing the enemy; at last, marching from Villamayor on Sesma, in the Ribera, where Lopez, with a column of 2,000 men, of which a large portion was cavalry, had advanced, I believe to collect provisions, Zumalacarregui had hoped to have cut him off as he retired; but informed of his approach, he speedily fell back again on Sesma, which, being on an eminence in the middle of the plain, was easily defensible by means of his artillery. Notwithstanding this, the place was attacked[86], a desultory fire being kept up all day. Some 20 or 30 men of the enemy's rear-guard were cut off, and, for the first time, we made use of the two mountain pieces taken at Vittoria; we had then, however, nothing but grenades to fire from them. After skirmishing all day, finding the place was too strong, at nightfall we retired. The loss on both sides was trifling, excepting that by some mismanagement the enemy's cavalry were for above ten minutes exposed in a street to the fire of our tirailleurs, who had crept along a bank; and in that short space of time they lost above 40 horses, and others might be seen galloping about riderless. Within cannon-shot of Sesma, there is by the roadside a large garden of vines and olives, surrounded by a high wall. Coming down from the rising ground, we had just reached this spot, which first brought us in sight of the place, when we discovered a party of horsemen, spurring for life or death across the wide plain before us. The cavalry was then considerably in the rear, and the general had detached all his escort of lancers, excepting 30; to this corps I then belonged, and happened to be by his side, as well as the captain of the troop. Don Tomas Reyna, his aide-de-camp, however, put himself at our head, and we followed,

---

[86] 5th. November 1834. The Carlist commander was Mendiry

165

scampering over vines and ditches, starting the game as we rushed along. We had not then time to count, but the party we were pursuing consisted of some lancers and the 5th. Light Dragoons, 35 in number, including a courser they were escorting; we were thus pretty evenly matched. Both armies paused, as if by mutual consent, and all eyes were turned towards the plain. The enemy did not, however, show fight, but made full gallop for the town, and several of our men got unseated, or were left, behind, and it was only within a long cannon-shot of the place we came so close upon them that their officers gave them the order to wheel about and form in battle. On the left this manoeuvre was executed with some confusion, and before their horses could be put into the trot, our line advancing full gallop burst upon them eleven were killed and eight taken.

I was then fortunate in being well mounted, and, with little urging, my horse carried me into what might have been rather dangerous company, if the enemy had not been too much alarmed to attend to anything but their own safety. I rode for above 50yds alongside a dragoon, trying to seize hold of him with the bridle-hand, which I at last effected without his having made any resistance. On applying my pistol to his cheek he dropped his arms, and shouted *"Viva el Rey!"* as a sign that he had surrendered. I called out to him to fall back, expecting that the men behind would secure him; they were still at some distance off; the first that reached him was my own servant for he never offered to move who, although seeing him unarmed, barbarously ran him through with his lance. Having again spurred on, I got alongside another of the same regiment, and called out to him to surrender, when he made a desperate cut at me: fortunately I had abandoned my pistol for my sabre for I doubt if I should have been able to have used the former, so sudden and unexpected was the blow. I was on his left side, and it was consequently what, in the broad-sword exercise, is known as cut 5, an awkward stroke to recover, if given with too much force on the gallop. Having fortunately parried it before he

166

could do so, I brought the point to his neck, when he instantly dropped his sword, and surrendered. Having hastily made him dismount, I gave him in charge to the serjeant, making the latter responsible for his safety.

I must mention that I had met a French infantry officer, named Aubert, who had only just reached headquarters that morning, and as I had then two horses, I dismounted my servant from one, and lent it to him to ride till he was placed; he was totally unarmed, and followed by my side, although I represented to him the folly of his charging with us. This horse, an old but spirited Andalusian, his rider being little of a horseman, and unable to rein it in, carried him with the fugitives right into Sesma. Led away by the heat of the pursuit, I found myself with Reyna at the very entrance of the place. We saw that it was high time to turn back, as our men and the captain had retired out of cannon-shot, and we called out to Aubert for God's sake to pull up - that he was going right into the jaws of the enemy. We fancied that we heard his horse's hoofs clattering for a moment behind us, but on turning round saw him in the distance, in the midst of the fugitives. We were obliged quickly to make off; as they were now no longer afraid of hurting their own people, they were plying us with grape and musketry. The courier escaped.

A few days after we heard of Aubert's death. As soon as his horse stopped, he found himself in the hands of his enemies. As he only spoke a few words of Spanish, and had come unarmed amongst them, the fugitives scarcely knew how, it was at first thought that he was a deserter. A French officer in the Queen's service, probably anxious to save him, came to interrogate him. He briefly stated that he was a Vendean; that if he found himself amongst them it was by some mistake; that he had come to Spain to serve Don Carlos and no other; and he concluded by exclaiming in Spanish, "*Viva Carlos Quinto*!" He was sentenced by a court-martial to be shot as a rebel, and his execution took place at sunset. He refused to kneel, and gave the signal for the fatal discharge by

167

throwing his hat in the air, and crying, "*Vive le Roi!*" He bequeathed to the curate of the village, after embracing it for the last time, a medal and a small coin, bearing the effigy of the Due de Bordeaux, given him by the Duchess of Berri, which he had always worn next his heart, and from which nothing but death could have parted him. I in vain attempted to obtain these articles afterwards to send to his family. The inhabitants were so struck with the gallantry of his death, that when the Christinos abandoned the place next day, they buried him with great pomp in the church.

It is true he did perhaps more good to the Carlist cause by his death than he would have done if he had survived, as he had already had his commission of ensign five months, and been with the Junta, without learning either his duty or anything of the Spanish language. His whole life had been but one tissue of misfortune. He was one of those examples of the dreary and sunless path some men seem destined to tread through existence, and nature appeared to have used him little kinder than man, he was short, thin, and pale, and wore a long beard, in imitation of the French officers who followed Bourmont to Portugal, and vowed never to shave their chins till the campaign was concluded. His father, who had been a wealthy *métayer* or farmer in La Vendée, had been killed by the republicans, and the paternal roof having been burned over his head, his mother was driven, with two children, in all the inclemency of a hard winter, to wander from house to house. She was afterwards carried to Nantes, and perished at one of the *noyades*, or republican marriages, as the Convention termed the tying their victims two by two and throwing them into the Seine[87].

He was adopted by a relation, who afterwards became impoverished and died. He had embraced a seafaring life, and was for some time superintendent of a fishery on the coast of

---

[87] The atrocities committed by the French revolution against the royalists of the Vendée were evidently well-known to Henningsen, but were covered up by successive republican governments, and only rediscovered by academics in relatively recent times.

Newfoundland. He abandoned those cheerless shores to be twice shipwrecked, and lose what little property he had amassed. On the movement which was made in La Vendée, in 1832, he had taken arms for Henri V, and was one of the defendants of the Chateau de la Pénissière, of which General Dermoncourt, in his account of Madame, speaks as having been so heroically defended. It may be remembered that it held out for many hours against several hundreds[88] of the National Guards and the line, and that when the roof and the ground-floor were in flames, the little garrison had sallied and cut their way through the besiegers. He had afterwards been hid for many months in the house of an old lady at Nantes, never venturing out but at night. He at last, under an assumed name, traversed France, and crossed the Pyrenees with such recommendations to Charles V, from the French noblemen of his district, that he received a commission of ensign of infantry. He had been placed in the Junta's guard; but the Junta's guard is like what the bodyguard in Spain was formerly, who would not condescend to fight and sully their swords with plebeian blood, unless the King in person took the field. The Junta's guard never fights unless the Junta fights, and this it was never their business or inclination to do. Their retinue and military force generally consisted of all the incapables, and those of very problematical courage.

He arrived with Lacour[89], who, after he had presented to the general his commission, and a letter from the Comte de Villemur, Minister of War, interpreted what they had to say, as Zumalacarregui spoke nothing but Spanish and Basque, and he had learned the Spanish when campaigning with the Due d'Angouleme in 1823. The general, finding that Aubert did not understand a syllable of the language of the country, shrugged up his shoulders, and said that, as he held the King's commission, which he was bound to respect, he should have his servant and rations, and the

---

[88] The Legitimists numbered possibly as few as 45; the Orleanists had about 1,200 men.
[89] Ensign Guetier de Lacour

treatment of an officer; but that until he had learned sufficient of the Spanish, he must be contented to carry a musket, as these were times when every man must be usefully employed. Aubert replied very starchly, that he considered that against the dignity of a commissioned officer. "Very well," said Zumalacarregui. He then questioned Lacour. He stated that he was of good family, and had been for several years serjeant-major and fencing-master in a regiment, from which he produced certificates; and that he knew how to instruct and command troops in Spanish as well as French. His tall military figure and bearing seemed to please the general. "Are you sure you know enough of Spanish?"

"It is easily tried," said Lacour, turning to a knot of staff and superior officers, supposing these gentlemen to be recruits.

"Agreed," said the general, who was highly amused, making a sign for them to obey. Lacour quickly went through the words of command, and ordered one to hold himself straight, another more backward, another more forward, as if they had been in reality so many recruits.

Zumalacarregui ordered a pass to be made out for Aubert to the Junta of Navarre, with orders to place him in their guard; and for Lacour a letter to the Commandant of 3rd. Battalion, pursuant to which, on delivering it, he found himself placed as ensign in the grenadier company.

Tired of the life he led with the Junta, whose business it was to escape before every detachment of the enemy, Aubert had again reached headquarters, in the hopes of getting placed in some corps on active service.

We had been informed that a large convoy, consisting of cartridges, cloth, shoes, leather, rice, and stock-fish, had arrived at Calahorra, in Old Castile, destined for the winter stores of the different garrisons. It was said to occupy a league of the road, and that 500 mules were laden with the various articles. This would have been a glorious prize for the Carlist army, as the rigorous season was coming on. Zumalacarregui kept hovering like a hawk in the environs between Calahorra and Pampeluna, whither they were shortly to direct it - sometimes marching away, as if taking a contrary direction, and then as suddenly returning: but the enemy was too wary. At last a column of 2,000 men was sent from Los Arcos, in the direction of Murieta, along the Ega, to attract the notice of the general, with orders to retire into the strong position which Zuñiga and Orbiso afford, and there await reinforcements from Los Arcos and Estella. Zumalacarregui, who saw well enough that their design was only to amuse him while they passed their convoy on to Pampeluna, affected to he deceived by the stratagem, and feigned an attack on the outlying division, which, on his approach, retired into Zuñiga and Orbiso.

It was nearly sunset when the firing commenced, and at nightfall we retired, lighting fires on the border of the wood, as if the army were bivouacking, and it were our intention to renew the attack next day: but in the middle of the night we silently marched in the direction of the river Arga. On the road we were joined by the King, but this in no way diminished the rapidity of our movements. We were, however, informed that the convoy had escaped us, shutting themselves up in Olite or Taffala, having evidently been made acquainted with our march. The King and the greater part of the army slept, I believe, in Berbinzano; and the squadron to which I belonged was sent on to Miranda (de l'Arga), the captain having received private instructions. I must here state that this man was a native of Miranda, a soldier of fortune, who had risen during the wars of the independence and the constitution; and that he had a cousin there who was the alcalde of the place, and one of the wealthiest inhabitants, but unable either to read or write. Whenever we passed through, the fatted calf had been killed for the captain, and he always looked forward with pleasure to lodging at Miranda, where he was sure of an excellent bed and good cheer. A sort of old servant or hanger-on, who had been a shepherd, and who now followed the army, as soon as we knew we were to march in the middle of the night, was despatched to

171

Miranda, to tell the alcalde to kill a couple of capons, as probably his cousin the captain would be able to pay him a visit, as he believed the army was marching that way. As this fellow knew the country well, and was an excellent walker, even in that country where all walk well, having two hours the start, he arrived a long while before us.

On reaching Miranda, the captain went up, and having had the tickets for quartering the general, his staff, and two battalions, who were coming, as well as his lancers - told his cousin he was sorry he must obey his orders and arrest him, but trusted there was only some misunderstanding: he also arrested an ecclesiastic and another individual. An hour or two after, Zumalacarregui and the Guides arrived. The next morning the march was beat before daybreak. It was cold, and in that season, being only 4 o'clock, pitch dark. We were formed on the other side of the bridge of the Arga, awaiting the General and his staff; I was standing beside the captain, who in very silent mood was puffing away his paper cigar, when three successive discharges, of several shots each, rung on the air, and we could distinctly see the flashes on the height on which
Miranda is built, in the darkness. "*A Dios!*" said the captain. "What is it?" I inquired. "The three we arrested yesterday, amongst them my cousin, departing this life the only relation I had in the world," and he recommended puffing away vehemently at his cigar. After indulging in some minutes' gravity, he seemed little discomposed during the remainder of the day.

It appears the alcalde had some time been bought over by the enemy, and had sold them the piece of intelligence which saved their convoy: being unable to write himself, he had dictated the letter to an ecclesiastic whom he knew to be of liberal opinions, and he had sent it by an equally trusty messenger. It was written in the morning, and the same evening, the three who planned it, who wrote it, and who carried it, were arrested, and never saw another sunrise. The mystery always remained how Zumalacarregui was

172

made acquainted with their treachery, as only one letter had been sent, and was evidently delivered; so that it is supposed he must have had some spy in the Christino ranks. So circumstantial was the accusation, that when they were tried during the night by the auditor of war, or grand provost of the army, they gave up all hopes of escaping, and confessed their guilt. The circumstance added another example to the many, of the singular certainty and rapidity with which the Carlist General always discovered the spies of the enemy, deterring those who might otherwise have been tempted by the high price they paid for all their information.

Having missed the convoy, we took the opportunity of destroying the fortified church of Villafranca, garrisoned by Urbanos, who, in the heart of the Rivera, fancying themselves out of the reach of the Carlists, had committed the greatest atrocities on the Royalists of the surrounding districts; and our being obliged to retire from Peralta a little time before, had given them greater confidence. To reach Villafranca which is that wide vale of the Rivera between the Arga and the Arragona, the latter river must be crossed a little above where it empties itself into the Ebro; at that place it is wide, but extremely rapid, and only to be crossed by a ford, which is generally perilous. We were guided by a little old man, dressed like a "bourgeois" of the country, with a fur cap, and mounted on a magnificent mule. This was Ximenes, a native of the place, and Zumalacarregui's chief spy. He once possessed there very considerable property, which was confiscated, on his having, with two of his sons, joined the Carlists; but the third, who had always been of a wayward disposition, had taken part with the Liberals, where he met with rapid advance merit, and was at this moment commanding the small garrison of 50 Urbanos shut up in the fortified church: against his own son he was, therefore, leading the Royalist battalions. It was at first hoped we should surprise the garrison in the village, from the secrecy and rapidity of our march: they had, however, retired into the old church, which was palisadoed and crenelled, and from whence they kept, up an

173

incessant fire. While the infantry was taking possession of the town, we went round at a full gallop to line the banks of the Ebro, and detain all the boats upon it, making it death for anyone to cross till the church was perceived to be burning. This was intended to prevent their receiving any succours from Calhahora and the other fortified places in Castille.

The garrison consisted of only 50 Urbanos, and were unimportant in every other point of view than that they prevented our levying rations, and terribly oppressed the inhabitants; unlike the generality of the Urbanos, who in Spain are drawn from the wealthier classes, they were mostly reprobates of the lower orders, of about the same stamp as the peseteros, and had only taken arms to have *carte-blanche* to plunder the neighbourhood. The week previous, they had levied 16,000 douros (nearly £4000). They were in the habit of arresting and executing, without trial or formality, any individuals suspected of Carlism, or who were obnoxious to them. The Queen's government made use of every kind of weapon, and discovered, too late, the immense injury it had received by the odium thus thrown over all its proceedings.

I must not omit a circumstance which struck me very forcibly. When the battalion of Guides arrived rather late in the evening for the 7th. and 2nd. had first invested the place it got bruited amongst the inhabitants that a column was advancing, and that the Carlists were about retiring. The people, mistaking the troops who were waiting to receive their billets for our army preparing to march, loudly reproached us for leaving the work undone. With all the vehemence of the Spanish character, they showed their mortal hatred of the Christinos, and the oppression they had endured from the *Brigands*, as they very unceremoniously styled the national guard of her most Catholic Majesty.

I shall never forget one old woman, almost in rags, her grey hair floating dishevelled about her neck, who came up to the captain of a company with whom I was in conversation, and probably mistaking him for a superior officer, doubled her

174

shrivelled hand in his face, and shrieked out a volley of insulting epithets, which she concluded by invoking *"La maldicion de Dios"* (the curse of God) on all our heads, if we retired like *falsos* (a word which it is difficult to translate according to the meaning attached to it in the provinces, and which means alike dastard and perfidious, and may perhaps be best rendered by false of heart), and left a single one of the *negros* alive. Having inquired of a bystander who was this fanatic, we were informed that she was an old weaver, of a neighbouring village, whose only son had been shot that day fortnight - having been dragged from his bed by some of the Urbanos, it was supposed, for having carried tobacco to the Carlists - the only transgression he had been guilty of. On account of the popular excitement against them, it became necessary to destroy the garrison at all sacrifices, unimportant as it was in any other point of view, lest the inhabitants might say that the Carlists could not afford them any protection against their tyrants, and levied rations upon them without utility.

With some difficulty, the two 4-pounders taken at Vittoria, and which at that time constituted all the artillery we possessed, were brought to bear on the church gates, which were lined with heavy sheets of iron. The gates having been burst open, with the loss only of three men wounded, the volunteers rushed into the church, but they were only able to surprise one or two of the enemy, the rest having retreated into the steeple, of which the staircase had been broken away, and where they had most strongly barricaded themselves. As they obstinately refused to surrender, and it would have taken too much time to undermine the massive walls of the old steeple - in which act the approach of a column would probably have interrupted us - it was resolved to set fire to it. Piles of wood, tow, goat-skins full of brandy, and other inflammable matter, were collected at the foot of the steeple; the Baron de Los Vallos, having just arrived with the King, had been entrusted with the commission of setting fire to it. The besieged had no doubt of being relieved before daybreak, and therefore were

175

loud in their jokes against the Carlists, to whom they called out, "Mountain thieves! sons of monks! rebels! you will soon have to run back to your mountains - the columns are advancing." Nor were the volunteers backward in replying according to their usual practice.

We now perceived, from the sound of voices, that they had women in the steeple; and, upon inquiry, were informed, that, independently of the 50 Urbanos, there were in the steeple eight women and eleven children of their own families, besides two women and two monks, their prisoners. Here was a striking picture of the horrors of civil war, even to ourselves, who had been accustomed to them for several months in every shape. Those which occurred during the burning of the church of Villafranca we had never pictured to ourselves even in imagination. At about 10 o'clock at night the tower was all in flames; but the garrison retreating higher and higher, still obstinately held out, and kept up an incessant fire on every object that presented itself. The shrieks of some, however, who had taken refuge in corners of the building where they were reached by the flames, as well as the women and children who saw the devouring element raging below, were now heard at intervals, and although orders were given to fire only on the men, it was often impossible to distinguish the dark figures that flitted before the light, endeavouring to obtain an instant breath of air out of the smoky atmosphere. It was repeatedly proposed to them to let the women and children out, but this they refused.

The bells had all fallen in, and packets of cartridges were constantly exploding; towards morning a few faint cries of *"Viva el Rey!"* were heard from the women, and the commandant of the tower inquired if quarter would be given them? He was answered, "No; the men had none to hope for." He then inquired if it was Zumalacarregui who had besieged them, and where was he? The General had just arrived, and most imprudently went beyond the corner of the church, exclaiming, *"Aqui estoy!"* "Here I am." The commandant said they could bear the heat and smoke no longer, and asked if they would be allowed the consolations of religion before they suffered death. Zumalacarregui replied, that the Carlists had never yet denied them that, but not to flatter themselves with the hope of mercy. The commandant then said that they surrendered. But how men who had defended themselves so deperately, and who had no chance for their lives, missed the opportunity of shooting the Carlist leader (who was not above 50yds from them) by firing downwards, when it is so much easier to aim, and a bullet carries so much straighter than in a horizontal direction, has always been a matter of surprise to me, particularly as several shots were fired by them afterwards.

The flames were by this time nearly extinguished, but the smoke had proved more intolerable than the fire. When ladders were placed to the church roof, and the volunteers went up to receive their arms, they shot one soldier, and an officer was wounded. The men who fired were bayoneted on the spot one in particular, who defended a narrow ledge, and was struck in the breast by a volunteer, fell from the top to the bottom of the steeple headlong at our feet: the rest made no resistance. Three women (one a prisoner) and four children had perished, and above 30 of the garrison, either in the church, by the smoke or the flames, or the shot of the assailants. Those that remained were so blackened by the smoke, that they presented a most ghastly appearance; with considerable difficulty they were got down over the roof of the church, which, although the steeple had been burning for ten or twelve hours, had never taken fire. The commandant, who only the day before had received his captaincy, and his lieutenant, were brought before the General, who inquired whether the garrison had been acting all along by his orders.

The commandant hesitated, but the ex-schoolmaster boldly replied, "Yes, they acted by our orders." The former was a short man, about 34, his form athletic, and his bones all thickly set; he was dressed in blue trowsers and a *zamarra*. The smoke to which he had been all night exposed had swollen his eyelids and darkened his face, giving his features, naturally coarse and repulsive, a still more forbidding appearance. This was the son of Ximenes; on the whole, he presented the idea of a bold and determined ruffian. The schoolmaster, who was also below the middle stature, had an open and prepossessing countenance, and he behaved in every respect with the firmness of a man; while the captain occasionally betrayed signs of weakness, which I should scarcely have expected after his gallant defence - for such it incontestably was.

"Have you anything to say in your defence?" inquired the general. The reply of the lieutenant was to the following effect, as nearly as I can remember:- That he neither begged for mercy, nor did he suppose it likely that pardon would be granted him. They might, however, do worse than let him live; he had no affection either for the Queen or for Don Carlos, but where chance had thrown him, that party, as they had seen, he would serve; and if they chose to try him, and let him live, he would serve the King like a soldier, and if they shot him, like a soldier he would die. "And you?" to the captain. "I only surrendered," replied the son of Ximenes, "because I was promised quarter; if not, I should have held out longer. You may judge, from my behaviour, whether I would not have perished in the tower if I had not distinctly understood so." "It is false," hastily interrupted the general; "whom did I speak to myself?" "To me," said the lieutenant. "And did you say to the commandant that I had offered quarter?" "No; I told him that you had refused us our lives, and we should both have perished there, only the smoke had grown intolerable: this is the truth, or you would not behold me here now." The general beckoned with his hand for them to be removed. "You will remember my father and brother?" said the captain imploringly; "if I have done the King wrong, they have served him faithfully."

The whining tone in which this appeal was made contrasted unfavourably with the bold and frank demeanour of his fellow captive. "If your brother had been taken," said the general, "his brother's treason would have been no palliation of his loyalty." The schoolmaster, I remember, held a paper cigar between his fingers (for at all times and seasons the Spaniards smoke), and was looking round for a light. The general took his own cigar from his mouth, and handed it to him to ignite his by; he bowed respectfully as he returned it to him. "Think on what I have said, general," cried he, as they were led away. It was evident that Zumalacarregui was strongly prepossessed in this man's favour; he gazed after him with that intense and penetrating look so peculiar to him, and muttered a few words, in which "Que lastima aquel muchacho!" "What a pity that lad!" were alone audible.

Liberals executing Carlist prisoners as traitors

CHAPTER XII.

Ximenes and his Son - Death of the Son - The Hermitage - C. Vicomte de Barrez - Defeat of Mendaça - An Emigrant - Death of Barrez - The Fifer Morriones.

The scene in the morning was extraordinary, when the volunteers were allowed to pillage the tower. Being unable to descend the ladders, all the lower part of the tower being still nearly red-hot, without losing hold of their booty, they threw what had not been consumed - corn, biscuits, powder, cartridges, chocolate, old guns, and muskets which had been taken from the peasantry, and many articles of value - down from the steeple to the ground. The dead bodies they met with, some half consumed, were also thrown down to be buried. There were amongst the number the corpses of several infants. Their heavy fall, 60 or 100 ft, had an appalling effect on the soldiers, intent as they were on scrambling for the spoil obtained by this melancholy expedition. The inhabitants of Villafranca, however, seemed to have no such feelings, and were with difficulty prevented from massacring the prisoners. The women, as I have generally remarked in those cases, were the most violent, and screeched out their divers grievances in the ears of the captured Christinos. Certainly, if one-tenth part of what they reproached them with were true, they richly deserved their fate. It has always been a matter of surprise to me, how a government wielding every engine of power, setting aside the injustice of the case, could be so imprudent and impolitic as to let loose upon a population a set of ruffians like those who composed this garrison, whose conduct alone was sufficient to indispose the inhabitants towards it, supposing even no previous dislike to have existed.

It was, I think, two or three days after this affair that we were at Sanguesse, on the frontier of Arragon, when my own lodging being of the worst possible kind, the weather too rainy to lounge at the door, and the house, which was of the poorest description, so smoky and dirty that it was impossible to remain in

181

it, I went in search of a particular friend, a captain of Guides, with whom I had formerly messed, and was in the habit of supping and sleeping if it chanced that his quarters were better than my own. He happened to be on guard with his company at the "Prevention," as the moveable prison was termed. The prisoners, as we had no depot, followed on the march between fixed bayonets, which distinguished those on that service, in which, turn by turn, they were employed from sunset to sunset. The spot fixed on for the prevention for the night was, in this instance, an old abandoned inn, without a stick of furniture. The captain informed me that the officers of the Urbanos of Villafranca were amongst the prisoners, and that the commandant had written to his father, Ximenes, requesting an interview, and that he was momentarily expected.

When we entered the room where the prisoners were confined, to the number of six or eight, all belonging to the garrison of Villafranca, the commandant was sitting in an alcove writing, and the lieutenant walking up and down, smoking; the former asked us repeatedly if we thought there was any chance of his life being spared. "I know that what weighs principally against me is having shot several peasants, but you know you use them very hardly yourselves, when they are at all opposed to you, and, as I have proved to the auditor of war, my orders on that point were very strict. We are in a different situation from you; having all the population against us, it is impossible to forego making some severe examples. My father's services ought to count for something, too." Convinced as we were that there was no chance of their lives being granted to the prisoners, who were Urbanos and volunteers, and who had besides acquired such an unfortunate celebrity for their treatment of the inhabitants, at a time when no quarter was given even to the line, who were supposed, being originally conscripts, to have been in some manner forced to fight against us, since after the 28th. October, when we had spared the lives of 600 men, the very next prisoners that fell into the hands of

182

the Christinos were immediately put to death, we pleaded entire ignorance as to the fate that, awaited them.

When I heard that Ximenes was come, I could not help feeling a thrill of horror, and we were all about retiring, when the prisoners begged us to remain. The meeting and the parting, the last time on this side of the grave, between the father and son - who, however divided in opinions, were still united in blood and in affections, which they in vain endeavoured to control - was a heart-rending scene. Ximenes had sacrificed two fortunes, and the ease and independence of his old age, to his duty, and he now saw his eldest and once his best-beloved son, about to suffer death, with the consciousness that, he had done his part to bring him to so bitter a punishment. He had resolved at first not to trust himself with an interview, but the prayer of his son, against whom all animosity was now extinct, he had been unable to refuse.

Ximenes, of whom I knew much both before and since, although advanced in the vale of years, is still hale and healthy, short in stature, sharp featured, and grey-haired. I shall never forget, when he entered the room, his son's throwing himself at his feet, and the expression of his countenance as the tears started to his grey eyes and rolled over his weather-beaten cheeks! In an instant they were locked in each other's embrace. Retiring into the alcove they conversed earnestly for some time, but not, from what I involuntarily gathered, until the last, about the possibility of saving him. As the father took leave of him, we heard him distinctly and earnestly say, "Is there no hope, then?" *"Pide usted a Dios!"* "You must pray for it to God!" replied the old man, as he tore himself away. When he was gone, we sent up the larger part of our supper to the prisoners, who had their rations, but which they could only get cooked in soldier-fashion. We had much conversation with them. The commandant seemed much more tranquil after this interview - and his lieutenant preserved the same sang-froid as at first. We lay down on the floor, a bed we were pretty well accustomed to. For my own part, being so unlucky in

183

the lodging that had fallen to me, it was not worthwhile to go through the dark and muddy streets for what I could find on the spot a place to stretch my cloak on.

A day or two after, having been tried by the auditor of war, the prisoners were shot. On inquiring after them, I was told that they had been *pasado por las armas*. I have often seen Ximenes since. He still continues to serve us with the same zeal, and has been on many and dangerous expeditions, but he is visibly altered, and has always a settled gloom and melancholy in his countenance. I have heard, but never authentically, that Lorenzo had offered him a large sum of money to gain him over; this had come to Zumalacarregui's knowledge by means of the communication he kept up in the heart of the adverse party, and he had reproached Ximenes with not having informed him of it. On account of this, it was said, he had been deterred from making any application to obtain the pardon of his son. This may or may not be the fact, and it signified little, as, under existing circumstances, it was out of the general's power to have granted it.

In the month of December, 1834, we were quartered in the villages of the Valley of Beruesa or San Gregorio; the General had then under him a considerable force, amongst which were my own corps and the Guides, who always followed him. This valley may be considered as neutral around between the mountains and the flat or undulating land of the Rivera, from which it is only divided by one chain. On the summit of the chain rises a lofty building, something in the Moorish style, and resembling one of those old castles which are scattered over the country, seeming to stand here and there as sentinels on the heights, whence they look on either side far over the plains below. The edifice in question is, however, the chapel of St. Gregory, whose relics are enshrined there in silver. Originally erected, probably, for warlike, rather than for religious purposes, it resembles a watch-tower more than a hermitage, the name it goes by in the country, where its reputation

184

is far spread, and is attested in time of peace by numerous yearly pilgrimages.

After the battle of Vittoria, the enemy had not seemed at all anxious to take the field; but a considerable period having elapsed in almost perfect inaction, the Queen's generals thought themselves in honour bound to attempt some movement, and for many days had been mustering strongly in the direction of Estella and Los Arcos, with the intention of forcing a passage by way of Zunia to the plains of Vittoria, on the other side of the Sierra de Andia.

The Carlist army, consisting of ten battalions, occupied Piedramillera and the valley, thus ready to give them battle at the first step. I had been sent in the morning with a few horse to place videttes on a height whence we could observe the road from Estella to Los Arcos. A considerable division had passed to the latter town. The day being miserably cold, I had a fire lighted, but the wind was so high and piercing, that I was, notwithstanding, almost frozen. An order was given me towards nightfall to return, after having spent eight or ten hours on my post. It was pitch dark, by the time I got back; and by the order and regularity with which we were challenged by the advanced guard, I recognised that it was commanded by a young French officer of the Guides, with whom I was particularly intimate; and whose friendship, if it had not been his fate to fall so early, I hope I should have still preserved.

Charles Vicomte de Barrez was the eldest of three brothers, their father one of the most determined Carlists of the south of France. In the earliest part of the war, with that chivalrous feeling which distinguished the old French nobles, he sent his three sons, with his blessing, to fight for a Bourbon who was struggling for his throne, in the hope, perhaps somewhat visionary, that his success might revive the fallen hopes of the same family in France. Young Barrez had been a lieutenant of artillery in his native country, but on the breaking out of the revolution which hurled the legitimate branch from the throne, had immediately resigned. As we at that time had only the two small field-pieces taken at Vittoria, and there

185

was, in consequence, nothing to do in this service, he begged to change to the infantry, and a few days before had entered the Guides. The three brothers, all of whom I knew well, were favourites in the army, and behaved with much gallantry; but the oldest, of a singularly prepossessing personal appearance - his limbs and features, though small, all delicately and regularly moulded, his brow high and noble - and his dark eyes with a thoughtful expression - was one of those original and sterling characters which, even upon first acquaintance, are distinguished from the common herd. A profound scholar, and an accomplished gentleman, he had cultivated both ornamental literature and mathematics, talents rarely united, with singular success. On English literature, with which he was perfectly acquainted as well as with his own, we were in the habit of conversing; he had also made several very useful and ingenious inventions for the service of the artillery, to the study of which he had devoted himself. I have mentioned the reasons which prevented him from following such a career in France.

Though only 27 years of age, he had seen much of the world, and was looked upon as a good companion in our revels. His disposition, however, was naturally serious and contemplative. Being the eldest son, and descended from an ancient and loyal family, he had considered it his duty to unsheath his sword for a cause which he deemed to be a just and sacred one, and to which he believed, when it was most abandoned, his honour most bound him to adhere. His brothers were gay and thoughtless, but he had reluctantly parted from his scientific pursuits, his mother and sisters, to embrace a life, not only of peril, but totally unsuited to his feelings and character. He behaved with the greatest valour; but the scenes of desolation and horror which we were daily called upon to witness seemed to leave a profound impression on his mind. Though very strict in everything regarding the service, he was beloved by all those under his orders; and when his company happened to be on guard at the "*prevention*," he used to devote his

186

time to the prisoners - writing their memorials, furnishing them at his own expense with a thousand little comforts, and listening to all they had to say - details to which, after marching all day, and from boors and soldiers who imagine their fate is in the hands of a subaltern - few men would have had the patience to attend.

The post made a fire under a sort of shed, their arms being piled against the wall, and under this Barrez had to pass the night. Having informed him that the enemy had effected a junction at Los Arcos, and that we should probably have an engagement next morning, we parted.

An hour or two later, after warming and refreshing myself, not feeling in the least disposed to sleep, I resolved to go and spend a few hours with him, as he was quite alone, and I had myself experienced in the morning the ennui of the service he was engaged in. I had sent forwards my servant with materials to make punch. Barrez seemed rather melancholy, which I was surprised at, as the prospect of an action, particularly when, after the affairs of the 27th. and 28th. October, we never doubted for a moment of success, had always had the effect of exhilarating our spirits. We talked at great length each of his home, so often the topic of the soldier in campaign, though, excepting for a toast, it is a remembrance he tries to banish in his hours of merriment. He had been in England, and his original description of the way in which the Modern Rome, her manners, her institutions, and her character had struck him, amused me so much, that it was two in the morning before we parted. He assured me that he was perfectly wearied and disgusted with his present mode of life, particularly as he thought the cause of Charles V was now doing well. All that he wished for was a wound, however severe, to have an excuse for returning home with honour. Throughout his conversation it was easy to discern a gloomy foreboding. The words he spoke are still fresh in my memory, and the minutest details of all that happened on the ensuing day, although bloodless in comparison with many others, have outlived, I know not why, many graver events in my recollection. To cheer my friend on parting I said, "We shall meet in London some day," (for he had expressed his intention to make a more thorough acquaintance with our island,) "and there we will laugh at our hardships and straw couches." "Je l'espère," said he, shaking his head. "We shall have an engagement tomorrow," said I, as I took his hand, "give the enemy a second representation of Vittoria, march on Madrid, and then we will re-cross the Pyrenees together." "If we have not the victory," replied Barrez, "I shall seek a wound, even if it he a mortal one; I am wearied of everything tout m'ennuie." We parted then and for ever! The wound he sought he received on the morrow and it was a mortal one!

The next morning, the 12th. December, we were in our saddles before daybreak; but it was not till eleven a.m., that I was sent with the captain of the troop and about 50 lancers to keep watch on the hill between Piedramillera and Los Arcos, which, from the hermitage of San Gregorio, we could see distinctly. The captain took to the right, and sent me with a detachment to watch the road. Having placed videttes by the side of the hermitage, as the wind was piercingly cold, I halted, and laid myself down under the portico of the church of Sorlada, a small village at the foot of the hill, whence a signal from the videttes could be distinctly seen. Our army was formed for action from Mendaça[90] to the gorges that lead to Zuñiga. It is difficult where on every side there are mountains and valleys, to describe the varieties of position. Generally, where there is one valley of considerable extent, there are others which appear almost like branches, or rather as if, in some convulsion of the earth, they had formed the beds of some rapid torrents, which had run into a vast lake. All the soil was removed save that portion adhering to the huge bones of the earth which even the torrent could not move. It is one of these tributary valleys, if I may be allowed the expression, which running out of, or according to my hypothesis, into that of the Beruesa, and narrowing into defiles as it enters the mountain, that affords the

---

[90] Mendaza, population today 300. The battle took place on 12th. December 1834.

188

passage to the famous bridge of Arquijas[91]. The entrance from thence into the Beruesa, is nearly opposite the hermitage; on one side is the village of Asarta; to the right Mendaça, at the foot of a rugged triangular-shaped mountain, one face of which flanks the valley of the Beruesa, the other the one you have just quitted. Piedramillera is also built almost against it, the steeple of its church reaching half-way up the bold and prominent rock. It is therefore necessary only to turn the angle in order to reach Mendaça.

This mountain, if properly defended, forms the chief strength of the position, if taken up at its foot, as it requires several hours and a considerable force to turn it. It is also advisable, if the enemy come from Los Arcos, to attack them immediately on their sallying from Sorlada, before they can extend their force. On a previous occasion, on our having advanced for that purpose, they had, however, kept themselves shut up in the village, which we could not attack on account of their artillery, and had retreated back on Los Arcos. Zumalacarregui, whose object was to entice them to an action if possible, and get them well into the plains, was therefore obliged to abandon all idea of this position, and formed only three battalions on the angle of the mountain, intending them to keep the rocks, and sending forward a battalion or two whose retreat would be supported by the cavalry, to entice them into the narrower valley, where they would be exposed and surrounded on three sides, as if in an amphitheatre.

At last old Ximenes on his mule passed me by at a brisk trot. "They are coming," said he. The videttes made signal almost at the same moment, and after communicating the intelligence we retired about half-way over the plain, between our own lines and the village, where we halted and watched them as they came down the road and into Sorlada, their force altogether, as near as I could calculate, with their cavalry, and a small column which came down another *puerto*, that of Mirafuentes, must have been between 10-12,000 men, commanded by Cordova. They advanced in two

---

[91] A narrow, single-span bridge.

columns, their artillery, eight or ten pieces, in the centre, and their cavalry, about 500 horse, on their left wing, which, with 2,000 infantry under the command of Lopez, composed the second column, which had three pieces of artillery. Zumalacarregui, instead of taking the command of the three battalions in front of Mendaça, in person *viz*., the Guides of Navarre, the 6th., and another which I forget left them with Ituralde. They were also above four hours awaiting the enemy, exposed to the cutting east wind till their teeth were chattering, which had the effect of considerably cooling their courage and enthusiasm. The first column was then divided into six, and commenced an impetuous attack on the three battalions. Ituralde, who is brave, but frequently rash and hasty, advanced a little instead of extending his line to the left, and a sharp engagement immediately commenced between the Guides and the masses of the enemy, who, from their superior numbers and their artillery, could not fail to drive them back, while, in the mean time, two of the subdivisions of the column were allowed quietly to climb up the mountain by Piedramillera, and advance, driving the 6th. battalion from the rocks, which they abandoned with the most scandalous precipitation. The other two were taken in flank and obliged to retire. Three battalions of Alavese, the 3rd. of Navarre, and the cavalry, were now sent forward to support their retreat; the Guides, who had behaved with their usual gallantry, alone being in anything like order. During this time I had been joined by the captain with nearly a troop of horse, and as we had always retired before the enemy at a short distance, we found ourselves in one of the hollows formed by the undulation of the ground; the fire of the two lines, who could not see us from the smoke by which they were enveloped, passing over our heads. Although grenades and shot were constantly falling around us, we had only two or three horses wounded; but to extricate ourselves we were obliged to follow up the sinuosities of the ravine. This we effected, and came up as the 3rd. Battalion was marching to support, the retreat of the first three and one of the Alavese, already in complete dispersion, against a division which was coming close upon them. At first they seemed to hesitate, but at length went boldly at them, singing their favourite song of the Requeté, and drove them back, though their loss was severe. This battalion, which was characterised by a mixture of waggery and decision, behaved on this occasion with great bravery, and prevented an immense loss, as upwards of 1,000 men came up in a state of dispersion, and were enabled to form and continue a retreat in some order, while they detained the enemy.

I remember seeing one of the fugitives throw down his musket on the ploughed field; I instantly threatened to cut him down if he did not pick it up. He said he was wounded; and though I did not perceive any blood upon him, as he was deadly pale and seemed quite exhausted, I let him pass on, and ordered a trooper to take it up. About 50yds farther on he staggered, fell down, and expired. Our cavalry had been ordered to charge that of the enemy, and had come up to a broad ditch where part of the infantry of Lopez was in ambuscade, who instantly commenced a rolling fire on them. Fortunately they all fired too high, the shot rattling amongst and splintering the lances. Just above 40 men and horses were killed or wounded. They were, however, obliged to retire precipitately, and this check so disheartened our horse, that if Lopez had not been afraid to charge them, they might have been routed without much difficulty, and the victory, on the part of the Queenites, would have been complete. Instead of this, they kept following up at a distance, their own infantry being afraid to push their advantage too far, while our cavalry still continued menacing them.

The cavalry of Castille and the first squadron, having been left considerably behind the others, were, however, charged, and, on giving way, hotly pursued, the former losing several men before they could reach the squadrons of Navarre. Amongst the killed was the Baron Louis de Lamidor, who was run through the body while gallantly defending himself. He was one of the old French emigrants who were with the Prince de Rohan when the latter was killed by the Republicans in Italy. He had eleven wounds, had made 16 campaigns, had been a Lt. Colonel in the Austrian service, and afterwards in that of Ferdinand VII. He had retired to France, but on hearing of the war in Navarre, although upwards of 60 years of age, he came to fight his last battle in that cause for which his whole life had been but one struggle.

He was universally beloved; his urbanity, and the vast fund of anecdote he had always at hand, rendering him a most pleasant and entertaining companion. The same morning, when we were complaining of the cold, we had been much amused to see the old soldier with his white hair, which had bleached in the fire of innumerable actions, dancing to show us the readiest mode of restoring circulation. "Take care," said he, during the action, "if we fight here today, not to get your horses' legs entangled in the vines, for it is very dangerous." Such were his last words to me, for he had always some useful admonition, drawn from his long experience, to mingle in his conversation. His only daughter is the Abbess of a convent near Mont de Marsan, in the Landes of Languedoc.

The difficulty of crossing a ditch caused several to fall into the hands of the enemy, who gave them no quarter. One volunteer told me he was so closely pressed, that, on hearing *"hai quartel!"* (there is quarter!) shouted by the pursuers, he was about giving up his lance; but, at the same instant, the cries of those they were butchering reaching his ear, he made a desperate effort, and scrambled through the ditch which his horse had at first refused. A Castillian officer was surrounded, but made his escape: he was a very powerful man, and with a single blow cleft the head of the cornet who had seized his rein to the chin, as if it had been an apple, and then spurred away. About 15, however, perished there. It must be remembered that, though the men were always very determined, our cavalry was not then what it subsequently became after the arrival of O'Donnel; and the successes it had hitherto met with

192

were attributable less to discipline than to chance and the terror their strange equipment, enormous lances, and wild impetuosity had inspired. When Ituralde saw his battalions taken in flank, and forced to give way, and observed the disorder of the Alavese sent up to reinforce them, he became like a madman, and rushed several times into the thickest of the fire, as if seeking for death. When the Guides retired, and his company was giving back, Barrez placed himself, sword in hand, followed by a single soldier, to attempt to rally the men in front of the advancing line of the enemy. The soldier fell first, and, an instant after, the young Vicomte received a shot through his cheek staggered, and fell into the arms of a French servant who went to drag him off- and instantly expired. The enemy was, however, so close upon him, that, after carrying the body a few yards, he was obliged to let it drop, and run.

A curious circumstance occurred to a captain of Guides, named Vedos. Being behind, to render the retreat of his company as orderly as possible, lie was so close pressed by the advancing enemy, that he was recognized by one of the pursuers, who, according to their custom, offered him quarter, which was never given, calling out to him by name *"Hai quartel por Usted, Vedos!"* (There is quarter for you, Vedos!) Vedos, snatching up the musket of a man who that instant fell at his side, paused one moment to take a deadly aim, and shot his friend on the spot. Whether he deserved his fate or not, it is difficult to determine.

The bravery of the 3rd. battalion, the approach of night, and the presence of Zumalacarregui, prevented the enemy from reaping any further fruit from their success, and enabled the army to retreat without greater loss on Zuñiga, Orbiso, and Santa-Cruz-de-Campezzu. It was not until the following morning that I learned the death of poor Charles de Barrez. Four officers had been killed and five wounded in the battalion of Guides. I should estimate our loss at between 400 killed and badly wounded; and, on account of the piercing cold of the weather, all those whose wounds were severe, as the frost had got into them, died. The enemy also suffered considerably. I must not here omit to mention the name and story of the gallant little fifer Morriones. Many months before, he had begged to be allowed to march with the Carlist volunteers, but was refused, on account of his extreme youth, not being above twelve years old. He then pointed to some drummers who, he said, were younger than himself; but was answered, that they at least knew how to beat the drum and play the fife, but he, being ignorant of either, would only be eating a useless ration. He retired, and a Christino column passing near the village a short time after, he joined it, enlisting as a fifer. After two or three months, when he had learned to play, he deserted to the Carlists, certain of being now received. In the early part of this action he received a bullet through his brain.

CHAPTER XIII.

The day after a defeat – Bézard - Position of Zuñiga - Battle of Arquijas and defeat of Cordova - Stripping of the Dead - Desertion of a Polish Officer - The Amescoas.

The day after the affair of Mendaça we were assembled at Zuñiga. Zumalacarregui bore an aspect as black as thunder, and gave out all his orders in a peculiarly ill-humoured tone. We were all looking at each other in that gloomy silence which usually prevails in an army after a defeat. From the countenance of the General down to the last drummer, it was easy to perceive in an instant that all was not right. The soldier was passing no jokes. The subalterns, particularly steady at their posts, neither gathered in knots nor even smoked their cigarillos. A cloud seemed hanging on every brow. We were looking anxiously for our friends as the battalion defiled; for the night only having elapsed, it was impossible to say who was killed or wounded. As he passed, the captain of his company informed me of the death of Barrez. In the long narrow street which runs through the town of Zuñiga - for it holds the rank of villa - I saw a young man, another friend, looking very pale; he had been wounded. Mr. Vial, whose father I believe was Spanish minister at the court of London, and who had behaved with great gallantry, was also wounded in the shoulder. An old Vendéan captain, named Bézard, with whom I was very intimate, also came limping along; he had received a shot through the calf of the leg. It would be an injustice to pass over this gallant old soldier without a word to his memory.

One of those original and enthusiastic characters of which the Bocage furnished so many examples, he had sacrificed everything to his loyalty; and at the age of 55 had given up his half-pay to go and fight the battles of legitimacy in Spain. In the time of Napoleon, he was one of those few young men who, undazzled by the glory which, in the eyes of the majority, legitimated his usurpation, always refused to serve the empire, and dissipated the

195

greater part of his small patrimony in furnishing five successive substitutes for the conscription, enormously as they were then paid. This he said was the least part of the sacrifice he made to his opinion - for, as the most loyal families had been carried away by the stream, his behaviour was only imputed to cowardice. The restoration at length arrived, and then the Hundred Days of Napoleon's second reign. Bezard put himself at the head of a handful of peasants, and attacked the nearest post. In this affair, I have heard him say - and he was a man whose word those who knew him never for an instant doubted - that he had killed, with his own hand, *thirteen* of the enemy. It is certain, although he had never served before, that, for the gallantry he displayed in this achievement, he received a captaincy, and a year or two before the revolution was placed on half-pay, being a captain still. It is difficult to account for the circumstance of a brave officer, thoroughly acquainted with his duty, and having made a campaign in Spain with the Duke D'Angoulême, never, during 20 years, having been promoted. It was, however, the ungrateful and foolish policy of the Bourbons[92] after the restoration, entirely to neglect the known Royalists, and only to court the favour of the Liberals - on the principle, that the first were already attached to them, and that they had to gain over the latter. If the birthplace of a petitioner was La Vendée, it was enough to ensure a refusal to his solicitations. The character of this wretched policy needs no comment, and has met with its own reward.

Bézard's regiment was a long time in garrison at Bayonne; and although his temper was rough and techy, I found that, on account of his sterling good qualities, he had acquired the friendship of the principal inhabitants, who all spoke of him in the highest terms. He had thrown up his half-pay as captain, and armed with a double-barrelled fowling piece - although, as I have mentioned already, advanced in the vale of years - he came to serve Don Carlos as a simple volunteer, having crossed the frontiers

---

[92] And of conservative governments generally, always and everywhere.

196

when on a shooting party. His countenance opened at once the whole tale of his high and enthusiastic spirit - it might have been called something Quixotic - as many may smile at a man so bigoted to his political opinions as to leave his home and comforts at an age when they become most alluring, to prove that he was not a mere talker. Let a man's principles be what they may, even though what I should consider erroneous, still if, from a feeling of their truth, abandoning his interests, he can brave hunger, fatigue, and death, to support them in a strange land, he seems to me always entitled to some admiration and esteem.

Bézard reached the army during an action, and was remarked foremost with the guerilla by Zumalacarregui, who, struck by his tall figure, his round hat, and long greatcoat, in the midst of the uncouth Navarrese, observed his behaviour, and inquired who he was: no one could inform him. Zumalacarregui sent for him after the action, and inquired if he was in any corps. He replied, in such Spanish as he could recall from his campaign in the war of the constitution, "That he had come to serve Don Carlos in any capacity which was allotted to him; and, as he had arrived during the action, he had thought that it was no use to seek the General then." So pleased was Zumalacarregui with his behaviour and appearance, that, on inquiring the rank he had held in France, and being answered captain, without further investigation, he placed him as captain in the Guides. This was far from being the General's habit; but he often took strong likings or dislikes on a first interview. He seems to have been a skilful physiognomist; as I believe he was deceived by few of those who had prepossessed him in their favour.

The bravery of Bézard, the deep interest he took in his company, and the strictness with which he attended to the service, it would have been difficult to surpass; and the cheerfulness with which he supported every privation without murmur, showed a man really fighting from principle. More than once, when I have been shivering on my horse, or soaked through, I have smiled to

197

see him bearing his 55 years and all the disagreeables of wind, cold, and rain, with a contented earnestness of countenance. His Roman nose and features, and tall, thin, and somewhat grotesque figure, mounted on his pony, and sitting quite erect, together with his ungartered stockings and short trowsers, showing his bare tanned legs, formed a striking and original picture. He had first seen most of the foreign officers at a sort of drinking party; and although, from his years of service, he must have been well accustomed to that sort of thing, he seemed to have been prejudiced. against them, and I was almost the only person with whom he was on terms of intimacy.

I recollect, two or three days before the affair of Mendaça, Barrez was absent from the parade of the Guides, who assembled on the platform of the church of Piedramillera; for all the usages of regular armies were, as far as possible, strictly enforced. I had the instant before been conversing with him, as I happened to be walking on the platform, and, hearing him called for - I said to Bézard, "Where is Barrez! he has gone somewhere just at the moment when wanted." "I do not know," said he; "it is so much the worse for him; it serves him right for absenting himself." Rather piqued, I ventured to say, that I found it a very extraordinary thing that amongst a handful of Frenchmen in the army, who ought to look upon each other as brethren, there should be nothing but ill-will, antipathy, and jealousy; and that he should consider a French officer getting into any sort of difficulty should be a matter of such perfect indifference. He seemed rather huffed, I thought, at this; but in the evening came to sup with me according to previous appointment. He was remarkably grave, and we both ate in silence: at last he interrupted it by saying, "You were right this morning in what you said; it is sometimes hard to bear a rebuke from those so much younger than ourselves; but you were right - quite right."

Cordova, after his victory, hearing that Zumalacarregui had only retired three miles, and was occupying Zuñiga, flushed with his first success, resolved on attacking him again. As his intention was such, I have never been able to learn why he delayed it till the 15th., retiring from the Beruesa to Los Arcos, and sallying again on the 14th., unless he calculated on still further damping the courage of the Carlists, by leaving them for two days formed during a piercing cold, which they were obliged to endure, as Los Arcos, where his own men were in comfortable quarters, is not above 2 ½ hours' march from the bridge of Arquijas. Zuñiga holds the rank of town, and is still surrounded by an old wall, although of inconsiderable extent: its position, and the inclosures of stone surrounding it, render it easy to be defended. It is in a sort of plain, or rather a piece of table-land, considerably higher than the Beruesa and the valley of Mendaça. To reach it, you must pass over some high and rugged hills, covered with a dense forest of arbutas and laurel, and other evergreens, whose tangled roots and branches twining amongst the rocks, independently of its steepness, render it almost impassable, excepting by the road. The chief obstacle, however, is the river Ega, which runs rapidly between high banks. Although of very inconsiderable breadth and depth, in many parts there are holes, and the stream rushes with such force, that it is very difficult to cross. On the other side the hill is so steep and covered, that you have not 3ft from the edge of the bank to form your men, who may be in a few minutes entirely destroyed from above. In short, excepting by the bridge of Arquijas and the fords about the little plain some 500yds long, extending from the bridge to the hermitage of that name on the opposite hill, if defended, it is impassable.

On the morning of the 15th. December 1834, the piercing cold still continuing, I was sent out reconnoitring with the lancers of the escort; we swept down the valley nearly as far as Mendaça, retiring at safe distance, as we saw all the column advancing. Having dispatched, one by one, the greater part of the detachment, to give notice of every movement of the enemy, or to collect all the information they could gather from the peasantry, we retired into the wood of *encina,* or evergreen oak, which commences on the plain. There were 25 men only, commanded by a sergeant, at least two miles from our advanced posts, standing very quietly round a large fire, although 4,000 or 5,000 men of the advancing column were marching straight in that direction, and were not above 600yds off. I inquired of the sergeant what his orders were? He said to fire a few shots and retreat across the rocks skirmishing. He had all chosen men with him, stout, active fellows, joking and snatching the acorns of the *encina* out of the hot embers with their fingers, taking the same amusement in it as children at snapdragon, and quite heedless of the impending action, and the dangerous situation in which, to the eyes of one unaccustomed to the agility of the guerillas, they seemed placed. "Come, take your muskets," said the sergeant to his men as we passed; "it is high time to post ourselves." This sergeant was a gallant fellow; he was a student at Pampeluna, whence he made his escape, entered the ranks, and was afterwards promoted to a commission when in the hospital where he died, having had his arm shattered by a musket ball about half an hour after we left him. Notwithstanding his wound, he led his men back in safety, having executed his commission with the greatest intrepidity and success. He killed and wounded several of the enemy before they reached the hermitage of Arquijas, and shot the horse of a field-officer under him.

The hermitage or chapel stands quite alone in the wilderness[93]; it something resembles that of William Tell at Cusnach. As our own advanced guard was at the bridge, we halted and dismounted, and a fire being still burning there, the men eagerly began their breakfast. My own was as frugal as theirs - a draught of brandy and some bread which my servant toasted in the embers. As I had eaten nothing since the previous midday, I never breakfasted with more appetite; and when an order came for us to withdraw immediately, which indeed it was high time for cavalry to do, as the shot were already beginning to whistle about our ears from the enemy's skirmishers, who were clearing the road, I

---

[93] Founded in the 13th. Century, rebuilt in the 16th., it houses the image of Our Lady of Arquijas.

remember abandoning another piece of crust, which was just warming, with considerable regret.

It was by this time half-past eleven. The 4th. battalion, and part of the 3rd. of Navarre, were stationed along the further bank of the Ega, where they were well sheltered by the trees. The rest of Zumalacarregui's force, amounting in all to 11 battalions, were distributed on the heights, or echeloned behind Zuñiga in reserve. 600 horse were formed in the plain, between Zuñiga, Orbiso, and Santa Cruz, which they entirely commanded. Cordova had sent forward one column under Oraa[94], by a long and tedious march, to attempt to take us in the rear by the Val de Llana. To let them gain time, he had delayed his attack till the hour I have mentioned. Zumalacarregui, who well knew that it would be four or five hours before there could be any danger from them, left there only a small force, the 1st., 2nd. and 3rd. of Alava, under Villareal, trusting to his cavalry, which was in high spirits, and burning to revenge the defeat of Mendaça, to command the plain. Zumalacarregui himself was before the gate of Zuñiga, with the large masses of his force. His intention, I firmly believe, from his disposition, was to have charged them before they had been able to form in the plain, between Zuñiga and the wood and ravine which leads down to the Ega, as I do not think he anticipated the obstinate defence the 4th. Battalion made of the passage of the river. Cordova, having reached the hermitage, planted there four field-pieces, and took possession of all the heights on his own side of the river, whence the firing soon became heavy between the enemy and our troops, who vigorously replied. Zumalacarregui now sent down the Guides and a battalion of Castille, incessant efforts being made by Cordova to gain a footing on the little plain at the foot of the hermitage, whence his men were instantly swept like chaff before the wind.

---

[94] Marcelino de Oraá Lecumberri (1788–1851), field marshal 1836; later Governor-General of the Philippines

For four hours the artillery of the enemy and the volleys rapidly succeeding each other were heard echoing amongst the hills like thunder. We rode three or four times to the scene of action, to see the wounded carried off and afford them assistance; our men were still firm at their post; once it was a very interesting moment - the enemy had succeeded in forming two battalions of carabineers on the small piece of open ground which I have mentioned, formed by the winding of the river and the surrounding hills into a sort of amphitheatre - and a tremendous fire had been opened under cover of it; they were making a desperate push to cross the river; the slaughter as they advanced was very great; but the foremost succeeded in crossing the bridge, when they were charged at the bayonet by the Guides, and driven back in the greatest disorder. The cries of about 14, who were cut off on this side of the river, I could distinctly hear from where I was standing, "*La vida! la vida! por la carita!*" "Quarter! quarter! in the name of charity!" - but no quarter was given. The enemy then retired for a moment; the bugles sounding through the din of action to cease the firing, and to prepare for fresh efforts. Before Zuñiga, as we returned with the General and his staff, a dead silence reigned.

The action was now to be decided at the bridge; and down the road two lines of troops were constantly moving, silently and in good order; one returning from the fire and bearing their wounded, and the other going to relieve the combatants. By this means Zumalacarregui constantly had fresh men entering the action. Amongst the wounded I shook hands, as he passed, he passed, with poor Bezard, who was carried by, the thigh bone of the same leg on which he had been wounded three days previously having been broken by a grape shot. He had persisted on entering the fight although very lame, and was struck as he was taking cartridges from the belt of a dead man, to give to one of his company, who complained he had no more.

In the cemetery of a ruined chapel they were burying two of our officers, who had died as they were bearing them to Zuñiga.

The bodies were not cold as they were stripped and wrapped in one cloak for a winding sheet. The stripping of both friends and foes, by the Carlist soldiers, was a striking feature of this war, where one army was armed, equipped, and clothed, from the spoils of the other. All the dead bodies that you met with were entirely naked, and, on account of the white and livid appearance of the flesh, exhibited a spectacle infinitely more ghastly than they would otherwise have presented. Almost the instant a man had breathed his last, the spoilers were upon him, and he was stripped with a dexterity and quickness scarcely conceivable. This spectacle was to be seen sometimes during the hottest fire of an action. Even on the little plain between the bridge and hermitage of Arquijas, stragglers of our volunteers might be seen busily engaged, although more than one paid the penalty of his hardihood.

This rapacity at first much disgusted me, and gave the idea of an unconquerable spirit of plunder; but after a little while it seemed natural enough. Clothes, ammunition, shoes, arms, money, everything they were accustomed to take from the enemy; from him only were they to be got. When they asked for them from their leaders, they were told, "There are the Christinos, take them!" This reply was more than once made to their complaints by Zumalacarregui himself. In other respects, I think I have mentioned already that, under such circumstances, perhaps never any army existed where so much honesty, sobriety, and order were to be found, on account of the extreme severity of discipline the Commander-in-Chief had introduced in that respect.

The firing, and the efforts of Cordova to cross the bridge, had been incessant till half past three in the afternoon: after being driven back over the bridge, he caused attempts to be made by fording. As soon as they reached the bank his men were, however, cut to pieces. The attack after this continued comparatively feeble, and, no doubt, the enemy, despairing of being able to pass, would have entirely desisted from it, had he not been awaiting the effect of Oraa's division, which already, by the *puerto* or defile of

203

Gastrain, was entering the Val de Llana, to take us in the rear. A small column had also gained Santa Cruz di Campezzu, of course without cavalry. As on the other side of Santa Cruz the ground is a level plain, and occupied by vineyards, three squadrons of cavalry were despatched thither, instead of being sent against Oraa.

Oraa meanwhile resolved on making a desperate push, and the Alavese, under Villareal, prevented only by the personal intrepidity of Ituralde from being routed, were giving back in some confusion, when Zumalacarregui himself, with the 1st. Battalion of Navarre, and the 1st. of Guipuscoas, hurried to the scene of action. His appearance changed directly the fortune of the day; Oraa was driven back in some confusion. The battalions which had exhausted their cartridges at the bridge immediately advanced by order of Zumalacarregui; upon which the Queen's general, who found his men unable to keep their ground against the impetuosity of the two fresh battalions now attacking them, was little disposed to wait the approach of a force which, for aught he knew, was well supplied with ammunition, and precipitately retreated. Cordova, also, when night came on, was glad to retrace his steps, and lighting fires in the mountains on the other side of the river, to make the Carlists believe that he intended passing the night there, fell back on Los Arcos, his army in a dreadful state of disorder, of which their own fatigue and the night coming on had prevented the Carlists from taking advantage. Cordova carried back with him 350 wounded, and left above that number of dead on the field.

Of the column of Oraa I cannot speak with certainty; but its loss is supposed to have been much more considerable, and in wounded must inevitably have been so; for at the bridge, although the firing was tremendous during so many hours, fresh troops coming up constantly to relieve each other on both sides, the loss was comparatively insignificant, as on each side they were greatly protected by the rock and wood. The whole loss of the Christinos, in killed, wounded, and missing, was estimated at 1,500; that of the Carlists, which, as I was constantly up and down the line where the

204

wounded were passing, I had some opportunity of calculating, I should estimate at 400. A great number of Christino officers perished in proportion to the number of men. Close by the hermitage of Arquijas, three that had fallen there had been buried.

A Polish officer - the only one in the service95 - this day deserted to the enemy. The manner in which he had been treated, on account of the interest the story he had told us created, rendered this still more unpardonable. He had served in the army of Miguel, as several of the French officers had known him in Portugal; and he immediately received his lieutenancy from the King. Zumalacarregui placed him in the 6th. Battalion of Navarre. He had taken, he told us, an active part in the Polish revolution, as well as his family: they had, in consequence, been sent to Siberia, he alone having been able to effect his escape. His object in serving a cause that little interested him was, to obtain an attestation from Don Carlos, as he had from Don Miguel, of having served him faithfully - which was the only reward he looked for; and, throwing himself at the feet of the Emperor of Russia with these credentials, he hoped to obtain his father's release. He pretended that he had come from the frontiers of Portugal by land, hiding by day, and travelling by night. He was a universal favourite; and we should all, I believe, have done anything to serve him. On his first disappearance, imagining him to have been taken prisoner, his loss was greatly lamented; and even Zumalacarregui, whom the story of his having come hundreds of leagues to fight in a strange land for a father's liberation had greatly interested, sent to Mina to make him offers of a most advantageous exchange, if his life were spared. A few days after, we were informed by the *confidentes* that he was well known by Mina, and had been all the time only a spy, who had fooled us all. He was then in some regiment in Pampeluna. When we knew this to be the case, we all wondered at our own stupidity, in not perceiving his falsehood at once, when he joined the army

---

[95] Some strains of Polish nationalism identified with the Carlist cause; however Poles fought on both sides of the war.

in a military undress, in which he pretended to have come from the frontiers of Portugal, sharp as the look-out on all strangers must have been by the police in the provinces through which he must have passed. This is the only foreign officer, I must in justice add, who in any way misbehaved himself; and on that account it was still more deeply felt.

In the dusk of the evening I met Lacour; he accosted me with "Your friend Bézard is wounded." "I know it," said I; "he has the same leg broken in which he was wounded three days ago down in the plain." "*Il en vouloit donc à cette malheureuse jambe il avoit juré de la laisser la.*" "He had a spite against that unfortunate limb; he had sworn to leave it there, it appears," said he, drily. I could not help smiling at his expression: he reminded me of the French soldier of fortune who was standing beside Charles XII of Sweden, at the siege of Fredericshal, when he received his death-wound, and said, very coolly, "*La pièce est joueé—allons maintenant souper."* "The piece is played out— let us to supper."

That night I slept at Orbiso on a table; it was desperately cold; and, in consequence, nearly all those who had received any severe wounds died. The cold and the snow, which was beginning to fall very fast, caused us to retire into the Amescoas, the enemy being shut up in Estella, Los Arcos, and Viana, which had been fortified after the defeat of Carandolet there in the month of August previous. Rest was peculiarly acceptable, there being 3ft of snow upon the ground; and, moreover, we could not have assumed the offensive for some time, from the want of ammunition; our manufactory in the Bastan and at Eckala, in the Amescoas, only producing a limited quantity daily, made from saltpetre and sulphur smuggled over the Pyrenees from France, by the *contrabandistas,* at 100% on the value. Gunpowder itself could not be got in France without so much risk of detection, that those who furnished us, entirely declined undertaking to send it in its manufactured state. This want of ammunition, which so often occurred, was another of those obstacles with which the great

Carlist Chieftain had to battle. The soldiers in so many instances had only had the cartridges distributed to them an hour before entering action, that it was never known in the army when they really did fail. In consequence, the enemy could not take advantage, which he might otherwise have done through his spies, of the critical situations in which this want had sometimes placed the Carlist army.

While we were in the Amescoas, learning by chance that Bézard was at Contrasta, I went thither to visit him. Although it was only nine miles, it took me nearly four hours, on account of the great depth of snow upon the roads, in most places from 4-6ft. My horse fell or floundered about in it repeatedly. The villages I passed through were full of wounded, who had all been very insufficiently attended to: at Contrasta they were almost entirely neglected. I found Bézard in a miserable room, of which the shutters had been closed to keep out the cold wind: he was stretched on a mattress of maize-straw. He was attended only by a half idiotic servant, whom he had always persisted in retaining. Although he was evidently in great pain, he bore his sufferings with a resignation I have but rarely witnessed. I was shocked to learn, that although five days had elapsed since the action, excepting a bandage put on on the field, his wound had never been dressed. The bed was full of blood, which was already in a putrid state; and the people of the house, like most of the peasantry, seemed afraid to meddle with his wound, though they expressed their good will, by bringing him quantities of food, which he could not touch. He said that he was well aware, from the neglect he had experienced, that his fate was sealed. "So," said he, "let the will of God be done." He did not repine; if things could happen over again, he would act, he said, as he had done; and although he had suffered much, he had no reason to regret death in such a cause. The day after his being wounded at Mendaça, he had received a letter, acquainting him with the death of his father, who had reached an extreme old age. In allusion to this, he observed, with a smile, "The saying of the old women in my country is true. When one misfortune follows close on the heels of another, the third and greatest is always near."

My first impulse was to return to Eulate as quickly as the road would permit me. I went straight to Zumalacarregui, to whom I related what I had seen. He flew into a violent passion. The head surgeon, to calm him, said that the person sent to dress his wound must have passed me on the road. This was untrue. He then wrote on a piece of paper an order, under *pena de la vida,* or pain of death, for all the surgeons I met to follow me. This order, given in his anger, showed how much he was carried away by his feelings; for, if I had chosen literally to make use of the mandate, and take with me all the medical attendants of the several hundred wounded in the intermediate villages to compensate one act of injustice and neglect, he would have forced them to commit many more.

Having taken up two surgeons on the road, and two servants, one of whom was a Frenchman, and an excellent nurse, I immediately returned to Bezard, although much fatigued, and almost frozen with cold. About half an hour after we had been there, the staff-surgeon and an aide-de camp came from the General; the latter to bring him a sum in case he should be in want of any money. The surgeons spoke with confidence to him, of curing his wound; but he was not deceived, and if they had been in earnest in their assertions, I had seen sufficient of their want of skill to know that it was a hopeless case. He begged of me constantly not to omit to learn how his company was going. I always answered, that we were too much interested about him to think of his company. The last words of the old soldier were, to beg of me not to forget to deliver to the colonel of the Guides, Torres, his message - reminding him that, at the last distribution of greatcoats (for the Guides were now regularly dressed), his company had received 21 less than their number: "the poor fellows," added he, "must want them in this weather."

208

The next day my duty called me on an expedition, to cut off a foraging party of horse peseteros in the vicinity of Estella. We succeeded in capturing four, but they escaped, on account of their horses being rough shod; and this precaution having been neglected as to ours, on attempting to pursue, several fell, and blocked up the road. We had two killed that day, by missing their footing and rolling down a ravine. Meanwhile, Bézard was removed to the regular hospital at Narque, in the Val De Rana, where, three days after, he expired. On account of several signal acts of bravery, and the interest his devotion to the cause had excited, he was made knight of San Fernando. The diploma, however, only arrived the day after his death; so that he had not the satisfaction of knowing anything about it.

The arrival of Mina, fourth on the list of generals who had failed in their efforts against the revolted provinces, when he came to throw the colossal reputation he enjoyed in those countries into the scale in favour of the Queen, created some apprehension in the Carlist party in Spain, and was considered, beyond the Pyrenees, as a decisive event. But Zumalacarregui, well acquainted with his character and the real extent of his talent, shared none of those forebodings, and spoke with a degree of confidence and assurance in which it was not his habit to indulge. He was generally very modest in the terms in which he expressed himself, either before or after an engagement. Sometimes when he first met with a new general in the field, he would express himself ironically nearly in the following terms:- "Ah, there is general such-a-one - I have heard much of him I do not doubt his superior talent at all - but we must try; perhaps some of us may escape from the action." When Mina took the command, he several times repeated, "I had rather have to deal with him than anybody; others give me much trouble in guessing their movements and combinations; those of Mina I know beforehand." Mina, indeed, was an old fox, but he had to deal with one who knew his earths well, and circumstances had widely changed since the War of Independence. Intimately

209

acquainted with the country, he has much talent as a guerrilla chief, and for a warfare carried on in the style of that which at this day Merino wages. But in the present conflict he was like a man skilful in the exercise of one weapon, wielding another to which he has never been accustomed; and found himself at the head of regular armies, playing the same game the French had played against himwhich, by experience, he knew to be a most hopeless one.

If Mina had found himself at the head of the Carlist insurrection, at the pitch to which Zumalacarregui had brought it after four or five months - although I doubt whether he would, before that period, have prevented it from being crushed in its cradle - he would probably have remained carrying on a more desultory mode of warfare to this day in the provinces, but without making those rapid advances in which the Guipuscoan General succeeded - advances not in point of territory, but of strength; for Zumalacarregui always looked upon the provinces as the arena where the quarrel, not only of legitimacy and usurpation, but of the partisans of the liberal form of government and of municipal tyranny against those of an absolute form and of municipal freedom and ancient privileges, was to be decided. From the very beginning, he said "that Navarre was the battlefield where Madrid must be won or lost;" and to that territory he confined himself, as the most favourable to his purpose. He commenced by defeating the smaller divisions of the enemy's army, assuming, day by day, a more imposing attitude, until he at last ventured to await all their combined force under Valdes, and ended by driving it so completely out of the field, that he was allowed to capture all those garrisons which could not escape, to St. Sebastian or Pampeluna, without an effort being made to prevent him. A feeble reserve, and some uncertain regiments, only interposed between him and Madrid. He then successively attacked and took the different fortified places, principally for the artillery and cartridges they contained, which were necessary for the long march he intended commencing on the capital; and such was the terror he had struck into the Queen's party, that he would probably have reached Madrid without a single shot being fired. 8,000 or 9,000 men might have kept Valdes and all the force of the provinces entirely in check; and he could have led 20,000 men through the two Castilles. His untimely end, besides the blow it was to his own party, restored to the enemy all their moral force. The army of Valdes, which, from its total demoralization and the discouragement that pervaded its ranks, was as useless as if entirely destroyed, became, as soon as Zumalacarregui's death was known, again an army nearly as formidable as before its defeat; it was as if 20,000 men for the Queen had started into life. While Zumalacarregui was alive, they were afraid to meet him again on any terms; but, after his death, they drove the Carlists from the ground at Mendigorria, on the 16th. July 1835.

All this proved, that in keeping for so many months so cautiously within the same circle, Zumalacarregui had judged well; and this has given rise to the idea, that he was a mere mountain chieftain - a second Mina. There was, however, a wide difference between the two. Mina, when placed at the head of a regular army, seemed entirely lost. I am not reproaching him with his want of success; for his knowledge of the kind of warfare carried on by the enemy tended only to discourage him, as it served to show the impossibility of all remedy against it. The nature of the country, and the devotion of the inhabitants, were formidable weapons, and he knew, full well, how to have used them, and how they were used against his army; but this was to him of no avail; for, against the popular cause, it was impossible for him ever to apply them. Most of the Queen's generals, indeed, were not ignorant of the reason why it became impracticable to pursue - to cut off - to surround - or to disperse, beyond a few minutes, the Carlists; but over these causes they had no control. Other officers, as well as Mina, possessed ample knowledge of the rapid modes of conveying despatches and orders, and thereby forming combinations; but that knowledge was of no use; they might give their *partes* or

211

despatches to the peasantry, but as there was no commanding the good will of the people, and as neither gold nor menaces could work on their stubborn dispositions, it was only giving their despatches into the hands of their enemies. The veterans of the Christinos knew every path and glen, but they dared not cross these with a few armed men, as in the times when they had the inhabitants in their favour, without the certainty of being cut off. Wherever they marched with a large force - men, women, and children dispersed as spies in every direction, and gave intelligence of their approach.

Mina, I therefore repeat, cannot be reproached with his want of success; but with having done less than any of the other generals. Zumalacarregui, instead of confining himself to the almost predatory warfare of the other chiefs and of Mina during his war against the French, in everything attempted to regularize his army, and only fought in the mountain because he was too weak yet to enter on the plain. His object was, not to maintain himself like Merino, but to form an army that might fight its way to Madrid, which was his grand object. Instead of risking his force in Castille, by advancing, he waited until they had been obliged to send everything against him in the provinces - to conquer them on his own ground, where he could fight the battle to such advantage. Until the defeat of Valdes, the destruction of the divisions of Oraa, Iriarte, and Espartero, at the siege of Villafranca, he had never really been in a situation prudently to take the plains of Castille; and then it was his intention to have marched on Madrid.

Mina did less than the other generals, from want of military talent, or at least military knowledge. Zumalacarregui, who, as colonel, was known to have studied deeply *la tactica Francesa,* as the tactics of a regular army are termed, was not kept in the mountains by ignorance in this respect, but from the superior number of his enemies - the difficulty of disciplining his troops - want of arms, ammunition, cavalry, and artillery - all indispensable in a flat country. These obstacles he had at last overcome, excepting the two last; and these he had in great part conquered. The reputation he has won was earned while he was forming an army; and at the moment that, from the spoils of his enemy, and the rude materials afforded him, he had fashioned one to his own hands, at the moment that, having fortunately struggled through difficulties almost unparalleled in the history of war, considering the means of success at his disposal - he died.

I forget which of the Christino generals it was, who, surprised at the discipline the Carlist troops displayed during some affair at an early stage of the war, said of him, "That man would make soldiers out of the trees, if he had no other materials." Mina also, whether to palliate his own disgrace, or from a nobler motive, on retiring from his command to Montpellier, did him justice. On hearing of his death, he said publicly, that, as a partisan, he rejoiced - but, as a Spaniard, he was inclined to weep; for Spain had lost a man upon whose like *"pour de longues années elle ne reverroi pas"* - for many a long year she would not look again. What had always given Zumalacarregui the greatest uneasiness during the first year of the war was the fear of French intervention. In that case, he said, he would assemble all his battalions, and disband them, excepting six, recommending each man, as he was a true Spaniard, to bury his musket against a future day. These six he would disperse into the mountains, and, leading a complete guerrilla life, wandering all over Spain from one chain to another, he doubted not of being able to escape all the efforts of his enemies to take him; and to be ready, as soon as the storm was over, and the foreign torrent had swept by, to recommence, and descend into a less inaccessible country to arouse that spirit of the Spanish people, which may be kept down, but never crushed - and would only glow the more intensely from the attempt to suppress it.

The Lancers of Navarre in which Henningsen served as a Captainat the age of 20

CHAPTER XIV

Conveyance of Despatches - Junction of the Christino Army - Disposition of Carlist Troops - Battle of Segura - Burying the Dead - A night Surprise – Lacour's promotion - Retreat of the 3rd. January - Destruction of the Regiment of Granada - Pursuit of the Enemy.

On 2nd. January 1835, we were in Villareal of Guipuscoa; so called, to distinguish it from Villareal of Alava, and innumerable other Villareals in Spain. We had spent there new year's day, and were, as usual, tolerably ignorant of the movements of the enemy. Indeed, the whole army had such confidence in the General, that there were few who interested themselves about what the enemy was doing, except when forming in battle. We, however, learned that a column had slept at Oñate, where at first it was supposed we were going, the day before. At 10 the march was beat, and cartridges distributed, which, joined to several other circumstances, occasioned a report that we were to have a brush; circumstances, indeed, rendered it probable. Zumalacarregui had quietly marched with only four battalions and a squadron of horse to a place near the vicinity of Bergara, Bilboa, St. Sebastian, and Villafranca, which were all strongly garrisoned, and could easily unite so overpowering a force, that it was unlikely they would allow him to return unmolested. We took the high road to Vittoria. The soldiers were in high spirits on leaving the province, where, as it produced no wine, they had only received half rations. The patronas were all at their doors and windows, waving their hands, and expressing their best wishes to their lodgers as they defiled.

On the road, several peasants came running up to the General; two of them delivering up the "*partes*," despatches of the Christinos, for which they obtained receipts, and departed. The Queen's generals, as I have stated, attempted the same mode for the conveyance of their orders and despatches as the Carlists; but in vain. The documents were usually given to the alcalde or regidor, to forward, on pain of death, from village to village, until they reached the division to which they were addressed. Obliged

215

to receive them, the peasant who was pitched upon as messenger, left the village, but went straight in search of the Carlists, gave his papers up, and asked for a certificate that he had been stopped. If he had been inclined to have acted otherwise, he would have feared that his own relations - nay, that the very stones would denounce him.

One of these *"partes"* announced, what the peasants confirmed to us, the junction of the four columns of Espartero, Jauregui, Lorenzo, and Carratala, uniting, in all, a force of upwards of 12,000 men. It was addressed to the governor of Vittoria, and concluded by stating, that the arch rebel was at last fairly hemmed in without possibility of an escape; and that he must perish inevitably with all his division, not amounting to 3,000 men. Certainly the Carlist force was not undervalued. Having reached the village of Ormaistegui, the birth-place of the General, we took to the right, and halted on the steep mountain which affords the only passage to the valley, at the further end of which is the small town of Segura. The hill, which is bold and steep, is entirely naked; but as it is used for pasture ground, it is divided into a number of fields, all surrounded by walls of loose stones, which separate the herds of cattle. Although it does not appear so at first sight, it is, in fact, a position of amazing strength, if held by an adequate number of men to defend it, as the walls form a succession of parapets and natural defences.

Here Zumalacarregui formed the Guides of Navarre and the 6th. Battalion, sending the 3rd. on to take possession of Segura, which, just touching the mountain on the opposite side of the valley, would have been vigorously defended if the position on the first mountain had been forced. The 4th. Battalion of Guipuscoa was on a hill to the right of the plain, between the two ridges, where they could alike prevent the possibility of the first being turned, or with the cavalry protect the retreat if it had become necessary, from one to the other. This, at first, would have appeared a difficult thing to have attempted without entire destruction, had it not been that

216

the road down was so steep that the enemy's cavalry could only have ome *pas à pas,* and Segura would have been reached before they were on level ground, where horse could pursue; whereas one squadron was quite enough to keep their infantry, disorderly as they must have been when they reached the bottom, in check, while unsupported. It was evident from all these dispositions that the General intended to make them pay for their passage dearly, and give them another repetition of the affair of the bridge of Arquijas. The disparity of numbers alone seemed startling. There were barely 1,700 men of the 3,000 who could be actually engaged, and the enemy, who by this time was in the village of Ormaistegui, and along the royal road, was above 12,000 in number, with artillery and mountain-pieces.

The soldiers seemed rather uneasy, and were wondering what could be the use of exposing them there, when Segura offered a position so near the mountains, and afforded so favourable a retreat. The General, however, had his private reasons for wishing to make as vigorous a stand as possible, there or thereabouts, as next day he expected Ituralde with a strong division on their rear from the Borunda.

The confidence and sang-froid which Zumalacarregui displayed, in some measure inspired the soldiers, as they saw the dark masses of the Christinos moving upwards from the road and taking possession of each side of the gorge. The fire had already been opened some time by the guerrillas, or tirailleurs, and ours had been gradually retiring as the enemy advanced, firmly but slowly. The columns of El Pastor or Jauregui and Espartero were those which attacked, I believe, on the right, where the Guides of Navarre were stationed, part in reserve, just sheltered by the brow of the hill, and the rest lining the stone walls on the left. In that it must have been Lorenzo and Carratala who attacked the 6th. Battalion, but their efforts were throughout feeble, compared with those which were made on the right, where a tremendous fire had now opened on both sides. Under continued volleys of musketry

217

and grape, the enemy, with some loss, got possession of several stone walls, which we had not men enough to defend, and the greatest exertions were made to carry the fences behind which part of the Guides were sheltered. Some of the Christino officers behaved on this occasion with the utmost bravery in attempting to lead on their men, who seemed emulating the peseteros, and other tag-rag of which El Pastor's column was composed. Three officers of one company were shot down successively in attempting to lead it across, as they presented themselves entirely uncovered, urging their men on sword in hand.

The Carlists kept up a rolling fire, and then *feu de peloton*, with a regularity and order almost incredible in such half-disciplined troops, and which I thought they would have been incapable of exhibiting during a review. Zumalacarregui, his whip in hand, for he seldom drew his sword, was galloping entirely exposed behind the lines, exhorting them to keep firm. *A ver que no passan, muchachos!* (Let us see that they do not pass, my lads!) *No passaran! No passaran!* (They shall not pass! they shall not pass!) replied the men. In the midst of the fire two captains of Guides and 14 men rushed down to take possession of a little piece of wall; 13 reached it, and being partly sheltered, kept up a galling fire at 30yds from the enemy, until only six returned, and those mostly wounded. The captain of the 1st. Company, Morrales, was killed, and Captain Sabatier wounded in the shoulder; the company were consequently obliged to retire. Finding that they were losing many men and only encouraging the enemy, the Christino Generals, who began to find that in catching "Uncle Tomas" they had caught a Tartar, ordered a simultaneous charge at the bayonet to be made on both sides, to force the position by one bold push. Accordingly the carabineros and peseteros of Jauregui's division ran in upon the Carlists with considerable fierceness and determination; but the fire of the Guides, which continued admirably regular, waxed warmer and warmer as they rushed forward. The commandant of the peseteros and numerous officers

218

fell, which occasioned a moment of indecision, and was immediately taken advantage of. A few voices amongst the Guides crying, "a la bayonetta," the tables were turned, and the whole battalion rushing down to meet them half way entirely dispersed them, retaking even to the lowest wall, and leaving more than 100 of the enemy, whom they bayoneted, dead on the space between. Having once drawn blood with cold steel, the Guides, as they were opposed chiefly to the peseteros and carabineers, who were held in particular terror and detestation, became so animated that three times during the successive efforts the Christinos made with reinforcements to regain their footing on the heights, where, in spite of the Carlist fire they formed in considerable masses, they were driven back and dispersed at the point of the bayonet with considerable slaughter, Zumalacarregui exhorting them "To spare the lead and use the iron." So effectual had been the third dispersion, that the enemy hastily moved his artillery from the opposite height, and the retreat was ordered - disorder and discouragement being evidently in his ranks. The Carlist General with difficulty restrained his men; but as, by this time, night was coming on, and they were fatigued, and almost without a cartridge, he feared the enemy's rallying further on, when he saw the immense disparity of numbers; and was on so much more favourable ground.

I must not here omit to mention the behaviour of a gallant little corneta (or bugleman) of the Battalion of the Guides, who, exposed to all the fire, considerably amused and encouraged the soldiers, by the rapid changes of the tunes he played. *Halto el fuego* - to stop the fire, when that of the enemy slackened; *Retirada,* or retreat, when they gave way; and when they attempted to storm the position, the "fandango."

On the left wing, the 6th. Battalion had been much more feebly attacked, but had stood their ground equally well. The horse of Pablo Sanz[96], the colonel, had been shot under him, as he was

[96] Pablo Sanz y Baeza (1801 - 1839)

219

talking to Zumalacarregui: it was one which had belonged to the grandee Via Manuel, taken prisoner at the rocks of St. Faustus. When the enemy attempted to force the whole line at the bayonet, the Regiment of St. Ferdinand advanced with considerable resolution; but, on being met half way by five companies which descended, the courage of the men failed them, and the whole regiment wavered, and gave way. Sanz, a number of officers, and about 100 men pursued them and if they had been seconded by the whole of the battalion-which, less daring than the Guides, was alarmed at the numerical superiority of the enemy, and seemed afraid to go too far from its old position - the whole regiment might have been destroyed. The handful who advanced with their officers, finding themselves unsupported, although quite close to the enemy, who was retiring in disorder, instead of completing it by striking with their bayonets, stopped to load and fire. It is true, *"à brule pourpoint"* from the enemy, who, rallied by their officers, effecting their retreat in something like order, at last obliged the Carlists to retire. Although judged imprudent to pursue, it was glorious for 1,700 men to have repulsed, after seven hours' hard fighting, more than eight times their number, commanded by four generals of some reputation, and leading some of the best troops of the Queen's army. Her generals, it is said, came to such high words, that it was reported two of them (Pastor and Espartero) even pulled each other by the hair, each attributing to the other the disgraceful issue of their intended capture of the Carlist chief, of which they were in confident expectation. He might have said, like the French dragoons at Lyons, or the bear to the hunters - *"Qu'il étoit promis, mais no pas encore livré."*[97] Determined, however, to attempt the passage again next day, they retired, and encamped in the village of Ormaistegui and along the royal road. The Carlists took up their quarters in Segura and Segama.

---

[97] On the entry of the allies into Lyons, the French dragoons, imagining that they had been sold by their generals, exclaimed, "Nous sommes vendus, mais pas encore livrés." CFH

At daybreak I was sent with a few lancers to see that the peasants buried the dead. Several trenches had already been filled; but opposite the right of our position two were covered up, in one of which were 90, and in the other 40 bodies, nearly all having been killed by bayonet wounds. I fancied that their countenances seemed more distorted than those who died from shot. They were nearly all stark naked. I recognized the commandant of peseteros, however, by his red trowsers, which, having been pierced in two places, and entirely saturated with blood, had not been taken off, but about the fob had been ripped open with a knife. He was a fine military looking man; his mouth, from which a stream of blood had flowed, was wide open, and his corpse exhibited a ghastly appearance. Most of those who had been shot during the action were carried off and buried by the enemy behind their lines, which accounted for our finding none in the places where their masses had been formed, and must have suffered terribly, but the earth, newly turned up in innumerable places, showed where they were at rest. From what I saw, and the number of places where our horses' feet had sunk in the mould, I should not estimate the loss of the enemy at less than 400 dead, and certainly 600 or 700 wounded. That of the Carlists, in killed and wounded, was about 350, the dead being more than 1/3 of the number; for, as behind the boundaries of stone, the head and shoulders only were exposed, a great proportion of the wounds were mortal. The General having sent to know how many dead the enemy had left on the field, his messenger counted 260 on the hill. Knowing how apt his people were to exaggeration, according to his custom, he said, "*Put half the number in the bulletin*" but as those who framed those documents were unwilling to allow the enemy this advantage, they made things square, by ridiculously diminishing our own loss, and often augmenting that of the enemy in wounded and prisoners, if they were not allowed to set down the largest number reported to have been slain. Amongst the wounded were three French officers, two of Guides, and one of the 4th. Battalion of Guipuscoa, which, considering the small number of French serving in the Carlist army-not exceeding 20 - is another proof, to add to the many I can give, of the gallantry with which they always behaved.

On returning, I met with a French ensign named Guetier de Lacour, who, out of compliment to the daring feat he had performed, had been invited to breakfast with the General. As I shall have more than once occasion to speak of this officer, and he is one of the well-known characters in the Carlist army, a word respecting his history may not be *mal-à-propos*. Of an ancient but poor family, he ran away from his home at an early age, enlisted, and, from the rank of drummer, rose to be maître d'armes and first serjeant. Being, unfortunately like many troopers, addicted to the bottle, this propensity alone retarded his promotion to the grade of commissioned officers, who, in the French army, are all raised from the ranks. He deserted from the 4th. Legion, which was then at Bayonne, on hearing of the war in Spain, and presented himself to Zumalacarregui, with whom I have already mentioned his first interview. At the surprise of Viana he placed himself almost touching the chasseurs of the guard, who were divided from him by a trench, and were all firing on him with their carbines and pistols, and discharged a musket which he had taken up, eight or ten times with deadly effect, going through the exercise while loading as precisely as if on parade - for the edification of his men. He afterwards distinguished himself by many acts of bravery; and as he was looked upon as a perfect desperado, he had been sent the night before, when the enemy had retired to Ormaistegui, at least five miles from our lines, to cut off their outposts, with 50 men; a thing which was rendered very dangerous from the number of free troops (Peseteros, Chapelgorries &c.) who were with Jauregui's column, and who, being intimately acquainted with the country, it was feared would intercept him. As he described it to me, having buckled on a cartridge belt, and taken a musket himself, he followed the road until in sight of the enemy, who, being scarcely able to lodge their staff-officers in the village, were scattered round

222

their bivouac fires all along the road. When he was within 300yds, he perceived two peasants descending into the village, who were challenged and admitted. The fear of their being spies who were giving information, considerably alarmed his men, which prevented Lacour from doing what he might otherwise have done, and obliged him, being determined, as he said, "not to leave without wishing them good night, to commence operations more precipitately than he had intended." Advancing through the field where, as it was already dark, they were enabled to march to within 50yds without being discovered; and, having exhorted the men to aim well at the dusky figures of soldiers, thrown out by the glare of their fires, he poured in a murderous volley. The confusion that followed may be imagined, several of the men falling dead with their faces on the hot ashes. As no shot could be fired, according to the regulation in the Christino army, without the order of their generals, the officers commenced by extinguishing the fires, kicking away the fagots and the pots which were ranged round them, and contained the soldiers' supper, in all directions. His men having fired six cartridges each, Lacour, who rightly judged that, as soon as the confusion had a little subsided, and they found that it had been such a partial discharge, they would detach the Chapelgorries after them, now precipitately retreated, passing, in spite of every obstacle, through the stream, and straight across the woods and ravines. If he had not done so, 1,000yds further on, the paths had all been cut off; but the enemy were afraid to pursue him. I must not omit to state, that Lacour had passed between their outposts, and opened fire on the main body of the troops that were bivouacking. He regained Segura without losing a man, having killed, as our spies next day informed us, 17 men, two serjeants, and a captain, besides the wounded. Lacour, on going to make his report, found Zumalacarregui at breakfast; he insisted on Lacour's joining him, and praised his courage, while he was pressing him to do justice to his repast.

"As I had scarcely drunk a pint of brandy," said Lacour, "to keep out the morning dew - eating without drinking was very dry work - so I gave my neighbour, whom fortune placed nearer the bottle, a hearty slap on the shoulder, saying, "Pour us out something to drink, my friend;" it was the General Guibelalde. Imagining I did not know him, he took the opportunity of telling me so afterwards; but as Zumalacarregui was smiling on me, of course all was sunshine. *"Lacour is a great favourite with us all,"* observed one, *"it is he who took four men and a corporal at Vittoria"* *"Lacour is a true soldier,"* said the General. *"Yes, General,"* replied he, *"it is Lacour here, and Lacour there, when there is anything to be done; but when it is to change the epaulette from the left shoulder to the right[98] - no Lacour then."* "I have taken care of you; you must have a little patience - your commission of lieutenant is with the King." "It has been with the King a long time," observed the ensign, drily. Zumalacarregui, who knew the truth of the observation, said something aside to his secretary; and the next evening he received his commission, and 10 pieces of gold to distribute to his men.

On the morning of the 3rd. January, about 10 o'clock, to our surprise, we were informed that the enemy's columns were again in motion. Two battalions were formed in battle on the plain; so that they could fall back on Segura, which was intended to have been vigorously defended. Zumalacarregui resolved to give in slowly, until he had brought the enemy to develop all his forces in the little plain. If he could have occupied him till the arrival of Ituralde, who would have taken the mountain in his rear (the one which had been the day before defended), and could cut him off from the royal road, the Christinos would have been completely hemmed in. The latter, finding the heights abandoned, hastily took possession of them, imagining, no doubt, that we must have suffered equally with themselves the previous day. Here they

---

[98] An ensign or 2nd. Lieutenant wore a single epaulette on the left shoulder, a Lieutenant on the right. A Captain had epaulettes on both shoulders.

deployed all their force in battle array; for more than three hours they did not venture to descend, and then not till they had, with some difficulty, cleared away our skirmishers, and driven back with their artillery several companies who had taken possession of a little chapel and a few houses, whence they could be annoyed. Suddenly, as we were expecting every minute that the game would begin in earnest, they precipitately retreated. The Christino generals, it appears, were informed just in time that, in two hours, they would have been taken in the rear, and now saw clearly through the plan of the Royalist General. Intelligence of the entire destruction of the Regiment of Provincials of Grenada, who were on their march to cross the Ebro, had also reached them; and the fear of its getting bruited amongst their men also added to their anxiety.

This regiment, of which the men were all volunteers, and of "Sans-culotte" opinions, had made themselves notorious by the massacre of the monks at Madrid, and afterwards, having begged to be sent against the Carlists, were marching northward. Zumalacarregui, having determined, at all hazards - knowing the effect it would have on the people - to strike a blow against them, despatched Eraso for that purpose, who, crossing the Ebro, succeeded in surprising them. Of the whole regiment, only 17, including the Count de Campo Verde, the colonel, escaped; and as it was said that he had taken the command after the massacre of Madrid, it was looked upon by the population of the north as an evident judgment; and it was said that the 17 who had escaped were innocent of the sacrilegious murders, 170 prisoners were brought, a day or two after, to Mondragon, where we were: they were all shot; amongst them were 13 officers. Several of these Eraso had executed at the further end of the Puente Nuevo, the bridge within gunshot of Bilboa. The peasantry, so exasperated were they, hung them up in their uniforms; and when Espartero was retreating on Bilboa, the first thing that met his vanguard were their bodies dangling on the trees: they were immediately cut down, and hidden in a hut, that the sight might not discourage the army.

Zumalacarregui, although disappointed - well knowing the cause of their retreat, and that it must be effected almost entirely along the high roadinstantly pursued them. The scene would have seemed a farce to any one who could have looked down from the mountain, as the Carlists, to the number of about 2,000, pursued on the rear of a column of 12,000 men, who were attempting to cover their masses on the road by now detached companies on the heights on either side. The squadron of the General's escort was ordered to pursue, and charged, advancing full gallop through the Guides and 1st. Battalion, who opened right and left to make way. The enemy, finding what confusion and dismay were in their rear, took advantage of an open space on their right and the winding of the highway, to rally the Regiment of El Principe, of which one battalion formed in a treble line - swept the road by such a sharp fire, that the pursuers were brought to a dead halt, and the stragglers were enabled to reach the shelter of their line. At this moment I saw Zumalacarregui, who, with his staff, the cavalry, and some footsoldiers of the 1st., was endeavouring to animate them on, struck by two bullets, one of which grazed his wrist, and the other went through his fur jacket. At this moment they were so plentifully bounding along the road, shivering the stones, and cutting the brushwood, that several times the soldiers were driven back as they attempted to form on turning the corner of the rock. Having given me the order to support the infantry, and to take a few determined men, I made the attempt with seven lancers, and was fortunate enough to succeed in my undertaking with the loss of two men, and three horses wounded. Dashing on full gallop, we took possession of two houses on the road, spearing the Chapelgorries who were defending it; the rest either fled or retired into the houses. A few footsoldiers quickly came up, and as we had taken so good position, the enemy thought proper rapidly to retreat. They were pursued till 10 o'clock at night, to the vicinity of

Bergara. The road was covered with many thousand shakos and innumerable knapsacks and muskets. Indeed, after passing through Villa Real, it became, from a defeat, changed into a perfect rout: unfortunately, there were too few Carlists to take advantage of it. The enemy having speedily abandoned another turn of the road, which they had at first made a show of defending - of which we were by no means sure, however, and unwilling to compromise the men with me, till the infantry, who were a few hundred paces behind, could come up - I galloped on to reconnoitre, and found that they had got on still further than I imagined, and in the distance I perceived a little band of about 40 men, who, with Lacour at their head, were crossing the rivulet. I joined them. We entered Villa Real while the enemy was yet in it, having previously dispersed at the point of the bayonet one detachment which endeavoured to sustain the retreat, and kept pursuing at last in total darkness, on the rear of the whole army, killing and making prisoners a considerable number. We ran at one time some risk from the Guides, who, finding Villa Real empty, and not aware that any Carlist force had passed through it, came down to the number of five companies, along the bank of the river, which, as the road turns off at right-angles to the left, is a shorter cut; and, in the twilight, mistaking us for a part of the enemy's rear-guard, opened a heavy fire on us. It was only by reiterated shouts of "Viva Carlos Quinto!" that we could undeceive them. One of the Christino divisions took to the right the road of Villafranca; and the rest, after sheltering in Bergara, next day marched on to Bilboa and St. Sebastian.

The result of the actions of the 2nd. and 3rd. must have furnished matter of some reflection to the Queen's generals; who found that, whether in Navarre or the other provinces, they had to do with something more than merely a guerrilla chief; and how dangerous it would be to face him with anything like even numbers. This battle also entirely dissipated the terror which still lingered in our troops, respecting the Peseteros, Chapelgorries, and Carabineros, who seemed to have thenceforth entirely lost their

227

spirit; as from that date ceased all the excursions they were in the habit of making about the country. For this action, Charles V, at the recommendation of Zumalacarregui, was pleased to confer on me the order of knighthood of St. Ferdinand.

CHAPTER XV

Attack on the heights of Orbiso - Colouring of Musket Barrels - A Day's Service with the Infantry - The Rout - Nocturnal Expedition - Casting of Cannon - Defeat of Oraa - Cruelty of Mina.

Towards the middle of January, 1835, the Carlists assembled in some force round Maëstu, as if for the purpose of investing it; while Zumalacarregui, with four battalions, kept about Santa Cruz and Orbiso, ready to occupy the position of Zuñiga and the bridge of Arquijas, where Cordova had been defeated on the 15th. December. His aim at this time was to entice the enemy into action as often as possible, merely for the sake of the loss their ranks would probably sustain. Contrary to all the usual rules of warfare, he had no further object immediately in view. There were no positions that he cared either to win or defend, excepting as far as the accidents of the ground sheltered his own men and rendered the destruction of his adversaries greater. His great skill, his knowledge of the country, and many other circumstances to which I have referred in other parts of this narrative, enabled him, in every case, to render the loss of the enemy infinitely greater than his own, even when he was defeated. Of this I shall give an example.

A considerable force, at least about 10,000 men, from Los Arcos, occupied the Beruesa, but seemed unwilling to attempt the passage of Arquijas so soon after their first defeat there. Zumalacarregui in consequence retired from Zuñiga to Orbiso, politely ceding them the passage. As he had foreseen, they immediately took possession of Zuñiga; and having once passed the formidable spot, had no hesitation in immediately attacking Zumalacarregui, who, they were informed, was with only four battalions, or 2,800 men, in Orbiso, something less than two miles off. Orbiso is separated from Zuñiga by a wide and fertile plain, covered with vines, excepting on the right, where it is skirted by a wood of *encina*. It stands at the foot of a rather steep hill, over which runs the road to Contrasta. To the right, mountains, which

229

are thickly covered with arbutus, bar the passage; on the left of the hill, which is covered with low shrubs, are also other inaccessible positions, divided from it by a fearful ravine or defile, where a host might be destroyed by only rolling down on them the rocks from above. His flanks thus protected, Zumalacarregui, with two battalions, took up his position on the hill. The other two he placed either in reserve, or with the object of exposing fewer men in action. The name of the leader of the adverse side, in this affair, has escaped my memory. I believe, however, it was Lorenzo. Whoever it was it matters little, for no general could have seen, with 10,000 men under his orders, such an insignificant force daring him to the fight, without attacking them. The Guides of Navarre and a battalion of Alavese had possession of the hill, expecting the fray with an indifference which never augured so well as when they were hot and enthusiastic. From Zuñiga to Orbiso, a plain, which occupies the space between, was entirely covered by the advancing column. The dark masses slowly crept along, and in the distance were only discernible by the glitter of their arms.

I must here observe that, unimportant as it may seem, the English mode of browning the musketbarrels, which most foreign armies keep bright, is of very great advantage in a campaign, although the polished barrel has, perhaps, a more martial appearance. The guns when browned are, in the first place, more easily kept in order; but especially the march of troops, which is often betrayed by the shining arms, when the troops themselves are not discernible to the naked eye, or even the telescope, is more easily concealed. In a mountainous country I have had oftener occasion to remark this circumstance than in a district of plains.

In front of Orbiso passes a rivulet which, if I remember rightly, I have during the summer seen dry, but which, swelled by the winter rains, attains the width of 30ft or more, as its bed of pebbles indicates. The enemy approached it without opposition, but here a company of the Guides, dispersed in guerrillas, disputed for a few minutes the passage. It was, however, quickly crossed by a squadron of cavalry, and we fancied for a moment that they had been cut off, as the plain was distant about a third of a mile from the village of Orbiso to the foot of the hill where we had taken up our position.

The instant the cavalry passed, 100 or 120 men climbed the walls which support the terraces and gardens and retired still firing. The cavalry were afraid to dash through the village until it had been reconnoitred by the infantry: by the time that was effected they reached the foot of the hill. Shortly after, the enemy having formed in three columns, and driven in our guerrillas, the attack commenced in earnest. The first shot that was fired from our side struck a superior officer from his horse. I afterwards learned from the captain of the company that it was fired by a French tailor, a deserter. He had signified his intention of aiming at him, although at the distance he fired, 250yds, it was of course a chance that he hit his mark. The fault of our disposition was, that we had not a sufficient number of men to cover so large a front. If the battalions that were in reserve on the heights of San Vicente, and in the valley of the lower Amescoas, had been with us, we might, perhaps, have kept our position all day. A defeat, however, would have been dangerous, and it was evidently the policy of our general not to run any risk.

The enemy seemed to attack with little confidence; for about an hour and a half we drove them back. At last some companies of the Alavese gave way, and a small column of the Christinos having gained a footing on the hill on our left, turned our position, and the Alavese were driven back in disorder. Valdespina, with his one arm, was galloping to and fro on his piebald mare in the thickest of the fire, retreating the last. My horse, the only one I had at that moment, having been for several days too lame to do cavalry service, I had followed with the Battalion of Guides, and when we prepared for action, I sent my servant with my horse some 100yds in the rear, with the strictest

231

orders not to move from beneath an old oak tree till the return of either myself or some of a company which (having but one effective officer, the others being in the hospital) I resolved to join. I hung my sabre on my horse, and, borrowing a musket and some cartridges, went forward with the lieutenant, whose name was Garcia, and who had previously been adjutant to the Guides. I was thus strict in my injunctions to my servant not to move, because, although lame, my steed was nothing like so much so as his rider; and in case of our being driven back, I knew I should have been under the necessity of mounting him, as I imagined myself to have been unable to walk 500yds. On seeing the Alavese give back, a general discouragement seemed to prevail, and the retreat commenced. The 6th. Company, with which I was, and which had been posted where a few pieces of rock and the broken ground afforded some slight shelter, now found itself the foremost of three that were ordered to sustain the retreat. We had been there about an hour, suffering considerable loss, when the Alavese having retired, nearly two battalions of the enemy had formed on the plateau. The men kept the ground tolerably well, but fired in a very disorderly manner.

It is a favourite saying of the old French soldiers, in allusion to the uncertainty of the aim taken with the musket, that if they were sure the enemy would not aim at any of their neighbours, and only point at them, they would be without the slightest fear in action. This is often strangely exemplified. The red caps being still, at the time of this action, worn exclusively by the Carlist officers, those of the Christinos might often be heard crying out to their men to mark them out. We found them in consequence a very unpleasant distinction, but those immediately around us only seemed to suffer; and above half the men hit in the company, which amounted to above a third of it, were about us. The easiest death from a gun-shot wound seems in general to be when it is in the head; it is attended by no pain - no convulsive start - no distortion of the muscles or writhing of the body. I had an opportunity of witnessing two instances very close to me. One was a recruit behind me, who was burning his cartridges much too quick to fire them very effectually, and by whom I momentarily expected to have my brains blown out in a mistake; for once or twice I felt the warmth of the musket flash upon my cheek. Between every shot he was shouting out very lustily. As soon as I found my hero silent at my elbow, I turned round, and saw how it had fared with him; he had not even said "oh!" Another in front of me was just kneeling against a block of stone when he was struck by a bullet in the same place. He fell back about 6in., still in the same position, and remained there as quiet as he is to this day. I should not have believed him to have been dead, only the blood bubbling out at the back of his head left no doubt of it. The fire had become so heavy, and the enemy was climbing the eminence so fast, that it was evident we could not hold out any longer, when the Lieutenant Garcia received a shot in his thigh, and another in the abdomen, and, falling on his back, kicked up his legs in the air so comically, that I really thought at first he was joking. I had him carried off, but the wound was mortal. I managed to keep the company about ten minutes longer there; when the two other companies, afraid of being surrounded, disbanded; and my own, notwithstanding all my efforts, quickly followed. About 200yds farther on, a few hundred men, taking advantage of the ground, had been echeloned, to cover the retreat, and on these we fell back. The servant whom I expected to find bere with my horse was gone. The road runs along the side of the mountain for about half a mile before it reaches the plain of San Vicente. Here Zumalacarregui had placed his reserve, in case of a mishap, and two squadrons of cavalry were drawn out; but the Alavese having given way, and the first position being turned, it became urgent for those who had been defending it to retire; and as the road, on account of the thaw, and the rock, which did not absorb the water, was one canal of thin mud 2ft in depth, we found it impossible to preserve any order. The rout became general. A guerilla, sheltered amongst the broken rocks above us, kept at bay the enemy, who, if he had pushed forward, might have made a terrible slaughter of the two battalions, and with 20 horses have trampled down a hundred. But he took no advantage of our confusion, and seemed afraid of our guerillas sweeping the road.

On this occasion, scarcely able to hobble along, and obliged to make my way through the slough, I found myself, very unintentionally, quite in the rear, and must inevitably have been taken, if the enemy had been a little more spirited in his pursuit. I heard the dismal cries of several of the wounded, who were abandoned, and who were shortly after dispatched by the enemy's bayonets; and my reflections were none of the most agreeable, when, not expecting that I should be able to proceed, I apprehended that I should share the same fate. I was at last so thoroughly exhausted and disheartened - for I then believed the defeat to be complete that I was on the point of sitting down on the road-side, when I perceived Zumalacarregui on foot, unattended by a single officer of his staff, his drawn sword in his hand, apostrophising, in his stern and authoritative voice, his men, who, as they passed him, fell into order, as if by magic, although a little farther on they began to hasten their steps. The plain and village of San Vicente shortly afterwards opened to view, where three battalions were formed at the foot of the opposite heights in battle; and a squadron of horse came up to protect the retreat of the fugitives across the plain Zumalacarregui had dispatched Tomas Reyna to take the command of these when the position was forced. "You must charge at all hazards, even if the whole squadron is sacrificed, should they descend en masse to pursue; for the reserve must not move." "It shall be done," said Reyna, "if we all perish." He had not occasion to charge, but we found him with about a 150 horse quite ready to do so. The enemy however, perhaps suspecting a stratagem, with their usual caution, only followed step by step, and cleared all that part of the mountain which was above the road and occupied by the guerillas. Thus the battalion that had been routed had plenty of time to form, and march in good order to the rear of the reserve,

234

which, to their astonishment, the enemy found ranged in order of battle. Several of the wounded whom we were carrying off died during the flight. One, as he expired, said "Viva el Rey!" I have often heard shouts of enthusiasm from the wounded, but seldom any, save commonplace expressions, so immediately before death.

It was 9 o'clock at night before we were quartered at Contrasta, where I found my horse and servant. He excused himself by saying that he had been forced to proceed with the rest. I got a little wine, but it was so late, no provision could be found. Zumalacarregui had, I believe, counted on maintaining his first position; in this he was defeated; but, at the same time, the loss on the side of the enemy was nearly double our own. On the lowest computation, they had 450 men put *hors de combat*.

300 of their wounded were slowly moved under escort to Los Arcos, together with some arms, horses, and two pieces of light artillery. Zumalacarregui, being informed of this by his spies, or judging that such would be the case, although he had been since daybreak in the saddle, marched out at midnight without beat of drum with 200 of his hardiest footsoldiers and 50 of the freshest horses, and by a long and circuitous route through sbat seemed impasse bie mountains, and, crossing the Egz, succeeded in reaching the rear of the enemy's army, which was quartered for the night is Orbiso and Zuñiga The enemy, therefore, thus lay betwen him and his own forces. He would have succeeded in his object, had not the order been countermanded, and the convoy stopped at Zuñiga. However, he surprised and cut to pieces a small party of horse, and returned safe before daybreak, his men half dead with fatigue. Even after the longest marches, he was constantly in the habit of striking terror into the enemy by these nocturnal expeditions. The moral effect, even of this partial success, on their ranks, was very great; as it showed them, that, even after a victory, and when they imagined the enemy to be farthest off, there was no safety for them, except under shelter of their columns. Amongst the wounded Christinos was an English major in the Queen's

service. I was informed of this afterwards at Orbiso, whither he was carried, and where he died. I was convinced the *patrona* was not mistaken as to his nation, although she was unable to remember his name; for she had perfectly learned to say "Gdnit," which she said he often made use of, but particularly when his wound was dressed, and which she supposed must mean something like Jesu-Maria! or Maria José! He had had both thighs broken.

In the military colleges of Spain the pupils are brought up with liberal ideas; consequently all the officers of artillery and engineers are republicans. Hence very few of them joined our army; indeed we had but two: one the Brig-General Montenegro[99], and the other a young man named Reyna, a brilliant exception. At the academy he was looked upon as the most clever of their scholars, and of his attainments in his profession he gave the greatest proofs. By birth a West-Indian - a native of Havannah - he was of a wealthy family, and a lieutenant of the artillery of the guard. On the death of Ferdinand he sacrificed a handsome property, and leaving his mother in Madrid, came with his younger brother, a cavalry officer, to join the Carlists. He was then the only artillery officer in the army.

Zumalacarregui, finding the want of artillery, and knowing the impossibility of procuring any battering pieces without having some to begin with; and aware also that, before he could hope to leave the provinces, it became necessary to sweep away the garrisons sprinkled over them, sent him to try if he could manufacture a mortar or two. With nothing but the theory he had acquired - obliged to study the smelting of metals, to instruct workmen, to have their tools manufactured after his own directions, and having only the metal which old coppers and kettles bought up all over the country afforded, he set about his task in the recesses of the mountains, where, during the first ten months, he was constantly disturbed by the flying columns of the enemy. His first efforts were unavailing; the pieces proved total failures; and

---

[99] José Pimentel Montenegro, marqués de Bóveda de Limia, (1786-1838)

236

the arrival of guns so long expected from the Bastan had become a byword in the army for anything improbable. Nothing daunted, however, he cast them again; and at last succeeded in making two seven-inch and two 13-in. mortars. In the first instance the usual order of things was reversed; the mortars were cast to the size of some shells that had been captured in a foundry in the commencement of the insurrection, and buried; but shortly after we were obliged to cast shells to the mortars. One of the larger mortars being afterwards lost in the Bastan (for it was the plan of the Carlists, until the defeat of Valdes, to bury all their heavy pieces, as they would have impeded that rapidity of march which became so formidable), he then cast another. The last, considering the difficulties he had to labour under, was really an extraordinary production; and only required the work of the file to render it as good a piece of workmanship as if it had been turned out of a regular foundry. When the Carlists were going to besiege a place the pieces were dug up; and Zumalacarregui made the officer who was charged with bringing them up responsible for their travelling a given distance in a given time. The officer exacted of such a village to take it on to the next; all the cattle, all the population, if necessary, were employed for the purpose. The guns, placed on wooden drays, were drawn by many pairs of oxen; where the ground would no longer admit of their assistance, manual labour was resorted to. The difficulties experienced in moving the guns over the roads, or rather sheeptracks, they had to pass would scarcely be credited. I am convinced that no French or British cavalry would have dreamed of, overcoming them. Such, however, was the enthusiasm of the soldiers and peasantry, and their confidence that all that Zumalacarregui ordered could and *must* be done, that they were daunted by no obstacles. These guns proceeded in general night and day with only a feeble escort.

Segastibelza had been long occupying the Bastan and blockading Elisondo. The mortars were first tried upon this place with perfect success; by]the letter intercepted from Zugaramurdi,

237

the commandant[100], great damage, it appears, was done there on that occasion. Oraa and Ocaña, with 3,000 men, were sent from Pampeluna to his relief, while the main army occupied Zumalacarregui. Reyna in consequence buried the pieces; but, in the Val de Lanz, Oraa, who had divided his force into two columns, found not only Segastibelza ready to dispute the passage, but a small division, detached by Zumalacarregui, succeeded in interposing itself between his two columns, forcing the second to retreat with great loss on Pampeluna, and entirely routing the first, which thus found itself between two fires, and obliged, after great slaughter, to throw itself into the miserable village of Ciga. Here the enemy fortified themselves, expecting assistance from Mina. Leaving the greater part of his army to prevent Cordoba from following on his rear, with a small division Zumalacarregui in person reached Ciga, and determined on bombarding it. The shells did great execution amongst the few niserable huts, in which the enemy, to the number of 1800, were entrenched. A flag of truce being hoisted, a messenger at length informed Zumalacarregui that the besieged had adopted the same resolution as the remains of O'Doyle's army after the battle of Salvatierra, and had made hostages of all the inhabitants, whom, if another shell were thrown in, they would begin by exterminating. Several of those whose families were within were allowed to go to the Carlist general, and by their tears and supplications at last prevailed on him to desist. The enemy were however without provisions; and their soldiers might be seen, braving the fire of our troops, coming out to take turnips and beet-root in the fields around it. Mina, on this emergency, collected all his disposable force, and made a movement which obliged Zumalacarregui to retire, not however without considerably harassing the forces of his opponent. Mina, after relieving Ocaña, destroyed the Carlist foundry at Dona Maria, and committed the greatest horrors. The Brigadier Varrena, under

---

[100] There is a village on the frontier of the same name. (CFH)

his orders, amongst other atrocities, murdered 40 wounded Carlists. His behaviour to the peasantry was only acting up to his declaration (in which it was difficult to say whether cruelty or cowardice predominated), that it was on the inhabitants, not the soldiers, on whom his first punishments should fall.

An impassive Zumalacarregui cheered by his men

CHAPTER XVI.

Second Battle of Arquijas - Mina shooting the Oxen - Attack on Los Arcos - Treatment of the Wounded - Ludicrous Alarm of a Friar - Check at Larraga - Action of Llaregui - Retreat of Mina.

As it was feared that Zumalacarregui, who was concentrating his force, might place himself between Pampeluna and the Bastan, Lorenzo, according to his instructions, having united under his orders the troops of Lopez and Oraa, in all 12,000 men, resolved on attacking Zumalacarregui in the position of Astarta and Mendaça, where Cordova had obtained his advantage on the 12th. December. Zumalacarregui precipitately retired beyond the Ega, hoping to draw him into the position where Cordova had been defeated on the heights of Arquijas. Attributing the retreat of the Carlists to discouragement, Lorenzo, whose instructions, by the bye, were intercepted, were found to be, if he succeeded in repulsing the Carlists, to force the passage of the Ega at any price. Fortunately for Lorenzo, the attack did not commence till midday. The Carlists were to the number of 14 battalions, or 8,500 men. The attack was made on three points - the bridge of Arquijas, Santa Cruz de Campezza, and Molinas de Santa Cruz; but the chief efforts were made at the first place, where Lorenzo commanded in person.

Although the firing lasted till near nightfall, this affair of Arquijas was not so bloody as the first. Finding their artillery had made an impression, one desperate effort was attempted, and a column of 1,000 men rushed on to charge with the bayonet. Zumalacarregui having seen his troops waver opposite to the bridge rushed down himself. When within a stone's throw the Carlists poured in a murderous volley, which killed a superior officer at the head of the column, and his two aidesde-camp, and threw it into inextricable confusion. Zumalacarregui with the Guides, and the commandant Tans, who was wounded himself, pursued. This took place on the little plain between the bridge and hermitage of Arquijas, and Lorenzo in consequence thought proper to retreat. The Carlists continued the pursuit, but not very vigorously, as far as the Beruesa, where they were quartered for the night, Lorenzo retreating with 360 wounded, having left 200 killed. The loss of the Carlists was 300 *hors de combat*. Lorenzo, fearful that Zumalacarregui, who made a demonstration towards the Bastan, would now overwhelm Mina, leaving a slight garrison in Los Arcos and Estella, marched precipitately on Pampeluna. Mina was in the Bastan at this time, making active researches for the pieces cast by Reyna, having previously succeeded in discovering one of the larger mortars.

It is astonishing that constantly as the Carlist artillery was buried, never excepting in this instance were any of their pieces or any part of their ammunition found out, although the strictest researches were made. Mina succeeded always in discovering the peasants who had been employed in the transport of them, but it was impossible for them to disclose anything, as, for the purposes such concealment, they were always taken out of their beds, and their eyes kept bandaged while the pieces were buried. Thus conducted, they were, notwithstanding, by his order unmercifully shot. This had only the effect of making all those who had been employed in the transport of the pieces dread the same fate, and of course escaping to the mountains whenever the Christinos approached. Mina, finding that in all the environs of Dona Maria where the guns were supposed to be concealed, they had fled out of reach of his vengeance, caused the oxen which had been used to drag the artillery to be shot. This reminds one of the lashes which the Persian king inflicted on the Hellespont.

Los Arcos, in the Riveira, which I have had more than once occasion to mention, and which is situated between Estella and Viana, had long been a great annoyance to the Carlists, by harbouring the Christino columns, and affording them a ready refuge in case of a defeat, as had occurred on the 5th. February, after the defeat of Lorenzo at Arquijas. A part only of the town, together with the hospital and the house called Aizcorbe, were fortified, and as the enemy were supposed to be far away, it had been left with the weakest possible garrison. Lorenzo, after his defeat, had taken away from it several pieces of cannon, so that it was now left without artillery. An attack had never been dreamt of, as it would speedily have been relieved by Mina or Lorenzo from Pampeluna, if the former had not been led into the Bastan by the circumstances I have detailed.

As it turned out, Los Arcos was taken while Mina was still searching for the guns, and shooting the peasantry to induce some of them to discover the other mortar and two howitzers which were actually bombarding it.

On the afternoon of 22nd. February 1835, that part of the town that was not fortified was taken by Ituralde with the 1st. Battalion of Navarrese. At 8 o'clock of the 23rd., our battery, consisting of a 13-inch mortar, two seven-inch howitzers, and an old and heavy 18-pounder of iron, guns dug up in Biscay, and above a century old, composing, with the exception of the two small fieldpieces taken at the battle of Vittoria, all our artillery, opened fire on the fortified houses from the height of Castillo. With one battering cannon only, although the shells did infinite damage, it became very difficult to effect a breach, and the enemy kept up a constant fire of musketry. Several houses were, however, at last taken, as well as the Aizcorbe. The enemy kept retiring from one defence to another, leaving behind them numbers of sick and wounded. The battery was then advanced to within pistolshot, and by nightfall everything had been taken excepting the hospital, whither they retired. This had also been attacked by Colonel Juan O'Donnel, who had made himself master of the outer wall and defences, but had been repulsed from the hospital itself, at the moment of entering, by the numerous hand-grenades thrown by the besieged. As night came on, while a heavy fire was kept up, an immense quantity of combustible matter was, with some loss, piled against their last hold-fagots, straw, skins filled with brandy, and bags of the red pimento: the smoke of this, which I believe is in

243

England called capsicum, is so intolerable, that it is impossible, if the wind carry it into a house, to bear it, and it is, perhaps, one of the most cruel expedients resorted to in Spanish warfare.

The pitch-dark night, and a tremendous tempest of wind and rain, which in that country sometimes pours in such torrents, and beats with such impetuosity, that those exposed to it find it impossible either to hear or see, suggested to the garrison the possibility of making their escape, which they effected at 2 o'clock in the morning, leaving behind them their sick and wounded, and even the sentinels, who were not apprized of their intentions. The storm and darkness prevented the Carlists from perceiving what had occurred till three hours after, when the cavalry was ordered out in pursuit. Towards morning they killed and captured about 50 of the garrison; amongst the prisoners were a lt. colonel and a lieutenant. About 400, however, made good their escape.

In the part they termed "Fort Isabella" were found 200 sick and wounded, and above 60 in the houses. All the baggage and equipments of the Regiment of Soria, 1,200 pairs of new trowsers, 500 muskets, 20 cases of ammunition, besides immense quantities of wine and corn, and every variety of accoutrements, were taken. The sick and wounded, amongst whom were a colonel and six officers, immediately received assurances of pardon and protection, although all the wounded and sick taken by Mina in the Bastan had been mercilessly butchered. In return for the humanity the Carlists displayed on this occasion, affording the Christinos every possible assistance, and allowing those who chose to depart when cured, in the following month Mina burned to the ground the village of Lecaros, and, making a fearful lottery of the blood of his fellowcreatures, shot one male inhabitant in every five, for having neglected to give him notice of the movements of the Carlists.

Don Carlos and his suite the next day entered Los Arcos; and, attended by Zumalacarregui, he went round to visit the wounded. The scene is said to have been truly affecting; so much so, that even: the stern leader of the Carlists could not help

244

shedding a tear, when the exclamation of "What, can that be the ferocious Zumalacarregui?" accompanied by a start of terror, burst from the lips of one of the wounded. "Yes," he replied, "I am the ferocious Zumalacarregui," and he observed to the King, "This is the way in which our enemies delude the soldier; your Majesty best knows whether I have been guilty of a single act of severity to which their example has not forced me; and whether, with your Majesty's consent, I have not set them often the example of mercy; and yet this is probably the character given me in the greater part of Spain." On quitting them, both the King and the General left with each of the wounded a small sum of money, and orders that every attention should be paid to them.

The seven officers, on recovering, were allowed to return to their own partisans, without even having been shackled by a promise not to take arms again. The lt. colonel and the lieutenant, named Echeverria and Alzaga, captured in endeavouring to make their escape to Lerin with the other prisoners, were, however, shot. This unflinching severity towards those taken with arms in their hands contrasts strangely with his treatment of the sick and disabled. But amidst a war which had become one of extermination, these instances of generosity were frequent on the part of Zumalacarregui; and those who condemn as unpardonable the putting to death of prisoners even by way of reprisals, must remember, that the former were the faults of his education, his country, and his peculiar position, not only as the leader of a party during a civil war, but of the weakest party, which could least afford to be magnanimous; whereas the latter were the impulses of his own noble nature alone. The loss of the Carlists was very trifling: the artillery had two killed, and several wounded; and the infantry some 20 or 30 wounded.

Here I may mention one of those ludicrous circumstances which, during a life like that we led, were not unfrequent, and which seem rather inven. tions than realities. I have, however, little occasion to trespass on the regions of fiction, with the recollection of so many amusing and lamentable facts still green in my memory, and of which in these pages I have scattered here and there such as rose soonest to my remembrance. A poor artilleryman, mortally wounded in the stomach, had expired in the lodging of some officers of the 3rd. Battalion, whither he had been transported. They were dining in the adjoining room, when they were alarmed by a loud shriek, and immediately after a mendicant friar rushed into the apartment, exclaiming that the man was not yet dead! "Dead," said one of the officers, "why dead and buried too; I saw him buried myself." "There he is breathing and moving, however," said the monk. His party hastened into the room, and found, indulging in his pleasant dreams, to their infinite amusement, a fat French tailor, one of their servants, who, being completely drunk on the rich wine of the Rivera, when the dead man had been carried out, had staggered to the bed, and immediately occupied the place of the deceased. The old half-blind friar having come somewhat tardily to perform his office, knelt down beside the bed, and for about two hours had been fervently praying for the soul of the dead man, when, by a sudden turn in his sleep, the intruder's arms swinging over, hit him on the head - and, starting up in alarm, the astonishment of the friar had Occasioned the scene I have mentioned.

On the 9th. March we experienced a check before Larraga. The Christino general Soane[101], with about 4,000 men, was suddenly attacked by Zumalacarregui, with all his cavalry and eight battalions. Unfortunately for the Carlists, they appeared in sight a little too soon; as Soane, who, quite unsuspicious, was about to leave the village, finding an enemy, dropped as if from the clouds - took every advantage of the walls and houses, and the river which protected him. As Zumalacarregui was unwilling to retire now that he had come so far, he attempted to force the passage of the bridge. The enemy, however, well defended it by several walls,

---

[101] Antonio Seoane Hoyos 1790-1862 was Minister of War the following year.

which served as a parapet, and defied all our efforts. Zumalacarregui himself in vain rode up to the bridge head; four of his staff were killed and wounded; and, towards nightfall, finding our efforts useless, particularly as attacking enemies behind intrenchments was a species of service our men were very ill calculated for, we retired on Sirauki and Mañeru. Our loss was about 300 killed and wounded; that of the enemy, as they were much sheltered, about 150. A French captain, who had served with Bourmont in Portugal, named Rafechol, who had only had the command of his company four hours previous to entering action, was mortally wounded, receiving two bullets through the body. The General's secretary, Colonel Vargas, also had his thigh broken.

The next morning - judging that Mina, as soon as he heard that Zumalacarregui was in the Rivera, would seize the opportunity of going unmolested to the Bastan, where Ocaña, with his division, much straightened for provisions, was shut up in Elisondo, which Segastibelza was preparing again to besiege - we marched on the Val de Ollo, with four battalions and a troop of lancers. Early on the morning of the 11th. Mina and Oraa, with two columns - the whole amounting to 4,500 men - sallied from Pampeluna. On approaching Elzaburu, the last village before entering the valley of Ulzama, where the route for 12 miles lies through thickly-wooded mountains and morass roads, without meeting with a human habitation they were attacked by a few companies of the 6th. Battalion on the height of Oraquieta; and as the day was far advanced, they encamped in the village, where, in the evening, the 4th. Battalion skirmished with them till nightfall.

We passed the night in the village of Llaregui. Zumalacarregui had with him, as I have said, only four battalions; the 3rd., 4th,, 6th,, and 10th, of Navarre - in all, about 2,600 men; but the 1st. of Navarre and 7th, of Guipuscoa had orders to march from Almandoy, to cut the enemy off from Donamaria, if they took that road. In case they retrograded on Pampeluna, five battalions would

247

have intercepted them, and three were marching to join us before night. The dreadful state of the roads alone prevented them from arriving in time to effect the entire destruction of Mina's column. One of Zumalacarregui's misfortunes was, that none of his divisions could advance with the same rapidity that he did himself; yet he was too apt to calculate on the contrary. With every exertion, however, of the other leaders, it was out of their power always to execute the orders they received: in this respect. Zumalacarregui said that such a distance must be done in the time he fixed, and that they must go so far; and such was his ascendeney over the minds of his men, that all that the human frame was capable of doing they voluntarily performed.

The action next day became highly interesting. It was between the great leader of the Royalists and the redoubtable Mina. Their forces were about equal, and they were about to meet on one of those wild spots which seemed a fitting theatre for such celebrated mountain-chiefs to hold encounter. Mina, on account of his being so well aware of the danger of the localities, betrayed more hesitation than perhaps another general would have done. As his interview with the Guipuscoan was so sudden and unexpected, he seemed afraid to trust to the information he received, of the small amount of his force. Zumalacarregui vigorously attacked his left flank, his small force being posted from Llaregui to the mountain of Lanamear, where his reserve was formed on the plateau. There were then 2ft of snow upon the ground; and, worse than all, it was fast thawing. Mina made many and desperate efforts to carry the heights on his left, which, if he could have accomplished, he might have made good his retreat without further loss. Once the enemy had even succeeded in driving back our skirmishers or guerrillas in great confusion; when the General, who could perceive everything from the plateau where he stood, in an angry fit of impatience spurred his horse, and leaving all his staff behind, came down to lead them on, waving his naked sword. This movement acted like electricity on the waverers; the enemy were repulsed with great loss; and although the greater part of our force was now on their rear, they having passed along the road, a squadron of cavalry which they had with them was cut to pieces; and the confusion was for a moment so great, that Mina himself was nearly taken.

A lt. colonel of his cavalry, whom I well knew, from having seen him on a beautiful white steed, exposing himself with the escort he commanded in several actions, and who, indeed, was often pointed out for his valour, was lying, when I passed, as well as his horse, dead across the road. Rider and horse had been struck in the head. I could bestow on him, as we passed, but the thought and the glance of a moment. It was, however, with a painful feeling, strange as it may seem, that I made this nearer acquaintance with the features of the gallant soldier. I remember at Orbiso hearing a soldier say, "Do you see that officer on the white horse? I will shoot him." Likely as it was to be an idle menace of the soldier, I could not help thinking of that admirable speech of Don Quixote, where, talking of the invention of gunpowder, he says, "A noble heart is pierced by a missile winged by a hand that trembles" and I said to the soldier, "Fire rather at those cowards that skulk behind him."

Had it not been for a rivulet with steep banks that intervened, Mina would have been taken: all his baggage, the two asses that followed to furnish him with their milk, as recommended by his doctors, and his cabriolet, fell into our hands. This last was a curious thing; perhaps I should more properly have described it by calling it a hood. It was placed on a mule, and entirely covered his person, with a glass window in front. His wife, a young and handsome Asturian, who followed him during this campaign, riding cavalier-fashion, and habited in male attire, was also with him in this action. By immense efforts, Mina contrived at last to effect his retreat in something like order; and in this he displayed considerable skill. Zumalacarregui pursued him with the 10th. and 6th. Battalions, without giving him breathing time. His men, obliged to abandon the road, were up to their knees in snow, and perishing with hunger and cold, were pursued till it was pitch dark. It was late at night, and owing to the battalions that should have cut them off only coming up an hour after the column had passed, they were able to reach Gastela and Legasa.

I had retired to a hill, where we were ordered to remain; and the 3rd. Battalion also was awaiting the return of the General, who, with his freshest men, was engaged in the pursuit. Perhaps it would have been impossible to pitch upon a spot whence a better view of an action could have been obtained than from the eminence where we were. The chase, which we had now leisure to look on, appeared to us as if it had been pictured on a map. But for the reflection of the snow, it would have been more than dusk; and at last, when the pursued and pursuers had dwindled into nothing, the fire might be seen on the distant brow of the mountain like flashes of lightning, although we eould no longer hear anything. We were wet through: our horses as well as their masters had been all day without food, and now we were left shivering in 2ft of snow. The infantry, however, at last cleared some away, and lit innumerable fires, piling them against the roots of old oaks and chestnuts, which, when their trunks were burned through, fell with a loud crash to the ground. The forest trees destroyed where a bivouac has been form one of the striking accessories to a picture of the ravages of war - the growth of a century having been often laid prostrate to cook a soldier's mess and light his cigar by. It was three in the morning, and, wet and cold as we were, we had enjoyed our first sleep on the snow, when we were despatched to some villages on our rear, to be again on foot at half-past five. Mina carried off with him 200 wounded, and left 400 men on the field. He might the next day have been tracked by the dead bodies of those killed during the pursuit, and the blood of the wounded on the snow. Our loss was about 100 killed and 100 wounded. Amongst the former were 40 men of a company of the 4th. battalion, who, posted in a certain position, by some mistake were not informed when to retire, and, being surrounded, were put to the sword on the spot. The army of Mina reached the Bastan, in such a dreadfully shattered condition, that Zumalacarregui, satisfied that it would be many days before he would venture to take the field again, inarched on the Borunda, to lay siege to Echari-Arenas, the strongest place between Pampeluna and Salvatierra.

CHAPTER XVII.

The "Ayuela"- Siege of Echari-Arenas - A Surprise - Carlist Art-illery - Narrow Escape - The Fort attempts to Capitulate - De-struction in it - Treatment of the Prisoners.

On the 14th March, breaking up the bridges of Evroy and Irurdiaga, in his rear, across the river Araquil, Zumalacarregui, with a large force, arrived in the valley of that name. About 12 o'clock we were before the fort of Echari-Arenas, the strongest in the Borunda. All the battering-train we had with us was one of the 7-inch mortars and the old Biscayan 18-pounder, which, from its ancient and decayed appearance, the soldiers called the *"ayuela"* or the grandmother. It was placed at the farther end of the street, and soon began to play upon the old fortified posada, round which redoubts had been thrown up. In Spain, the shell of all the houses is built with such solidity, that they are so many fortalices formed to the hand of those who choose to defend them. Zumalacarregui well knew, that with one cannon there was little probability of his being able to make an effectual breach; but he calculated on amusing them till his purpose should be effected by means of a mine. The mortar was more useful; for as, in fortifying all the places, the intention had been to resist a *coup de main,* or a siege carried on with light pieces, and the use of shells by the insurgents was never anticipated, they were not in any way casemated. This observation applies to all the forts they established, and was one principal reason why Zumalacarregui attached so much importance to Reyna's casting a mortar or two. The one we had there threw in, during the four days the şiege lasted, 300 7-inch shells.

The *ayuela*, however, was doing some damage, by knocking down a part of a tambour, and dismounting one of the enemy's guns, when it burst at the mouth, severely injuring one of the artillerymen. Our shells, too, as most of our artillerymen were novices, were very ill pegged up, or the *fusées* were bad, for several burst while going out of the piece, and killed some of our

253

artillerymen. When we entered the village, the enemy, exclusive of the fort, were in possession of eight or ten houses: these they set fire to and abandoned. I was, during the siege, quartered at Urbissu, nearly a mile from the place. I used to gallop thither 5-6 times a day. One striking feature of the scene was, the crowd of peasants who came from miles round to witness the destruction of their tyrants; for as such they were everywhere regarded. They generally shouted with joy when the red dust was seen, if any of the shells struck on the roofs. At every place we afterwards besieged this was the case. As the sparrows gather round an owl by daylight, thousands and thousands of the inhabitants - old women, children, and old men, all in their best attire, as on a day of rejoicing, thronged all the heights around us constantly expressing their hopes that it would be taken, or their fears that the "columns," as the Christino army was termed, would force us to raise the siege. Every time I passed to and fro hundreds were making anxious inquiries "How goes the siege, *Señor Militar, Monsieur le Militaire,* or *Señor Official?*" (Sir Officer.) The only way of satisfying them was, by stating that it would surrender before morning.

I had on one occasion advanced along the high road, and tying my horse to a tree, was attentively examining with a telescope that part of the fort which overlooked the road, our attack being entirely directed on the other side. I knew they had placed their four pieces there, and as it was far for musketry, they would probably take no notice of me. I was suddenly joined by two jolly farmers and a student on their mules, with badger-skin caparisons and huge wooden stirrups; they were all proceeding in high glee down the road, when I called out to them to know where they were going. "To Echari-Arenas, to be sure," said one of the party. "But, my good friend," said I, "if you go that way the enemy will soon let you know that the road is not free; they are firing already; do you not hear the whistling of the bullets?" I could not help smiling as I saw the consternation depicted on their countenances at this piece of intelligence. One of the group upon this thought that I was quizzing them, and they were just proceeding, when the enemy, seeing three mules and a horse on the road, although they had taken no notice of one, now imagined that it was cavalry, and swinging round a gun, fired at us. Just as the spokesman was persuading them to proceed, the shot whizzing over his head struck in the bank and covered us with dust. As if they had received an electric shock, they all three clapped spurs to their mules, and although 20yds farther would have placed them out of the possibility of being hit, I could see them at every undulation of the road riding as if for their lives all the way to Urbissu, and I am by no means satisfied that even there they considered themselves in safety.

The garrison still fancying that Mina was in Pampeluna, and would shortly come to their assistance, had not the remotest thoughts of surrendering. Meanwhile the mine from one of the houses the enemy had burned was silently working its way, under the superintendence of Lacour, who was well acquainted with that branch of service as well as most others. The old gun had been cut a foot shorter, and burst a second time again at the mouth. Another piece was, however, amputated, and although a considerable flaw might be distinctly seen, it was tightly bound round with thick rope, and recommenced firing more actively than ever. Zumalacarregui himself directed the mortar the greater part of the time, but it always played with surprising accuracy, considering the workmen and the tools, for the only artillery-officer we had, Reyna, was busy casting other pieces, as this bad been cast, out of old copper kettles and brazen utensils collected in the villages.

It was in vain that Montenegro represented to Zumalacarregui the inutility of his esposing himself to the bursting of our own shells, which could not be depended on. We were all standing round him, to the number of about 20 officers, when another of these missiles, exploding at 4ft from the mouth of the mortar, struck down the two artillerymen next him, wounding one mortally, and almost carrying away the head of the other. The

General never even started, and only exclaimed, *"Que majaderos estos artilleros!"* (What bunglers those artillerymen are!) - alluding to those who were filling the shells.

The wide and principal street which runs through the village was entirely clear, being swept by the grape and musketry of the fort. Our volunteers were amusing themselves sticking out their caps from the windows of the houses, or the corners of the lanes, to deceive the enemy, who instantly fired. Our 18-pounder, maimed and mutilated, was now approached to within 60yds of the fossé, but the enemy kept up such a constant fire of grape and musketry into the embrasure, that it could only be discharged five or six times during the whole day. Our soldiers were all making their quaint observations on the venerable piece of ordnance as it was dragged up. "The grandmother is like the nights," said one "they are both shortening fast." "They say we are to attack all the garrisons in the Borunda: the *ayuela* will be no longer than a pistol before we have done," said another; and thus the joke passed on.

What principally amused me, however, was to observe the tribulation of an old couple whose pig was wandering up and down the wide street, where the carcasses of more than one of its kind showed the malicious pleasure the Christinos took in converting them from swine into pork. They were both, and with much reason, afraid to step beyond the sheltering angle of the houses, and only ceased abusing each other while they tried to coax back the pig; but in vain they threw down maize and turnips; the wayward animal, as if taking a pleasure in tormenting them, resisted all their eloquence and insinuations, and, seeming to prefer the glory of ranging the forbidden spot to all they could offer him, turned his tail towards them and sauntered down the street. The lamentations of Sancho for his ass were nothing to those of the old man for his pig. The epithets he applied to it were most amusingly ridiculous: he called it his soul, his beloved, and a thousand other names which I do not remember. Whether he had eventually to mourn the loss of this interesting animal I never learned.

256

The mine had been carried under the fossé, and another was rapidly advancing on another side. At the time that the first was ready to be sprung, the enemy discovered it, and immediately set about countermining with great activity. Lacour had already placed two barrels of powder, and was busily employed in directing the final operations before lighting the fuse. They could distinctly hear the enemy working in the countermine above them, and therefore, although it was already known that the effect of it would be comparatively trifling, it was necessary to spring it as soon as possible. At this moment a quantity of earth fell on the head of one of the miners, and a candle, lowered by a string, came through the aperture right over a quantity of loose powder. It seems unaccountable how the enemy could be guilty of this piece of imprudence, as, if a single spark had fallen, it would have blown them up together. A lantern would have obviated all the danger. Lacour, the officer directing the mine, seized hold of the candle and extinguished it, and then fled with his men, as, hearing their voices, they were fearful that the Christinos might fire through the aperture, which would decidedly have been fatal.

In the first moment of anger at seeing them all scamper out of the mine, General Ituralde, who was standing behind the house in which it had been opened, observed to Lacour that he was surprised to see him amongst those flying. "I am not afraid of being killed, General," said the veteran, "but I never bargained for being killed and buried all at once." After a short interval he returned and finished laying the train. The enemy, as it had been calculated, finding that the countermine had reached the mine, and that the explosion from the free passage given to the inflamed air would be comparatively harmless, retired. About 10 o'clock in the evening it was sprung, and blowing up the palisades, the wall, and three houses, filled up the ditch and made a breach that was practicable, and with some loss which the assailants would probably have met with, left the place at their mercy. As it was reported that the other mine would be ready in six hours, it was not intended to storm the place till then. At 6 o'clock in the morning the train was laid. Before lighting it, an officer was sent with a flag of truce into the fort, giving them notice that if they did not surrender at discretion in ten minutes, another mine would be spring, and the battalions were all under arms for the storm.

The commandant, an old Navarrese officer, well aware that he had nothing for it, attempted to capitulate. He was answered, that he must surrender unconditionally, and throw himself on the mercy of the King, as the train would be instantly lighted. When our men knew that an officer with a flag of truce had been sent in, suspecting that some capitulation would be effected, they were loud in their outcries, and shouting that not a single life ought to be spared, demanded to be allowed to attack the place instantly.

It soon became, however, no longer in the power of the officers to await the last extremity, if such had been their intention. Eight of the garrison, leaping down over the ruins where the breach had been made, ran over to us; and although they passed through a storm of bullets from their own people, two only were wounded. They informed us that the soldiers within were reduced to the last extremity. They would have held out notwithstanding, had it not been for the mine, which had blown up 40 men in the houses. Our soldiers having cried out to them that another would be sprung, they were thrown into the greatest consternation. Shortly after above 20 more escaped, and came from another part of the fort to surrender. Before the commandant had given his answer, the men were rushing out in every direction, so that he had no alternative. The fort was surrendered; the 2nd. Battalion entering to take possession, and receiving the arms of the garrison, who were formed, to the number of 438, including the officers, in the wide street, between the fixed bayonets of the soldiery. This was about half-past 7 o'clock in the morning.

I was amongst the first who visited the fortification. One of the houses, all the front of which alone had been rent away by the mine, presented the spectacle of many mutilated bodies. One man had his two legs completely blown off; another corpse was hanging downwards, only held back by a beam of the roof that had fallen on his leg. There were also several blackened and bleeding masses, which it was difficult to fancy were the severed trunks or the limbs of human bodies. In the interior every thing had been dashed to pieces by the shells. We were all obliged to admit that the defence had been a most gallant one. The men, it appears, had been ordered to lie down on the first floor of the houses, so that the shells, sinking down to the earth, burst on the ground floor; and the chief risk had been from the tiles or beams, excepting in the rare instances where these missiles exploded before reaching the ground, or fell directly upon them. All the roofs had been so completely torn up that during the rain, which for two days was almost incessant, the greater part of the men were wet through; their muskets were covered with rust; and from the numbers crammed together in the sheltered spots, the men were in the most miserable plight. The powder-magazine resisted our 7-inch shells; but if the larger mortar had been used, I do not think it would have been proof against those of 13-inch diameter.

The prisoners were still in a dreadful state of anxiety and suspense as to their fate. Zumalacarregui was a long time irresolute as to how he should dispose of them. The manner in which Mina had requited the mercy shown at Los Arcos was no encouragement towards the performance of a similar act. Persuaded, however, that, having now some artillery, and his army having considerably increased, it would be impossible for him to continue the system of shooting, although in reprisal, all that fell into his hands - or, moved by one of those sudden impulses of generosity which in the hour of success seemed to direct his actions, he resolved to grant to all, not only their lives, but a free and unconditional pardon, and to allow them to go where they pleased. This order was accordingly read to them, they being drawn out in line. They had already been fraternising with our men, who, although a few minutes before calling out for vengeance and the blood of their enemies, eagerly pressed through the guard to share their rations with them, bringing meat, bread, and wine. So different did they find this treatment from what they expected, that they all answered by loud cries of "Viva Carlos Quinto!" and loudly demanded arms to fight his battles.

Zumalacarregui replied, that he did not wish them to be carried away by any momentary impulse; he would give them an hour to consider on what steps they would take. He pledged his word that officers and men should have his permission to depart, and safe conduct to the nearest garrison. From those who should go he exacted no promise; he left it to their own hearts whether they would again take arms against the sovereign in whose name he gave them pardon. When several of his officers observed on the imprudence of this measure, and said, "The officers will take arms again," "Let them," said the General. "You ought at least to take their word of honour that they will not. If their gratitude does not prevent them, I should confide very little in their word."

The men were directly allowed their liberty; and the nine officers, including the chaplain and a cadet, were invited to dine at the General's own table. They were all of the Regiment of Provincials of Valladolid. The commandant Mesquinez, with whom I conversed, spoke very good French. He was a native of Pampeluna, and distantly related to Mina. A few minutes before the parlementary entered, he was struck on the breast by a musket-shot, which had gone through the padding of his coat and a handkerchief, which had so far deadened it, that the wound was not of sufficient consequence to prevent his going to the General's. He seemed a very gentlemanly and well-informed man - tall and thin, and between 50 and 60 years of age, but with a most hideous countenance, more resembling that of an ourang outang than of a human being.

The General allowed them to retain their baggage; and on their requesting to be forwarded to Pampeluna, gave the commandant a certificate in his own handwriting of having done all that a brave man could do in his defence of Echari-Arenas[102]; and after dinner dispatched them with an escort commanded by the Captain of the *Partida* of Echari. The soldiers, to a man, refused to follow their officers, and only two of their servants could be prevailed upon to go with them. On approaching the gates of Pampeluna, a detachment of lancers sallied, and, without regarding the representations of the officers they were accompanying, killed one man of the escort, wounded the captain slightly, and carried them all into Pampeluna, where they remained in its dungeons until liberated by Valdes, at Lord Eliot's earnest solicitation.

Thus was Zumalacarregui rewarded for his clemency, at least as far as it depended on his enemies to requite him; for, on the other hand, the men who took arms for us as did indeed all the prisoners whose lives were spared, fought faithfully and well. They were incorporated with the 2nd. Castiile, which was commanded by Colonel Juan O'Donnel, the younger brother of Carlos. One 8-pounder, two 6-pounders - all in excellent order, great quantities of ammunition and provisions, were taken; and the Carlists marched to lay siege to Olzagutias, a few miles farther on the road to Vittoria. Although not taken, it suffered so much, that when Mina, recovering from his stupor, approached with the force he could muster, and the siege was raised, he found that it had been so nearly

---

[102] The following is a copy of this certificate:-"Don Tomas Zumalacarregui, commander-in-chief of the armies of his Majesty Don Carlos the Fifth, hereby certifies that Don Joaquin Mesquinez, commander of a battalion in the rebel army, and governor of this fort of Echari-Arenas, defended it with the greatest bravery, with his men, composed of four companies of Provincials of Valladolid and one of artillery of the guard, from the 14th. of the month to the present day, notwithstanding the explosion of more than 300 shells in the fort itself, 200 cannonshot, and a considerable breach, the effect of a mine. Don Joaquin Mesquinez, as a military man, defended with honour his post, and only surrendered when the fort was all in ruins. That his bravery, and the skill with which he defended it, may be appreciated and remain recorded, I have thought proper to give this certificate, at my headquarters of Echari-Arenas, this 19th. day of March, 1835. (Signed)

"Tomas ZUMALACARREGUI."

so, that he destroyed the fortification, and caused the garrison to evacuate it.

The capture of Echari completed Mina's disgrace. To give a brief account of his career, he had 41,000 men under arms, exclusive of 10,000 garrisoning Taffala, Lerin, Lodosa, Logroño, and Viana, and all the experience of a consummate guerrilla chief. Zumalacarregui had under his orders something less than 18,000, including the troops he was obliged to leave with the King, and those engaged in blockading 20 garrisons. A division under Ocana was beaten in the Bastan, and that general obliged to shut himself up in Ciga, whence he was with difficulty saved. Four divisions under Lorenzo were beaten at Arquijas. Mina was led by stratagem into the Bastan, and Zumalacarregui took Los Arcos. He attacked the columns of Soane, which induced Mina to march to the relief of Elisondo with a small division. He found the Carlist leader ready to meet him at Elzaburu; was defeated; and would have perished with all his division, had it not been for one of those circumstances against which no human foresight can provide - the sudden thaw, which prevented the expected battalions from coming up in time. Before he had recovered from his defeat Echari-Arenas had fallen.

CHAPTER XVIII.

The Guides of Navarre - The 3rd. and 6th. Battalions – Cavalry - Challenge of O'Donnel - Lopez and O'Donnel - Anecdote of Lopez - Bravery of O'Donnel - Slaughter of the Christinos.

The Guias de Navarra, or Guides of Navarre, which I have had occasion to mention so often before, were a chosen corps which always followed the Commander-in-Chief since their formation, having the preference in equipment and accommodation, and having been looked upon as *our* guards are in the army. They were termed Guides, not from any peculiar knowledge of the country which they might be supposed to possess, but because they were expected to lead the way in action. It was an appellation which, by the bye, they well deserved, as their steady bravery, and the destruction which prevailed in this corps, who were in the heat of every engagement, rendered a promotion to it, though considered a mark of distinction to both the officers and men who had earned it, a dangerous honour. Their original force was one battalion of 600 men; afterwards it averaged 1,000; but so constantly had they been exposed, and sometimes, it might have been said, sacrificed by Zumalacarregui, had he not always shared their danger, that it has been calculated that upwards of 1,500 men had been killed or wounded in that battalion since its formation. Not 100 of those who first composed it were now existing in its ranks, and the greater part of these were wounded.

Of three successive Colonels, Torres, Taus, and Campillo, the two former had been twice wounded. The officers who entered were either rapidly killed or promoted. I was well acquainted with almost every officer in the battalion, and before the affair at Mendaça, of the 12th. December, 1834, I happened to note down their names. Four months after, in looking through the list, only five of those I had known were in the battalion, the rest were either killed or in the hospital; a few promoted out of the battalion. Of five French officers, three, Captain Bézard, Captain Raffechol, and

263

Vicomte de Barrez, Ensign, were killed. Sabatier and Monginot were each twice wounded.

The gallantry which this corps has always displayed has induced me to mention these proofs of its behaviour, as I have often heard, since my return to England, the opinion expressed, that the engagements in this civil war had been limited to a few skirmishes, where neither danger could be run nor laurels reaped. The progress of the Carlists, too, was ascribed to the cowardice of their adversaries; and it was added, that the former had advanced simply because the others had retreated without a struggle. To prove that their advantages were not won bloodlessly, and considering it incumbent on me to do justice to so many brave companions in arms, who have fallen in the fields of Navarre and the provinces, and that they may not "unrecorded die," I am induced to dwell more at length on this subject than perhaps I might otherwise have done.

It would be impossible for me now to recall the names of all those who perished in this battalion, although the greater number were my personal friends; I must therefore pass over the names of many with whom I have spent more than one hour of pleasure and hardship - fellows of excellent companionship, who have gone to their last home with glory. Let me be permitted to mention only the rapid changes which took place in the 3rd. Company, which now occur to me, although that company was by no means singularly unfortunate. Solana, the first captain, was wounded and promoted to be Lt. Colonel of the 4th. Battalion of Navarre, his lieutenant was killed at Orbiso, his ensign at Mendaça. The captain who succeeded him at Arquijas was wounded. Of *his* two successors, one was wounded, the other killed at Larraga. Another ensign was killed in the Riveira. This was a company, too, which never had above three officers at a time. The Guides were distinguished from the other corps by their uniform; in the first instance they were all dressed in greyish-blue coats with yellow facings on the breast. As these wore out they, however, equipped themselves from the spoils of the dead, like the rest of the army. They were again dressed uniformly in January, 1835, with blue jackets with a red binding, and grey trowsers. In a short time their costume began again to vary, but they were always known by their red caps, which at first had been only worn by the officers. But it being found that the caps rendered us only so many targets in an engagement, they were then given to the Battalion of Guides, and afterwards to the cavalry, the rest of the army wearing blue caps as before.

The Guides of Biscay (for there were Guides of every province, but not reputed so highly as those of Navarre) wore white. Any soldier who distinguished himself might enter the Guides, and although at first composed only of Navarrese, afterwards two-thirds of the battalion consisted of soldiers of the Spanish Guards, either deserters, or the prisoners who had been intrusted with arms, and who, strange to say, always fought with a fidelity and courage far surpassing that of the peasantry. They were mostly natives of Castille and Leon.

As the greater part of the Guides were men who had served before, and always immediately under the eye of Zumalacarregui, whose favourite corps they were, there was nothing in the rest of the army to compare with them in discipline. They were, together with the 3rd. Battalion of Navarre (surnamed the *Requeté*,[103] from a song they were always singing), the two on which he could most depend.

The 6th. Battalion of Navarre was also a favourite with the General. I could never divine why. They behaved with great unsteadiness; what feats of valour they did perform were solely owing to the gallantry of the Colonel and Lt. Colonel, Pablo Sanz, whose jaw was fractured by a musketball at the defeat of Valdes in the Amescoas, and of Campillo, who succeeded Taus in the command of the Guides.

---

[103] In later wars this became the term for any Carlist unit.

The foreign officers in the service of Don Carlos, mostly French, are deserving of some mention. The strangers in the service were 22 at the commencement. Of these, 16 have been killed and wounded, results which will speak as to their behaviour. Others have joined the Carlist ranks latterly, so that the number of foreign officers is still about the same. But as that rapid succession of murderous engagements which took place while Zumalacarregui was struggling to play the offensive part have now ceased, the mortality amongst the last comers has been infinitely less than it was at first. In the early part of the war, the battalions only were paid, the others being merely dressed and fed; afterwards they all received the same pay - the soldiers one *real de vellon,* or about 3d. per diem, from which nothing was deducted. The officers received only one-third of their pay, the arrears to be given them on the conclusion of the war. After every action a certain number of *premios*, or pensions of a *real* per diem for life, were distributed to the soldiers who had distinguished themselves. One soldier might be the holder of several premios; many in the Guides have as many as three or four.

About the latter end of January we were joined by Colonel Carlos O'Donnel, who had been imprisoned at Paris, and tried for travelling with a false passport. He had made his own defence in French, and, having been acquitted, contrived to make his escape to Bayonne, and thence across the Pyrenees. Zumalacarregui gave him the command of the cavalry. A little while after his brother Juan, who has since been made prisoner, came also with several cavalry officers of the royal guard and a number of the gardes-du-corps.

Carlos seriously undertook to discipline and form the squadrons. There were many officers who had earned their rank by the circumstances of the war - by a reputation, sometimes usurped, of bravery; for I have often seen those who in a flight gave no quarter, striking on the armed and the unarmed alike, and then coming back, their swords dripping with blood, called *Valientes* by

266

those who did not know how they had stained their weapons. Many of the old school of Mina, and who had served in the army of the faith, could not separate their notions of valour from barbarity; and unfortunately this was the case with most of the guerrilla heroes. These looked with great jealousyon O'Donnel, who was still a young man, and also on the officers of the regular army, into whose hands, he was obliged to give the direction of every thing, to teach his regiment the ordinary manoeuvres, in which he found them deplorably ignorant. The guerrilleros were constantly sneering at "the men who wore new uniforms and pared their nails," and saying they were anxious to see them before the enemy, and under his fire.

O'Donnel having had time, as no encounter had taken place for a considerable period, to form his cavalry, and having obtained Zumalacarregui's permission, wrote to Lopez, whom he had formerly known, leaving the letter with a mistress of his at Sesma, to the effect that, as they had been so long without obtaining any opportunity of winning those laurels which are the object of the soldier's career, why not revive an ancient usage of chivalry, and fix on a place of rencontre, each giving his word of honour that no treachery should be practised, and none but the combatants should assemble? He offered, with 400 men of his Lancers of Navarre, to meet Lopez when and where he chose in the kingdom of Navarre. Lopez replied that "with the permission of his superiors, he would desire nothing more than to meet him with 100 men less, confident in the valour of the invincible cavalry of Isabella the Second." To this O'Donnel answered, that he would admit of no challenge save on equal terms; and that, if it suited him better, he would meet him with 100 men against 100, or 50 Carlist officers against any 50 of the liberals of Spain; and that it rested with him, within the fortnight, to appoint the place and time: but if this were refused, nothing could prevent Lopez himself, who had insulted him by proposing to fight him with inferior numbers, from meeting him alone with lance, sword, or any arms he chose. The combat would have been interesting, if it had taken place, as Lopez piqued himself on being the most dexterous with the lance, and O'Donnel was the best swordsman in Spain. It was long thought that one of these propositions, so suitable to both their characters, would have been accepted by Lopez. No answer was, however, returned. The fault was rather, I believe, with the Viceroy than with the cavalry general, who knew the policy of making the world believe that the Carlists were only a few bigoted and sanguinary peasants; and wished to avoid the inquiries such a duel might give rise to, and the attention it would attract. I have also heard that Lopez was severely reprimanded for having answered the first challenge at all.

Lopez and O'Donnel had both distinguished themselves by very daring achievements. The former, who is a South American, being in the Spanish army during the struggle for American independence, in the capacity of aide-de-camp, paid his addresses, as the story goes, to one of the wealthiest heiresses of all the southern continent. She, however, declared that she would never marry any one but a hero. Lopez had no resource, therefore, but in wooing her, like Othello, with his glory. One day he played the mad prank of giving false orders to several regiments to attack the enemy's line. Being unsupported, they soon found themselves in very serious difficulties; but by the singular valour and good fortune of the young aide-de-camp, the enemy were driven from their positions. The affair terminated advantageously; and as success makes the difference between the Cæsar and the Catiline, Lopez, who would have been shot if he had failed, was declared to have acted from private instructions, extolled to the skies, and received a rapid advancement, and what he more coveted even than that, the hand of the heiress. The termination of the affair was however less romantic, as he very speedily gambled away her immense fortune, and quarrelled with his wife.

Charles O'Donnel was known as having performed, when less than five-and-twenty, the most brilliant feat in the Constitutional war. He was then captain of a troop of Navarrese lancers, which he had himself trained and disciplined, and whose condition formed a striking contrast to the miserable state of the army of the faith. The troops of Ferdinand had already been retreating two days before the republicans, by whom they were purgued. The former had just been passing an immense plain in Old Castille, and were all entering the mountains, excepting the rear guard, who had only reached a little wood surrounded by a deep ditch, when 600 men of the cavalry of the liberals, with two pieces of flying artillery and a company of light infantry, appeared on the farther end of the plain. The rear guard, which was commanded by his father, was fatigued, discouraged, and without a cartridge. O'Donnel, finding that escape was impossible, resolved to sell his life dearly, and formed his 60 lancers so as to guard the entrance of the road into the wood. The enemy, seeing such a contemptible force, neither attempted to take him in flank, nor awaited their infantry and artillery, but came galloping on in column, a troop abreast, so as not to have the trouble of altering their order for the passage of the defile (as in military phrase it is termed), after they had crushed the handful of lancers. O'Donnel, seeing this egregious fault, pointed out to his men that their only chance of salvation was to overthrow the head of the column by one furious onset. As soon as the enemy came so near that he only just had time to put his horses to the trot and gallop, he charged, bearing down and cutting his way through the first lines; the third turned back upon the fourth, the fourth on the fifth, and so on, from there not being sufficient interval between them, till all was inextricable confusion. The infantry in the rear were crushed by the cavalry, and thrown into disorder, and the Navarrese lancers pursued, as the French term it, *l'épée dans les reins;* and, aware that they must give them no breathing time, making a tremendous slaughter. Not only was the cavalry entirely routed, and an immense number killed, but 200 royalists they were dragging with them as prisoners were released, and the two pieces of artillery taken. The infantry, rushing from the wood, afforded a useful

269

assistance, till the reinforcements from the retreating army arrived just in time to prevent the enemy from rallying. O'Donnel, for this action, was made chevalier of the military order of St. Ferdinand. The feat is well known in Spain. I had, at my request, the description from his own lips, but unfortunately I cannot remember the name of the spot where it took place.

CHAPTER XIX.

Valdes assumes the command - His projects - Enters the Amescoas - Rapid march of Zumalacarregui - Valdes retires - Amescoas.

Valdes, after declaiming loudly in the Chambers against Rodil and Mina, assumed, for the second time, the command of the army of the North, vowing that he would drive the Carlists either into the sea or across the Pyrenees. At Madrid he found it an easy task to quell the insurrection, and he now came to put his theory into practice. So certain was he of success, that he is said to have written to General Harispe, to be prepared to receive and disarm the Carlists, who would be forced to fly across the frontier. So calmly, however, did Zumalacarregui await the result of his efforts, that he in nowise concentrated his forces more than he had previously done, and left, as usual, above half his force observing and blockading the Bastan and all the fortified places.

The plan of Valdes was to unite so large a force, that the Carlists, unable to take the field, would fall back on the inaccessible part of the country: here he resolved to follow them up, after having swept through the Amescoas and the Sierra de Andia, which, because the Carlists had so often retired to them, and had established their trifling manufactories and hospitals, he imagined to be their most important strongholds. If his entrance were resisted, on which he calculated, he intended to force his way; and if he drove back the enemy, he resolved not to allow them to recover from their defeat, but to follow them up day after day, wherever they went, until he totally dispersed Zumalacarregui's army. He was under the impression that his predecessors had erred in not concentrating sufficiently all their force; so that they constantly risked being beaten back, or, if they drove the Carlists from the field, allowed them to recover entirely from their defeat, by suspending all operations for several days. He did not calculate that, even when the Carlists were driven back, the roads, the want of provisions, and the numerous wounded, always put it entirely out of their adversaries' power to follow up their successes, and

271

that a pursuit would in most cases have entailed upon them certain destruction.

Valdes, during his former vice-royalty, had been distinguished for his humanity. In the interval, however, the feelings of both parties were considerably embittered. Mortified by their defeats, the Christino generals constantly refused to discontinue the sanguinary warfare they now carried on, although Zumalacarregui made many overtures, by setting them examples of mercy, which, if they had only been requited by a demonstration of similar feeling, would have established tacitly that convention afterwards brought about by the exertions of Lord Eliot. Probably also the injunctions from the Queen's government to treat her enemies as strict: otherwise it is difficult to understand why they did not come to an arrangement, by which they would have been so decidedly the gainers, as the Carlists always took, at the lowest computation, 20 prisoners for one captured from them by the Christinos.

Valdes, on his first passage through the Amescoas, finding in Contrasta a number of wounded Carlists burned, indeed, the hospital and several houses of the village, as well as all their corn; shot some of the peasantry, and killed their cattle; but at the same time he caused the wounded to be carefully removed, and gave to each man a douro (five shillings) from his private purse. Mina always gave lead or cold steel instead of silver. Such conduct on the part of Valdes showed that his personal dispositions were by no means in unison with the orders which he received.

The new viceroy, having under his command about 9,000 men, made his first movement by entering the Amescoas, where he penetrated as far as Eulate. After burning the old castle, in which a powder manufactory was established, he seems not to have considered himself secure, as he precipitately retreated as soon as he was informed of the sudden approach of Zumalacarregui. We were on the other side of Lecumberri; and dreadful as the roads were which we had to traverse during a march of 35 miles, we arrived at nightfall, half our men having lost their sandals in the mud, and not having had time to pause on the road either for eating or drinking. Notwithstanding the piercing cold, we found ourselves on the rear of the enemy, where some skirnishing took place. Our sudden appearance seemed to have surprised the columns of Valdes, whose retreat was conducted in very bad order; and had not our men been prevented, not so much by the fatigue of the day's march as by the unfavourable state of the weather, from pursuing the enemy, they might have suffered severely. Valdes, however, had only retired on Vittoria to effect a junction with all the remainder of the disposable force in the provinces; and, at the head of 30 battalions, including the divisions of Cordova and Alama, on the night of the 20th bivouacked in Contrasta, the first village of the lower Amescoas, determined to penetrate into the upper, or narrower part of the valley. His force might amount to between 17,000 and 20,000 men.

The Amescoas is a long and wild valley, stretching parallel with the Borunda, from which it is divided by a sierra, or chain of mountains, high and wooded. This chain is called the Sierra de Andia; the summit is chiefly table-land; in the centre is a wide space, perfectly level, where, on an immense pasture-ground, a few flocks of sheep and some herds of half-wild mountain colts and mares may be seen roaming about. In the middle rises a solitary human habitation - an old castle, with four round turrets, now converted by the farmer who occupies it into a venta, or inn, for the accommodation of those who travel that way; and as the traveller has four leagues to go without finding another house in crossing the Sierra, he is glad to put up with the miserable accommodation it affords for man and beast. The soil is, I believe, crown land; the old castle is called the Venta, or inn, of Urbassa, and looks the very picture of desolation. The wood by which it is surrounded has much of the appearance of the primeval forests of America; the trees, with their branches, are covered with moss; some are perishing from old age, their wild gnarled roots twisting like snakes amidst the craggy pieces of rock that pierce through the surface, and their wild overgrown branches presenting innumerable obstacles to the passage of troops. The Amescoas, running between this sierra and another which divides it from the Val de Lana, is flanked on that side by a dense wood.

On the left side, in ascending the valley, that is to say, the one bordered by the Sierra de Andia, immense masses of granite, rolled down from the wall of rock above and imbec!ded in the side of the mountains, afford a complete shelter to guerrilla parties stationed to prevent the approach of an army into the valley. They can retreat from rock to rock, and hover round an enemy like vultures, till the main force chooses to give battle.

The system of Zumalacarregui, as I have already mentioned, was neither to abolish nor to adopt the guerrilla system entirely, but to combine it, as far as possible, with the method of fighting used by disciplined armies, using either, as the case demanded, and most frequently both. His successes are wonderful, considering what he had to contend with; and may, in some degree, be attributed to the circumstance, that all the chiefs in either army were men bigoted to one system or another, predetermined either to do every thing according to the ordinary rules of warfare, or every thing as guerrilleros, but unable to avail himself of each, and quite at a loss, when required to adopt the method which was not his own.

Along the narrow and lengthened valley rise at intervals some eight or ten small and miserable villages, which produce little more than suffices for the consumption of the inhabitants, with the exception of *garbanzos* and *lentechas*[104] (peculiar sorts of pea, the former as large as a pistol-bullet, the latter small and flat), which are much esteemed in Navarre. Here, out of the way of every road, and separated from the rest even of the uncivilized world of Navarre, the inhabitants lead or rather led, for war has introduced sad changes into their peaceful habitations - quite a primitive life,

---

[104] Chickpeas and lentils

varied only by the muleteers, who went to fetch wine from more genial districts, and by the hunters, who carried to Pampeluna or Estella the heads of their wolves, to receive the reward offered by government for such prizes. A great portion of the male population devoted themselves to the chace of these animals, peculiarly destructive in a country where so much cattle roam about almost unguarded. The inhabitants rarely went beyond their own villages until the death of Ferdinand took place, when a strong sympathy for Don Carlos induced many of the young men immediately to join him. The remaining inhabitants, whose feeling in his favour could thus only be strengthened, in common with all the Navarrese, aroused by persecution, like the steed beneath the lash, at last became such enthusiastic partisans, that even those whose age or sex incapacitated them from taking arms seemed to make a sport of sacrificing their lives, their families, and their homes.

As we passed through the different villages, on the track of the Queen's army, everywhere the traces of the savage vengeance of the latter were discernible. On first descending through the defile, we observed rising from four or five villages strong columns of smoke. As we approached them, we saw before the ruins of about a quarter of the houses which had been consumed, the families of the wretched owners searching amongst the ashes for any trifling articles that had not been destroyed by the flames. Other busy groups were endeavouring, in the streets, to gather up a little scorched corn, the enemy having collected all the grain, straw, and every article of provision from the inhabitants, saying they served to feed the factious, and, piling them up in the streets, set them on fire, as they could not carry them away.

Pigs, bullocks, and oxen were lying shot or with their throats cut in the streets; some had been partly cut up for rations; but as they had a choice, the soldiers of course only carried away the daintier morsels. Fortunately for the Amescoanos, the greater part of their cattle was in the mountains. Several of the inhabitants had been shot. There were, however, but few of the male inhabitants who had not fled on the approach of the Christinos, the proud and stubborn spirit of the Amescoanos not allowing them to bend to the carrying of burthens beneath the blows of the enemy, which they would have had to submit to if they had remained. When we entered Contrasta, in the lower valley, not a soul was to be seen in the streets. All the men had fled, and the women were in the houses sitting sullenly at their spinning wheels.

The Carlist hospital had been burned; but the wounded, as I have already stated, were well treated by Valdes. On retiring, they forced women and children to drive the baggage mules, asses, and ponies; many were compelled to carry burthens themselves. But as Zumalacarregui advanced so rapidly on their rear, they were obliged to release them. One boy of 14, after having been struck repeatedly by a carabinero for not advancing faster with a donkey laden with coin, had his brains at last blown out when he refused to proceed farther. The houses had been robbed of all their linen; their cooking utensils were broken, and their furniture burned. A very intelligent man, who was amongst the wounded at Contrasta, said that scarcely was the enemy's rear at a few hundred yards from the place, when the women, like harpies, were yelling after them *"Mueran los Christinos!"* and *"Viva el Rey!"*

Now that the second advance of Valdes was announced, the villages were entirely deserted. All the inhabitants, with their families, cattle, poultry, and chattels, took refuge in the Sierra, flying before the spoilers who came to establish the maternal and enlightened government of the Queen! Here a woman might be seen driving before her a sow-litter, a child on her back, and another following with an immense bundle on her head, the matron directing and sharing her anxiety between the wayward animals and children. The old and decrepit, with their little all, and baskets containing fowls, chickens, and turkeys, which had been carefully concealed in the vicinity, mingled their exclamations and varied noises as they trooped along. Such articles as they had not been able to carry away they buried, so that nothing but the bare walls were left for the Christinos. Here and there a voice might be heard chaunting the Carlist warsong, which, strange to say, speaks most of peace:

"Viva la paz! viva l'union!
Viva la paz y Don Carlos Borbon!"

Wrapped up in my cloak, and before a huge fire, I was shivering with cold, so piercing was the wind, which either carried the flame and heat one way, or suddenly veering round dispersed all the group by blowing the flame and sparks in our faces; yet many of the poor women and children were going along with bare legs, and clad in scanty garments of homespun linen, to pass the night without a shelter for their heads. I had several times slept without a cloak in the open air, even in the month of October; and knew, by experience, although the days are often very hot then, how great is the suffering sustained by night, even by those who are well-cloaked, and beside the large fires of the bivouac. Well do I remember when awaking at about three in the morning, the fire slumbering in its ashes, and our apparel soaked through by the rain or dew, how miserably cold is the feeling, even though we possessed the advantages of youth, brandy, and covering. I could not help, therefore, reflecting on the miseries of those poor wretches who had hunger, age, and nakedness to add to their other privations, uncheered by the enthusiasm which stimulates the energies of the soldier, and having before them no prospect save that of returning to a ruined hearth. "The enemy will soon be here," said I to an old woman who was loitering behind. *"Que vengan! Que vengan!"* "Let them come, let them come!" said she with exultation. "They will meet with *Uncle Tomas* this time."

On 20th. April, Valdes bivouacked again in Contrasta and its environs. At about a mile from him, in the village of Aranarache, with seven battalions and 150 horse, Zumalacarregui spent the night. In the meantime we were joined by four battalions more. Early on 21st. Valdes advanced in close columns up the valley, but could only proceed step by step, we retreating almost out of sight before him. About half the Battalion of Guides dispersed as skirmishers, rendering his advance very slow. Towards the afternoon Zumalacarregui attacked Valdes when he reached San Martin, with three battalions, and some sharp skirmishing took place. Valdes, finding that the Carlists were full of enthusiasm, and no longer the wild mountaineers he had met before, everything having been done with greater order and precision than in his own army, now began to find his mistake in imagining that he could sweep the narrow valley without great loss. Night approached, too, and either the fear of being attacked during the darkness, in the deserted villages, or the determination to advance always along the heights, whence he could not be commanded, induced him to ascend the Sierra, and encamp in the wide pasture ground round the Venta de Urbassu. Zumalacarregui, with three battalions, kept harassing his rear till late at night. Valdes thus found himself obliged to remain in the open air with his army; bitterly cold it was even in the valley, which was comparatively sheltered, sleet, snow, and rain succeeding each other till morning. We rested not the most comfortably in the world, since nothing but the bare walls were left; but still under shelter of a roof in the villages of the valley - Zudaire, Baqaindano, Gollano, Artasa, San Martin, and Eckala. The greater part of the enemy's mules, laden with provision, were either captured or forced to be abandoned.

Early on the morning of the 22nd., they recommenced their march, burning on their way the miserable huts of the shepherds, but much discontented by the want of provision, and the comfortless and disturbed night they had spent. Aware that they must eventually retreat on Estella, the mass of the Carlist forces kept between them and that city, Zumalacarregui in person attacked their right flank with four battalions of his lightest troops, all fresh men, and acting excellently as skirmishers. Convinced that if delayed much longer in the Sierra his men must perish from hunger, and that the main body of the enemy was before him, Valdes was obliged to continue his march, his troops suffering much from our attack. If a halt were made and a sufficient force collected to overawe the skirmishers, they retired. Thus the march was delayed, and the instant it was resumed the skirmishers reappeared, and were as spirited as ever in their movements. Under these circumstances Valdes found his 30 battalions rather embarrassing than useful.

As the road became more difficult, parts of the Christino force were thrown into great confusion, which, by the efforts of Valdes and his generals, was with difficulty repaired. Whether merely a feint, or that a division or the whole of the Christino army were disposed to descend by the puerto of Gollano, into the valley that runs along the banks of the river, I know not, but they certainly made a demonstration of coming down that way. Five of our battalions were in excellent position, and as sufficient of their force could not deploy to dislodge them before nightfall, they continued their march on the Sierra. We were brought up, but not in time to charge the enemy's rear on the tableland; the opportunity of their having been thrown into confusion by the Guides was lost. This was the only time I saw the enemy the whole of this day.

Valdes encamped in some villages in the mountains, which all night were attacked by *partidas*, or small detachments to the number of 20 or 30, consisting of about the third of a company. Finding himself, without having fought a battle fairly, unable to hold out another day in the Amescoas, where his men were starving; convinced that the vigorous pursuit, which it was easy to talk of in the cameras of Madrid, was totally impracticable in a country like Navarre, and with troops such as those against which he was contending, and aware, moreover, that by another day of harassing march and privations, similar to that he had already endured, his army would be destroyed, he determined to retreat on Estella. In performing this operation he found, however, the Carlists, who had been so formidable as guerrillas, regularly drawn

279

up to intercept his passage. He had kept entirely on the heights, so as not to be commanded; but the enemy now would not suffer him to come down. Attempting to reach Artasa, he discovered Zumalacarregui with the Guides, the 4th. and 6th. of Navarre, and a small cavalry force, opposite the defile. Although the heights were all gleaming with the arms of the enemy, through this puerto only could they come down, walls of rock rendering the passage downwards anywhere else impossible. When we saw the little force destined to stop him, and knew that if we were routed the torrent rolling down into this valley must entail certain destruction on us all, we could not help looking forward to the issue with anxious interest.

At the foot of the Sierra is a rising ground thinly covered with trees. This was taken possession of by the Guides and the 4th., who thus swept the road; the 6th was ranged in reserve, and we were placed so as to charge the first masses of the enemy if they should force their way down, in order to enable our infantry to save themselves. The fire was commenced by the Guides, who for two hours bore the whole brunt of the attack, two mountainpieces and two howitzers plying them incessantly. The Guides fell back about 200yds on the 4th., which then entered action. This position they maintained for above two hours more. About 200 men forced their way down, but were driven back by the Guides; they seemed to have approached each other by mutual consent, and when they poured in their volleys, they could not have been at more than 15yds asunder; their muskets, indeed, seemed almost touching each other. About 40 of the enemy fell, and perhaps half the number of the Guides; the former were, however, entirely dispersed. I was afterwards informed that these companies had allowed them to approach, being reduced to their last cartridge; and the Christinos were making a desperate rush with the bayonet. Certainly it was not ten minutes after, when the Guides retired, led back in the most perfect order by Zumalacarregui, having entered the action with 40 cartridges; and on a fresh distribution being

280

made, their ammunition was found reduced to one a piece; they had besides suffered greatly.

The 6th. now marched up to take their place. The road was so thickly strewed with dead that the Christinos could not descend without trampling over the bodies. 260 were next day buried there; besides this, I believe all the wounded led into Estella, to the number of 300 or 350, to have been wounded on this spot, as they were obliged to abandon nearly all those that were so in the attacks of the other battalions on their rear and flanks. Pablo Sanz, colonel of the 6th., led his battalion gallantly into the fire, driving the enemy, who during this manoeuvre had made some advance, back again. Almost immediately after, however, his jaw was fractured by a musket-bullet, which remained in the throat, and a captain fell by his side. He was carried off, and his battalion immediately gave way in great disorder. In an instant about 4,000 men forced their passage down; and the 4th. Battalion, by the flight of the 6th., was thrown into the greatest confusion and fell back. All this took place so suddenly that our charging, from the numbers who had already forced their way down, would have been worse than useless. Notwithstanding the firmness of the Guides, I thought for a moment that we should all have been cut to pieces.

About 800yds from this defile is another passage, where the road leads by a steep descent to the valley along the bank of the river, forming, as it were, a second step to the defile where the struggle had taken place. Here, with a part of the 4th. Battalion and half the Guides, Zumalacarregui made a stand. In that moment of danger the calm of his countenance, and the confidence it seemed to display, breathed a fresh spirit into all his men. The captains of companies were on horseback, but Zumalacarregui not only remained on foot according to his wont, but sent away his horse and remained behind with his drawn sword, which only in cases of extreme peril was unsheathed. Excepting part of the Guides and the 4th., we all, according to order, retreated. This was particularly necessary for the cavalry, as without proceeding with great care,

281

the descent became very dangerous. Even as it was, several times the horses, although led, were rolling over the men, and obstructing the passage of the infantry and wounded men in the winding road. I confess I feared much that, however gallant was the defence made by Zumalacarregui and those protecting our retreat, they would shortly fall a sacrifice, as there was now a free passage from the first defile for the overwhelming force of the enemy. He, however, was well aware of the importance of keeping his position for a short time, knowing what was to follow.

A few minutes after, distant but heavy discharges were heard. It was the Alavese battalions attacking the enemy vigorously on the rear. Zumalacarregui, knowing that all was safe, then retreated down the road and joined the dispersed battalions which had been reinforced, and with whom we were formed in order of battle on the plain, through which runs a branch of the Ega. The enemy's skirmishers only came to the position Zumalacarregui had abandoned, having, probably, reported that a force was ready to receive them below. Valdes, whose rear and flank were suffering horribly, little dreamed of renewing an effort which had cost him already so much loss. Taking, therefore, more to the left he retreated on Estella by a more circuitous road.

Zumalacarregui, who was indefatigable, nowy placed himself at the head of two fresh battalions, to reach a pass between the enemy and Estella: he was about a quarter of an hour too late, as it had been already occupied. If the dispersion of the 6th. Battalion had not upset his plans, and he could have delayed the retreat of the column in the Sierra till nightfall, or if he had had fresh cartridges to distribute, the carnage would have been terrific. We continued with this small force harassing them till 10 o'clock at night. When approaching Estella, the rout must have been like that of the passage of the Beresina. It may be judged of by the circumstance, that nearly 3,000 muskets were thrown away. All the baggage was lost; for upwards of a mile the road was covered with shakos; and the officers had their epaulettes stolen and their pockets turned out by their own men. Half famished, covered with mud, their clothes torn, bare-headed, and many bare-footed, they entered Estella pell-mell. Colonel Vigo wisely retired with 2,000 men to Abarsussa, where he spent the night: being on the rear, he might have lost two-thirds of his men, and could only have added to the confusion. At Abarsussa he had the chance of capitulating, or being relieved. A day or two after, Cordova brought him into Estella.

The loss of the enemy was much greater than was at first imagined. Judging from what I had seen myself, I estimated it at 400 killed; and we were told by our spies, that only between 300 and 400 wounded had been carried into Estella. This, a few days after, I gave as my opinion to Lt. Colonel Gurwood; but, on comparing notes with other officers and the peasantry, when I repassed the scene of action, I found this to be considerably under the number of killed, although I still believe pretty correct as to those actually slain fighting. All the wounded, excepting those at the defile near Artasa, where the 6th. Battalion was routed, had been abandoned, and numbers lost and dispersed in the Sierra, were afterwards taken, or murdered without pity, by the enraged peasantry, whose cottages were still smoking. I know positively, that above 200 privates and officers perished in this manner; and on one side of the Amescoas, from the extent of the ground that was the scene of action, I believe at least double that number to have fallen a sacrifice to the fury of the people.

Already reduced for one day to half-rations of bread - the next without bread or wine - wet through - benumbed by the piercing cold of the mountains, if Valdes could have been kept another night in the Sierra, his 16,000 men would have surrendered without firing a shot. Those who were killed by the peasantry had suffered so much, that they made no resistance; though bearing loaded muskets in their hands, they were killed with clubs and stones. I saw a young shepherd, who showed us his knotted stick, bloodied at the end, with which he boasted of having killed, separately, three soldiers, who, lost in the mountains, had been driven from their concealment by hunger. He seemed to take as much pride in the deed as if he had been destroying wolves of his own forests, and was surprised when I turned away with an expression of disgust. Five men and a captain had surrendered to two peasants, armed, one with a fowling-piece, the other with a loaded stick. Strange as this may seem, hunger, cold, and fatigue will so wear down men's spirits, that they allow themselves to be massacred without resistance. This feeling of despondency I have myself experienced; having been in a situation in which, to save my life, I should not have gone 20yds out of the way, nor should I scarcely, I believe, have taken the trouble of warding off a blow. Until I had experienced this state of mind, I could not understand it - it is the simple effect of privations on our moral as well as on our physical strength.

Including those who afterwards perished, I therefore believe the loss of Valdes, during the three days, to have been 800 or 1000 men, besides the 300 wounded, and some 80 prisoners, which altogether is the full amount of those that were taken, so unmerciful was the spirit which animated our men. Above 3500 were found missing: this circumstance carried terror into the army, which had reached Estella; at first, it was thought that Vigo and his men had perished; and about 500 of those who had been dispersed made their way again to the garrisons. Although many circumstances had combined to render the loss of Valdes comparatively trifling in men, the moral effect of it on both armies was immense. The Christino soldiers openly admitted, at Estella, that they could not make head against Zumalacarregui and the Carlists - saying, that whether he was the devil or not, they neither knew nor cared, but they were determined not to quit their garrisons again to fight the factions against whom nothing was to be hoped, and everything to be feared. All the baggage, 3500 muskets, and 300 horses and mules, were captured.

The high expectations entertained both in London and Madrid, of what Valdes was to do against the *faction*, were crushed by this unfortunate *debút;* particularly when it was known that Zumalacarregui had overthrown him with eleven battalions, having in the provinces 28 under his command, if he had chosen to bring them up; but that while he effected this, every fortified place was as strictly blockaded as ever. Between 20-30 houses failed in consequence in the city of London, where, no doubt, those philanthropic speculators - who never weigh the misery or oppression they are entailing on a nation against the furtherance of their own interests, or care if their gold is wrung from the heart's-blood of a people met with a sincerer condolence than they could expect from one who has seen, as I have, at what price their filthy lucre is earned, or rather at what price they hoped to earn it.

CHAPTER XX.

We reposed for a day or two in the environs of Asarta and Vendaca - a branch of the wide valley between the hermitage of San Gregorio and Piedramillera, and the direct road to the famous bridge of Arquijas. This was after three days' hard work, during our affair with Valdes in the Amescoas. His 30 battalions being beaten out of the field, there was nothing but the walls of their fortifications to oppose the Royalist General. In this state of things it puzzled everyone to comprehend why Zumala-carregui did not take advantage of the terror he had struck into the enemy, and, encamping before Estella and Lerin, where the Queen's army was shut up, attack and destroy them. They had been already forced to sally out from want of provisions, as so many men could not fail speedily to consume the scanty magazines collected for a small garrison. Had he vigorously assailed them, he might have at once marched on Madrid. To take this view of the subject, however, would be to censure him for not doing that which was out of his power. He was then in a singular position. He had beaten his enemy, and might have annihilated them, if they had again ventured to take the field; so great was the discouragement which prevailed in the ranks of the Christinos. But, in beating them, he had expended almost the last cartridge in his army. Had they known that circumstance, and attacked him, he had scarcely wherewith to have defended himself for half an hour. The powder-mills were set to work; but all this took time; and Valdes, to his infinite surprise, found that he was allowed quietly to escape.

We had heard of Lord Eliot's arrival, accompanied by Colonel Gurwood, at the Royal quarters. Colonel Wylde, the day before the attack, had supped with Zumalacarregui at Eulate, on his way to join Lord Eliot. An order was given me at Mirafuentes, to go to the General, who was with a few companies of the Guides quartered at Asarta, about two miles off. On arriving, I learned that I had been sent for on account of the presence of Lord Eliot and Colonel Gurwood, who had reached the General's quarters the previous night. I was speedily introduced to the noble Lord and Colonel Gurwood - both agreeable and gentlemanly men. They spoke perfectly the French and Spanish languages, and seemed admirably well calculated for the office they had undertaken, by their conciliating manners and a thorough acquaintance with the country, which one had acquired during a diplomatic, the other during a military career. As they had seen the King - to whom Lord Eliot's mission was of course more particularly directedhe had only been referred to Zumalacarregui to endeavour to effect some arrangement which might put an end to the barbarous system of shooting the prisoners taken on both sides. To this Zumalacarregui, as far as regarded himself, gladly acceded - as mutually sparing the lives of those who survived the slaughter of the field, had always been with him an object which he anxiously sought to effect; and, with that view, had often, though uselessly, set an example of clemency, until the painful necessity of retaliation had become a duty and an act of justice to his own army.

Few prisoners had been taken during the actions of the Amescoas; the Royalists, being exasperated at the ravages of Valdes had committed in the villages of this wild valley, had given no quarter. A few of those, however, who, on the dispersion, took refuge in the mountains, and afterwards fell into the hands of soldiers or peasants, were conducted to headquarters, and a part, as usual, suffered death. Lord Eliot, on seeing the remainder, and being informed of the circumstance, begged their lives of Zumalacarregui, who instantly granted his request - observing, that if he had arrived a day earlier, he would have pardoned the others. The men came afterwards, and threw themselves at Lord Eliot's feet, to thank him for his intercession. I had one of them as servant afterwards; and, to judge of the rest by him, they were far from

288

being ungrateful towards the memory of the foreigner who had so providentially delivered them. I believe they were 27 in number.

The General was particularly pleased with a present which Lord Eliot made him of a telescope. It had been used by the Duke of Wellington in several of his actions. Zumalacarregui set a particular store by it, and always carried it about him. As the convention for the exchange of prisoners was agreed to, and signed by Zumalacarregui, Lord Eliot was anxious immediately to proceed to the headquarters of Valdes. The General having evinced his intention of escorting the Commissioners in person as far as prudence would permit, we all started, - Zumalacarregui, Ituralde, about 20 of his suite, and Charles O'Donnel, the colonel of the Regiment of Navarre, with an *escorte d'honneur* of 25 of the lancers of Alva. Lord Eliot was on the right hand of the General, who led the way, and whom I had never seen so full of spirits. He was much pleased both with his Lordship and Colonel Gurwood: being a man little accustomed to disguise his feelings, whatever they might be, had he felt otherwise, he would certainly have given them a very different reception.

The Commissioners did not conceal their surprise at finding the Carlists in such a position - so erroneous were the ideas which had been entertained by people who ought to have been the best informed. From the reports which they had read in the newspapers, they scarcely expected to find on our side anything in the shape of an army. Colonel Wylde also, on passing through the Amescoas - although he had been for months in Pampeluna evinced his astonishment on seeing the real state of the Carlist force: while he was within the walls he had been kept in total ignorance of our numbers and equipment. The Guides in their red caps, and the 4th. Battalion, were drawn out in line above the village of Piedramillera, through which we passed; but these were all that Zumalacarregui displayed of his troops, at which I was much surprised, as he had all his cavalry and eight battalions in the adjacent villages of the valley, all in excellent order; and it would

289

certainly have been politic to show them. This very useful piece of ostentation would have been, however, quite contrary to bis character, which was decidedly opposed to anything is the shape of humbug, even to that which is necessary sometimes to the soldier as well as the statesman.

Estella was about 10 miles off - more than eight from our advanced posts - so that we breakfasted in a small village, and then proceeded to the content of Irachi. Zumalacarregui having proposed that they should visit it, and take chocolate there, Lord Eliot said that he was anxious to join Valdes as soon as possible, and that he could not spare time. This was, however, overruled by the General, who told them that Valdes was in Lerin, and that they must sleep in Estella that night, which was only half an hour off. Besides, there were some very handsome nuns, whom he would introduce them to; and they made excellent chocolate: O'Donnel alone remained on horseback with his 25 lancers; but we all went up into the parlour, where the superior and the nuns were delighted to see, for the first time, the Carlist leader, whose reputation in that country had rendered him the theme of every tongue. He introduced to them Lord Eliot and the Colonel. The former entered into a long conversation with some of the nuns, through the iron grating which divided us from them, and them for ever from the world, if the Carlists succeeded; and yet they were quite voluntary prisoners, for they heartily wished us success against the party who would ease them both of their vows and property. Sweets, chocolate, coffee, and every kind of refreshment were produced; and, after remaining 20 minutes, we took leave of the community. At the gate we parted with Lord Eliot and his secretary; my interview with whom, being the first of my countrymen I had seen for many months, afforded me very great pleasure; and to this feeling, the consciousness that they had come on so noble a mission did not add a little. With a king's messenger and several servants, they went forward, guided by a boy, to Estella; and we, on having mounted, galloped a mile or two on our road homewards, not without good reason; for when Lord Eliot had gone a few yards farther, he must have seen Estella beneath his feet, in which were then 26 battalions of the enemy. In five minutes, had they detached any cavalry, they might have reached - for I have often galloped it since in less than that time - and they would have found Zumalacarregui himself with only 40 horsemen, at more than six miles from any succour. Although they would scarcely have taken him or any of his suite alive, that was little to the purpose. On telling Zumalacarregui that Lt. Colonel Gurwood had led the forlorn hope at Ciudad Rodrigo, he said that in everything he gave him the idea of a soldier. It was a source of great satisfaction to me to perceive the favourable impression my countrymen had made, and the glowing terms in which the Spaniards, who are not wont to think highly of strangers, spoke of them. It must have been afterwards equally so to Lord Eliot to have been the means of saving the lives of above 5,000 of his fellow-creatures.

In accomplishing this part of his mission, his lordship undoubtedly had rather a difficult card to play, as both parties, I believe, were rather unbending - the Carlists being flushed in the hour of success, and Valdes, although well aware of the necessity of complying, fearful of being disgraced by his government if he acceded to it. Such subsequently turned out to be the case, although, I believe, the intrigues of Cordova were mainly effectual in bringing about his recall. The capitulation was signed by both generals without the names of their sovereigns being mentioned, to avoid all allusion to their respective pretensions.

Colonel Gurwood and the Brig. General Montenegro went into Logroño together, where crowds rushed to see a Carlist chief. Unfortunately, being a little man, *pour le physique*, he was not well calculated to make a favourable impression. I was at that time absent for a day or two from headquarters, and therefore missed the pleasure of seeing him on his second visit.

Having, by the defeat of Valdes, obtained the free and uncontrolled range of the country, we immediately laid siege to Irurzun, the next fortified village to Echari-Arenas on the Pampeluna side, and of importance as commanding that road, as well as the passage from thence into the road from the latter place to Bayonne. As invariably happened whenever we attempted to besiege a place, we had the most wretched weather possible, the rain pouring in incessant torrents. While I was in a small village, before reaching Irurzun, I learned that an Englishman had arrived. General Bellingero requested me to visit the stranger with him, as no one could understand him. He turned out to be a young surgeon, named Frederick Burgess[105], who had excellent certificates from Sir Astley Cooper[106], and had gone through two examinations at St. John's Hospital, but he had come without any further recommendations, and unfortunately spoke no Spanish and very little French. He had brought plenty of surgical instruments with him; and although it is natural to the Spaniards to be suspicious, and I had had no knowledge of him previously, on observing, that, as we had plenty of wounded, the value of his services might very promptly be estimated, Zumalacarregui gave orders for him to follow us. A day or two after, while besieging Irurzun, an artilleryman was struck by a four-pound shot on the kneecap, leaving the leg hanging only by a little flesh. The man evinced his readiness to have the amputation effected by the stranger, and the latter performed this operation, as well as two others, with so much skill and success, that he was immediately received into our ranks. He has since met with rapid and deserved advancement in the service; and if success should attend the arms of Don Carlos, has a right to look forward to one of the highest offices of the medical department. When I left, I had the satisfaction of seeing him

---

[105] He also studied at Guy's. He wrote accounts of several events in this war and in 1870 told the historian William Bollaert that he believed he might have saved Zumalacarregui if he had been allowed to operate on him as soon as he was hit.
[106] 1768-1841. He was President of the Royal College of Surgeons. He successfully removed a sebaceous cyst from the head of George IV.

universally acknowledged by the army as by far the most skilful of their surgeons; and nothing but the numerous and successful cures he performed, in cases when there was a certainty of death with their own people, could have wrung this concession from the Spaniards, one marked feature of whose character is an overweening self-conceit, and a dislike to everything foreign, which is too apt to blind them to any merit in a stranger - although, when once awakened to a sense of it, they are too just and too generous not to acknowledge it, painful as the effort seems to be to their pride.

The torrents of rain rendering our operations very difficult to carry on, Zumalacarregui resolved on raising the siege, and on retiring to the farther end of the Borunda, aware that Valdes would, as soon as he was gone, march from Pampeluna to disengage the garrison. Moreover, as Irurzun contained few stores, as long as the place was evacuated, it was not worth while, for the sake of capturing 300 men, to waste ammunition which might be employed to greater advantage in attacking more important forts. Before our raising the siege I was witness to a singular scene. I had just been sent for by the General, when I saw a company which had advanced at night to the ruins of a farm within pistol-shot of Irurzun, all scampering before about 20 of the garrison who had made a sortie. It appears they had fallen asleep on their post; and the alarm being given, all hurried out helter skelter. The General unfortunately himself was witness to this disgraceful flight. I reached the village a little above. Irurzun at the moment that the battalion was assembled (the 3rd. Navarre); the men were all formed on the little square; and by the dead silence that reigned, it was easy to see that something had happened. The General was on horseback in the midst of them, with looks as stormy as the weather. He degraded the officers of the company, and broke the serjeants and corporals, when an ensign, a Spaniard by birth, but of Swiss family, answered him, it is true, rather insolently "What!" said the General; "do you add insolence to your cowardice?" and instantly struck him on the head with the edge of his sabre. The blood trickled down; and, although the wound was slight, I did not feel less indignation for the cruelty of this treatment. A dead silence followed; he dashed his sword into the scabbard, and they all marched down to the high road. I have given more than one noble trait of Zumalacarregui, and I am aware that the good far surpasses the evil in his character. Stern as it was his wont to be, I have every reason to remember his treatment of with gratitude. I met with proofs of friendship on his part which I had no right to expect, and which are deeply and ineffaceably engraven on my memory. I claimed no introduction to or acquaintance with him, but that gained before the enemy; and yet experienced from him kindnesses it would be difficult ever to forget. This feeling, however, I trust has not diminished my impartiality. If I had not been well aware that the good in his character counter balanced the evil, I would never have penned these passages of the scenes of excitement which I passed with him during the last year of his life, but have left the whole, as far as on me depended, in obscurity.

As it was expected, Valdes instantly sallied from Pampeluna, and led back the garrison within shelter of its walls, which, to the Carlists, were, and continued to be, impregnable. At Echari-Arenas we received the intelligence of the brilliant victory gained by Brig. General Gomez[107] at Guernica over Iriarte, where he had totally dispersed his column, taking 500 prisoners and two pieces of cannon. A part of those who had escaped from the action were shut up in a convent, from whence they were afterwards

---

[107] Miguel Gómez Damas (1785-1849) was the Carlists' ablest general after Zumalacarregui. Following the latter's death, in 1836 he marched his 3000 men westwards in order to open a new front. Pursued by Espartero with twice the force, he took town after town. Surprised and defeated by Espartero, he regrouped and marched on Madrid, sweeping aside all resistance; but he calculated that he could not hold the capital. Several victories followed and he took important cities, igniting Carlism all over Spain in what is known as the Long March. In the end he succumbed to weight of arms. Misjudged by Don Carlos, he was arrested for disobeying orders and falsely claiming royal authority, both of which were true. Nonetheless, after his release, he covered Don Carlos' flight to France and himself lived out the rest of his life with his wife in penury in Bordeaux, declining an offer of a million reales if he would only acknowledge Isabella as Queen.

relieved by Espartero. A messenger was instantly dispatched to inform the Carlist chief of the arrangement made with Valdes. It was feared that he would scarcely arrive in time to save the lives of all the prisoners.

We were now again tolerably provided with ammunition, on account of the want of which the golden opportunity was lost of destroying the whole Christino army at one stroke. After repeatedly offering them battle under the walls of Vittoria, we marched on Treviño, a small town, capital of the county of Treviño, appertaining to the kingdom of Old Castille; it stands on the map like an islet in the midst of the province of Alava[108]. It is also on the road from the former city to Penacerrada and Castille. Thus we contrived to isolate Vittoria still more, Salvatierra, and Estella, which had not been attacked, because we were already informed that the enemy were destroying the works to evacuate them. Maestu was already abandoned. All these results were the fruits of the victory over Valdes.

Treviño is overlooked by an old Moorish watchtower on a hill which is seen from a great distance in the plain. The fortified houses and outworks were speedily taken, and the old church so battered, that the garrison of 420 men were obliged to surrender at discretion on the third day. They had as yet heard nothing of the capitulation effected by Lord Eliot for giving reciprocally quarter, although the order had been read at the head of every company in our army; and they were agreeably surprised at the intelligence that they had nothing to fear for their lives. An aide-de-camp of the General's, named Martinez, passing a narrow street in the town before the surrender, received five bullets, probably fired from a wall-piece, in the two thighs; three entered in one, and the limb which the other two entered was broken in two places. The Spanish surgeons insisted on amputation of both limbs. Burgess, however, still entertained hopes; and the patient, being called upon to decide, fixed upon my countryman. The event showed that he had not

---

[108] It remains an enclave to this day

misplaced his confidence, as a complete cure was effected. At the latter end of July, it was expected that in a couple of months he would be again on horseback.

We had marched as it was supposed, and there was a report circulated to that effect, although this circumstance was no proof of Zumalacarregui's intention, to attack Puenta la Reyna, when a division of 3,000 men and some cavalry sallied from Pampeluna. They were too feeble to attack anything but our vanguard, and were, I should therefore have apprehended, destined either to escort a convoy to Taffala, or marching to effect a junction with the forces in that city. Pampeluna lies at the farther end of a large plain on the road from Puenta la Reyna. This plain, over which lie scattered upwards of 20 villages, may be about eight or ten miles in length, but on every side surrounded by high mountains. Between two of these the high road to the latter place has been excavated. We were at least two hours' march, with about two battalions and 500 horse, before the rest of the army, when we learned from the peasantry, who every instant came running to us over the mountains, of the advance of this column. Zumalacarregui led us to the first defile, which is formed as the road winds into the mountain; here right and left of it he posted his infantry, and we were formed so as to be concealed by the undulating ground, ready to charge down the road and cut the enemy to pieces in the plain the moment they should make a retrograde movement, which they would not fail of doing as soon as they found the pass occupied. We had dismounted and were peeping over the brow of the hill, and gazing with intense interest on the black mass that came nioving up, apparently unconscious of the destruction that awaited them. Suddenly we saw them pause and form, their squadrons and battalions seeming no larger in the distance than black beetles crawling below. They then rapidly commenced their retreat, having been accidentally apprised of the lurking danger.

The instant Zumalacarregui perceived it, he gave orders for both infantry and cavalry to pursue and endeavour to cut them off

296

before they could reach Pampeluna. They were, however, three miles in advance of us: in vain we spurred on, as they got under the guns of that city before we could come up with them. Two companies, which had been detached on discovery, finding their retreat intercepted, had taken refuge in a village where cavalry could do nothing against them; but the infantry coming up made 70 of them prisoners, and killed the remainder.

The enemy never confronted us till under shelter of their guns, when our cavalry was ranged challenging the whole force assembled in Pampeluna to battle, which, as they had not above 200 horse, they were afraid to risk on such even ground. It was the first time, since a very early stage of the war, that the Carlists had been within sight of the city, and we could distinguish thousands thronging the walls to look with their telescopes on the red caps, red lances, and black flags of the *factious*, waving under their very walls. A little beyond the last venta or inn, along the road, about a mile from Pampeluna, there is a little bridge: here they had placed a piquet of 24 horsemen. We were afraid to rush upon them, because it was within range of their heavy artillery, and they would instantly have given back, leaving us exposed to the shot for our pains. O'Donnel, baulked of his prey, was riding impatiently up and down in front of his regiment: he was followed by his orderly, a serjeant, a trumpeter, and had with him five officers, when he suddenly exclaimed, pointing to the piquet at the bridge, "Look at those fellows! they are as far from their own squadron as from us; we are nine, let us drive them from the bridge," and spurred full upon them. The enemy, who were not regulars but peseteros, remained firm at their post, as they saw that they had only nine adversaries, and they were themselves more than twice the number. But when the Carlists were close upon them, they lost heart and fled. O'Donnel came up with one who was behind the rest, and might have cut down the man with ease; but instead of doing so he called out to him to surrender. The man replied by firing his carbine at him, which piercing through his saddlebow entered the abdomen: the *pesetero* was instantly cut down, the orderlies running him through and through with their lances. O'Donnel, although mortally wounded, struggled to keep his seat on horseback until he was taken off and carried to the venta, when I immediately fetched Mr. Burgess, who examined the wound, and caused him to be placed on a brancard. He was thus carried on to Echauri, a large village at the farther end of the plain, about which our army, as well as the reinforcements that had joined us, were quartered. As Mr. Burgess, who had been appointed full surgeon, was yet unacquainted with the Spanish language, although unwell at the time myself, I assisted at the operation of sewing up the wound, and spent the night on a mattress in O'Donnel's chamber, in the house of the apothecary of Echauri, the best in the village, whither he had been carried. Several other surgeons and medical men were present, but both O'Donnel and his brother expressed a preference for my countryman, who, however, immediately gave it as his opinion that the wound was mortal, for the peritoneum was cut through, and the gut injured, and in his opinion the patient had not 48 hours to live. He seemed to be suffering horribly, and was occasionally delirious. By a singular fatality, for the first time during the campaign, his servant had neglected to strap his cloak in front of the saddle; if it had been there, he would have escaped unharmed. The only observations he made were, when we inquired whether he suffered much, "I almost wish some one would send a bullet through me," and although his danger had been hitherto concealed from him, he observed, "I feel that I must say farewell to the world. I can have but a short time to lite. Already three O'Donnels are gone in this war! their blood has been shed on the right side as well as on the wrong."

The O'Donnels had indeed been strangely divided; cousin against cousin, and brother against brother; and an equal fatality seemed to attend them on both sides. Leopold, his cousin, bad been taken at Alsassua and shot by the Carlists. His second brother also, in the ranks of the Queen's army, had lost his leg at Arquijas, and was said to be dying of it. Carlos was then stretched on a bed from which he never rose, and his brother Juan, who was then attending him, by that singular fatality which seemed to hang over the devoted race, was wounded on the 16th. July, at Mendigorria, and being since made prisoner in Catalonia, was barbarously murdered by the mob at Barcelona, with 160 of his fellow-captives. The atrocities committed on his body, which was torn to shreds, and parts actually devoured by those fiends in human shape, while his head became the football of the rabble, have been given, in all their revolting details, in the public papers.

He was, to judge from his appearance, about 30, and had left his wife in France; his brother, by a few years his elder, had also left his lady at Madrid. I had been acquainted with Carlos long before he was wounded, but after that fatal circumstance became much more intimate, and, in proportion as I knew him, felt my esteem grow for his character. He was then commanding the 2nd. Battalion of Castille, formed of the prisoners who had voluntarily taken arms after the capture of Echari-Arenas.

The officers around Zumalacarregui were debating on the manner of distributing them amongst the other corps, from fear that they might not be sincere in their conversion and pass over to the enemy. Zumalacarregui stated that he thought they would do better together. "But who will venture to command them?" said one of his generals. "I will," said O'Donnel, who was Lt. Colonel, and waiting to be employed. Zumalacarregui immediately appointed him to the command of the new battalion.

These men, being fully equipped, had each a new coat and great coat, one of which the officers of the other corps insisted on their parting with, as many of their soldiers were in a most ragged state. O'Donnel, after many a tough battle with his superiors, managed, however, to retain them. If any of them had been at all wavering in their attachment to the side they had embraced, the kindness of their colonel fully attached them to it, and they always behaved with the utmost gallantry under his orders. At

299

Mendigorria, their cartridges being expended, they saw two companies of the guards, who grounded their arms, and cried out that they surrendered. On approaching, they, however, snatched them up and poured in a murderous volley. O'Donnel himself was wounded; but his men, enraged at this act of treachery, surrounded and bayoneted them all. Juan O'Donnel had always behaved with particular humanity towards those of the enemy that fell into his hands, when, after the capture of Echari-Arenas, the Christinos wounded and took prisoners the very men who were escorting to Pampeluna the officers of the Regiment of Valladolid, to whom Zumalacarregui had generously given their lives and liberties. Two soldiers and a serjeant of the garrison of that city were taken, and the excitement of party feeling being very high in the Carlist camp, at finding all their acts of mercy so ill requited, they were condemned to be immediately shot. Juan, showever, begged, and with the greatest difficulty obtained their lives, and incorporated them in his own battalion; and this was the man who was afterwards murdered in cold blood, and in the face of a solemn treaty, of which the adverse party first reaped the benefit! It appears that when taken he broke his sword across his knee rather than surrender it. Before Lord Eliot's convention, I think I saw sufficient of his character to know that he would not have been taken alive, and it had been well if he had not been.

Carlos died at about 10 o'clock the next night, and early on the following morning was opened by Burgess, who had differed in opinion with the other doctors as to whether suppuration or inflammation had been the immediate cause of his death; the result proved him to have been right. The bullet, after piercing the peritoneum in three places, cutting the gut and injuring the spine, had made a hole as big as a halfpenny in the blade-bone, from which it was extracted, as well as a small piece of brass, and leather, and cloth of the saddle, which it had previously gone through. He was no sooner dead, than his brother, who was greatly distressed, was obliged to rejoin his battalion; many others of his friends who were around him were also under the necessity of repairing to their respective corps, and we were but few who attended his remains to the grave.

He was buried without parade in the church at Echauri; he had, it is true, a rude oaken coffin, which was carried by six dismounted lancers; his sword and red cap were laid upon it. While the service was going through, the march was beat, and when we had seen a little earth shovelled on his grave, we departed with the regret it was impossible for all not to feel, some for having lost a friend, others fa skilful and daring officer. Thus ended the career of the chivalrous O'Donnel; he was worthy of a better fate than to have been the victim of such a paltry fray, although receiving his death-stroke the sword in his hand, and his feet in the stirrups - a death which no soldier should lament, when his last hour is irrevocably fixed - as I believe it to be, yet to perish by an act of rashness and temerity rendered him liable to be reproached for folly, although his hardihood would otherwise have met with praise.

I may here be pardoned for recalling a circumstance which, when I saw him lifted bleeding from the saddle, rushed forcibly to my recollection. I was a few days before with the Marquis de Broissia, a French nobleman in the service, conversing with O'Donnel on the losses those exiled from Madrid must have sustained, and upon their probable fate, in the event of the cause not succeeding, when he quoted, with considerable emphasis, the following lines:

"Quand on n'a plus d'espoir,
Vivre est un opprobre et mourir un devoir."

O'Donnel had borne the reputation in the Spanish army of being one of the best, if not the best, cavalry officer, as General Sarsfield was deemed to be the best officer of infantry.

CHAPTER XXI.

The Carlists in Estella - Defeat of Oraa - Val de Lena - Neglect of the Wounded - An Escape - Siege of Villafranca - The Forlorn Hope - Captain Lathchica - Sudden movement of Espartero - Defeat of Espartero - Surrender of Villafranca - Surrender of Bergara - Evacuation of Salvatierra - Attack on Ochandiano - Fall of Ochandiano - Gloom of Uncle Tomas.

Early the same morning Thomas Reyna, who commanded the 4th. squadron of the Lancers of Navarre, which had been detached, haying received no orders to march from the village in which he was quartered, and rations of straw being short (in all the north of Spain there is no hay, and the horses are chiefly fed on chopped straw and barley), had ordered the saddles to be taken off, when the peasantry came to inform him that two-and-twenty carabineros had passed along the road to Taffalla.

Leaving the squadron in command of the first captain, he had the "*boute en selle*" sounded; and with the first 16 men that assembled pursued. The enemy were so much in advance, that they followed them above two hours along the high road full gallop, until they found themselves almost within gunshot of Taffalla, where they overtook them. Reyna charged them fearlessly; took nine prisoners, besides those who were left upon the road, five only escaping into the town: they then made off rapidly before a horse could be saddled in the place. Amongst the prisoners was the lieutenant commanding the detachment. "You are a fortunate man," said he to Reyna, "only in the success you have hitherto had, but in the good fortune that must inevitably befall you. The courier, with important papers and a large sum of money, is to pass on this very road in half an hour, with a very feeble escort, and you cannot fail of meeting him." Reyna, little disposed to trust to the advice of an enemy, took off to the right, in which he acted well; for the lieutenant had endeavoured to entice him to follow the road, in the hopes that he would have fallen in with the column, which he knew was to sally from Pampeluna, and which had been so quickly obliged to retrograde.

From hence with our prisoners, we marched on Estella, which immediately on the fall of Trevino had been abandoned. Here, in the second city of Navarre, we made our triumphant entry, amidst the ringing of bells, the scattering of flowers, and the phrenzied joy of the inhabitants. According to the custom in Spain, in any great rejoicing, or when a procession passes, banners, shawls, handkerchiefs, and even old curtains and bed-covers, were hung out of the windows; and in the evening the place was illuminated. This city, which had been fortified by the Christinos ever since the beginning of the war, is situated along the banks of the Ega, and is overlooked by high and steep rocks. On one side rises the chapel of *Nuestra Señora de Dolores,* or Our Lady of Woe. On the other is also an old church, its grey spire not reaching to the full height of the rocks. As the city lies completely in a hollow, now that the Carlists were in possession of artillery, the town might in a day have been reduced to ashes, unless forts had been built on all the surrounding heights; but for this, very extensive works, and a more numerous garrison than the enemy could afford, would have been necessary. In consequence it was abandoned. Scarcely a young man was to be seen in the place, nearly all having joined Zumalacarregui at an early period of the war; and the crowds of anxious mothers, sisters, and relatives rushing through our ranks, and inquiring for or meeting with those from whom they had been so long parted, offered a very affecting scene. Up to the time of the defeat of Valdes they had been in a dreadful state of uncertainty; as the Christinos had always boldly asserted that the Carlists were beaten in every direction, although the hundreds of wounded brought in after different actions in the vicinity contradicted this statement. It was the first time they were assured that the Royalists were victorious, as the Christinos were pursued to the very gates where the firing was heard; and near 3,000 men returned, covered with mud, sans muskets, sans chakos, and many sans shoes and sans anything. On this occasion, they frankly admitted, that if the daylight had lasted a few hours longer, they would all have perished. They had been lodged by whole companies; and the *patrons,* or masters of the houses, had been forced to find food for their famishing guests. The garrison had only received six hours' notice to prepare for evacuating the place, after a residence of many months, when it was feared Zumalacarregui would march upon it. The few Urbanos and their families had consequently been obliged to leave the greater part of their property behind, which was seized and confiscated for the benefit of the Carlists, who had been similarly served by the Queen's partisans.

We here received the intelligence of the defeat of Oraa, at the Seven Fountains of Elzaburu, with the loss of a 1,000 men. He had been beaten by Cuevillas and Elio, ho had formed a junction with Segastibelza and the 5th. Battalion from the Bastan. Elisondo, Urdax, San Esteban, and Irun had consequently been abandoned, and the country, from the frontier of France to Pampeluna, was entirely cleared. From hence we marched on Villafranca of Guipuscoa, a town which, for an irregular fortification, was passably strong. It was the intention of Zumalacarregui, as I have every reason to believe, to have attacked this place, and then Bergara, for the stores they contained, and then to besiege Vittoria, which must either have fallen, or have led to a general action; which, so great was the demoralization of the enemy, they would never have risked, or, if they had, the confidence of his men, increased by their treading the very soil celebrated for two previous victories, left no doubt as to the result. We were now in possession of nine guns - the *ayuela,* a 13-inch mortar, two 7-inch mortars; an 8-pounder; two 6-pounders taken at Echari-Arenas, and two 4-pounders taken on 27th. October.

As I was rather unwell, I obtained leave of absence, and remained behind in the village of Acedo, with two servants, for a few days. When I next joined headquarters, it was at the moment that the siege of Villafranca had been raised, or rather was interrupted, on account of the rainy weather, which seemed to persecute the Carlists whenever they attempted to besiege a place. These few days of rest were far from unacceptable to me. I lodged, I remember, in the old Palacio; a square heavy brick building, with a sort of pigeon-house on the top of the roof. This was the property of some French count, whose name does not occur to me, and who had married the heiress of the rich domain to which the mansion belonged. It was now inhabited by the vicar of the place, whom I had known from having been quartered there previously. He much amused us by the vehemence of his protestations, when accused by one of the inhabitants of having, in conformity to the orders issued by the enemy, prayed in his mass for Queen Isabella II. I took up my quarters in a large hall, where I found an old picture of *Nuestra Señora de la Vela* or Our Lady of the Taper, whose aid to those who pray for her interference was, half-poetically, half-grotesquely, represented on the canvass. A Count of Oñate, a crusader, by the red cross on his breast, is seen in a frail galley on a stormy sea, and is clasping his hands as the image of our Lady of the Taper appears through the clouds, and assures him of safety. A mother is seen on her knees by the sick bed of a dying child, imploring her protection, when the image of Our Lady of the Taper appears to assure her of recovery. The criminal, or perhaps the guiltlessly condemned, about to mount the scaffold, is praying for *Nuestra Señora de la Vela's* intercession; and, as she is visible on one side, the messenger is seen spurring up with a reprieve. Lastly, concludes this illustrated legend "more than once the tapers lighted in her honour have burned without being consumed nay, have been even known to augment." At the door of a cottage in the little square before the church, I saw a family apparently in great grief. I instantly recognised a middle-aged woman to be the same, who, coming to inquire for her son in the Lancers of Navarre, as we were passing through some months before, was informed that he had been killed at the surprise of Viana. On inquiring the cause of her present distress, she informed me that her other only surviving son had fallen on the 23rd., in the Battalion of Guides -

the day of the defeat of Valdes. It was but a melancholy satisfaction to her, when I observed to the poor matron, that they had both fallen in the hour of victory. Here, as everywhere, the peasant seemed to take a deep and thrilling interest in our success.

I do not know if I have already mentioned that when - particularly in the early part of the campaign - we had been obliged to retire before the steadiness or superior numbers of the enemy, men and women might be seen at their doors, as we passed by, in tears; and when we were successful they seemed to share the glories of our victory - bitter as were too often the fruits which either victory or defeat entailed upon the peasant. As the village, having already given all their oats and barley, could only furnish me with Indian corn - which, although we were too often obliged to make use of it, is so hard that it inflames the mouth of a horse - I took the opportunity of riding over to our hospitals in the Val de Lena, to obtain rations of barley from the infirmary, whither I sent a servant every morning with a mule to fetch them.

About four miles off the road is a gentle ascent through a dense wood of encina and arbutus. On the side of the long narrow valley which spreads beneath your feet, rise the bleak grey rocks which must be passed to enter the Amescoas, and run parallel with it. Below, were the villages of Narqué, Ulibarri, and Vittoria; the two former were full of our wounded, to the number of perhaps 500; the latter place, being also an infirmiary for horses, contained about 100 wounded and sick. The men suffering from trifling wounds or from sickness were not sent to the hospital, but placed in the private houses of villages, where they were always treated with the greatest kindness; and it was but rarely, even if the enemy passed through - although perhaps not less than 1000 men were scattered over the country, that any of them were surprised. The approach of a column was always known hours beforehand by the peasantry; and the disabled Carlists were removed to the *casarios,* or isolated houses in the mountains. To visit all places of that description near which the Christinos passed was

307

impossible, as it was dangerous for them to send off even the most trifling detachment for such a purpose. The wounded whom I saw in the hospital, on account of every house in the three villages containing several, were much less attended to than in the other places; besides which, the constant sight of suffering had hardened the feelings of the inhabitants; and the thousand little attentions which, useless or useful, soothe so much a bed of sickness, seemed omitted. In point of medical assistance, perhaps they were better off; but as the surgeons were little superior to village barbers, this was not much to their advantage: three-fourths of those who were severely wounded, even if they had only arms or legs broken, perished. I saw here many of my friends; amongst others Torres, the colonel of the Guides, who was convalescent. So great, from the want of surgical skill, was the mortality which prevailed, that when we heard of any one having gone to the hospital, the natural exclamation was "*Poor fellow!*" and we were always surprised to see any one return from it, unless his wound was very trivial.

To penetrate into the valley in which these villages are situated was rather a difficult thing: it was always so well watched, that an entrance was never but once effected, though two or three times threatened, when the wounded were all carried into the mountains for safety. The scene is said to have been heart-rending; and yet, until the second time that Valdes assumed the command, our wounded even were never in security; when they had been surprised by Quesada, Rodil, and Mina, they were almost invariably butchered.

I had previously, during the campaign, reposed from its fatigues for a few days, and had more than once been to and fro between the Ebro and the frontiers where the principal points on all the roads were occupied by Christino garrisons. Although repeatedly sleeping within 10 or 20 minutes of their fortified places, secure in the devotedness of the peasantry and the vigilance of the *partidas*, I had on one or two occasions found myself obliged to escape on notice that was inconveniently short; yet I never ran a greater risk of being taken than I did when the country was comparatively clear of the enemy, who, excepting a small flying column of Lopez and Gurrea in the Rivera, was shut up in Pampeluna, Vittoria, and Viana. I had gone one evening to Estella, to take the baths; and as it was a long time since we had been in a large town, this offered many attractions, which at another time would have been passed over.

So rapidly had it been evacuated, that the enemy had abandoned 140 invalids, leaving their own surgeon; and until, pursuant to the capitulation effected by Lord Eliot, some place for the mutual security of the sick had been agreed to, we removed many of our wounded there, those of the enemy being hostages against any treachery on their part. A governor had consequently been appointed, and the place was thronged with a number of the ailing and the idle of our own army. Now that the lives of the prisoners were to be respected, the incaution of our own people was striking, and caused more than one capture.

I had spent several days at Estella very agreeably, never rising till 12 o'clock; and as the good people of the house in which I was quartered seldom rose till ten, we were admirably suited to each other. One morning, however, by a great chance, unable to sleep, I dressed at 8 o'clock, and went to the lodgings of a friend who was quartered at an inn on the marketplace, the *patrona*, or mistress, of which was noted as one of the few Christinos in the place. I observed some bustle in the streets, and heard some talk of the Christinos coming; but as this was repeated every day, and I had been accustomed always to hear march beat, not having been more particularly informed of the approach of danger, and as I saw no preparations for the departure of the sick and wounded, I had resolved on remaining. I took no notice, but went to rouse my friend out of his sleep, trying to persuade him that he had overslept himself, and that it was past twelve. We took chocolate, the *patrona* smiling and seeming in high glee, when, on going to the balcony, the servant of my host rushed up stairs, and informed me

309

that the column of Lopez, which had encamped the previous night, was close by, and that when the last peasant left them, the cavalry of the vanguard were at the distance of only a mile-and-a-half, and the road along the river was as smooth as a table. Above 200 housekeepers, who, on the evacuation of the place, had made demonstrations of royalism which would have compromised them, had already fled.

To mend the matter, my servant was so alarmed, that he made innumerable mistakes in saddling. Our anxiety was lest the enemy should enter before we were ready. Once on horseback, we had little to fear. The gay and cheerful aspect of the place in an instant vanished; all the stalls from the wellfurnished market were cleared. This spoke volumes as to the difference of honesty, or at least the severity of discipline on that point, between the enemy's columns and our own. Half the shutters were shut; the inhabitants retired from their doors; and it became almost like a city of the dead.

Having galloped as fast as was safe along the pavement, we took the road to the mountain, and reached an eminence which it takes about ten minutes to ascend, but from whence you look into every street as plainly as from its own steeple, when we saw a troop of carabineros enter. They went straight to the market-place at a brisk trot. About 10 minutes' ride farther on a curious spectacle presented itself. The good citizens, who did not find it wise or profitable to await the arrival of Lopez, with their wives on mules or on the little mountain horses, were here anxiously watching the result. We reassured them, by repeating what they had already been told, that the column could not remain above a few hours, as Ituralde was advancing with four battalions, and that they must speedily retire; which was a fact, and turned out as we predicted. From this spot they could see everything going on in Estella; and if the enemy passed through the other gate, we could escape by a dozen different roads, without the possibility of being overtaken, as the most spirited horse can go no faster than a mule on the broken pathways that lead up to it. As the siege of Villafranca was continuing, I started to regain headquarters. We travelled all day through torrents of rain, and as we passed the table-land round the Venta de Urbassa, the wind was so high, that I was obliged to take off my cloak, and work my way up against it by going in a zigzag direction, as the torrents of water beat with such violence against my face that it was impossible to see if going straight against it; and my horse had already stumbled several times in the holes and ditches which the rain had filled with water.

I lodged in a village of the Borunda, where, in the evening, three or four of the members of the *consejo,* or council, came to smoke their cigarillos, and to inquire the news. Since we had cleared the Borunda of its garrisons, the inhabitants had been pretty free from rations; but three squadrons of our cavalry and several battalions now quartered there, which again made them open their purse-strings, made them all outrageous; and we had a violent discussion, they declaring that the peasant could stand the rations he was obliged to furnish no longer. In all the districts which had been the principal theatre of war I was accustomed to these expressions of discontent; and never did the inhabitants complain so vehemently as during the first two or three months that I was with the army. Experience taught me the way of silencing their murmurs. I appeared at last to chime in with them. "You are quite right, my friends; the peasant cannot stand the exactions any longer; we shall be obliged to give up to the Christinos." This instantly elicited all their patriotism and party spirit. "Give up to the Christinos? Never! We Navarros - we who have beat them so often-give up? They shall burn our houses over our heads - take our last cow, and our last sheaf of corn or stalk of maize - before ever we acknowledge any but Don Carlos, or give up to the Christina!" to whom, *en passant,* they applied no very polite epithets. This was invariably the case: Often those who complained most bitterly were the most violent Carlists. This feeling of devotion to their cause absorbs every other even that of vengeance.

311

A peasant of Eulate, in the Amescoas, had been beaten with the flat of his sword by an officer, for his unbearable and uncourteous behaviour. The peasant vowed revenge. Two months after, the officer being wounded, was surprised at finding the same individual come to the village where he was, to apprise him that he was in danger, for which purpose. he had come after nightfall several miles. When the officer thanked him, he told him to thank not him, but heaven, that he was a Carlist; and refused to take any reward. When the wounded man observed that he was in great pain with his shoulder, he very coolly observed "*Mi alegro*" - I am glad of it - and went his way.

On reaching headquarters, the siege of Villafranca, which had lasted five days, had been interrupted on account of the weather, but was however speedily resumed. Villafranca is a small town, some leagues to the south of Tolosa and east of Bergara, situated in a plain, through which winds the river Orrio, and on the high road from Bayonne to Burgos. Previously to taking Tolosa, this place was invested. Like most of the towns in the northern provinces, the houses are high, and the streets narrow, so that the place covers but little ground. The whole was surrounded by a high and massive wall, round which a fosse had been dug, and the gates blocked up with planks laid edgewise and filled up with mud, besides a double ditch and *chevaux-de-frise*. Here all the Christinos of the surrounding country had retired; those who were suspected of royalism had been driven out, the newcomers without ceremony taking possession of their homes: consequently its present inhabitants consisted of all who were most obnoxious in the country, who had taken refuge there. The garrison consisted of 300 of the line, and about 300 Urbanos. Such was the number of men within the place; and from their known attachment to the contrary opinions, and the muskets that were found dirtied, although, on the surrender of the place, they endeavoured to make it appear that only 40 were Urbanos, there is no doubt but that all were under arms. On one side Villafranca is overlooked by a steep hill.

312

Without this circumstance, it might have baffled the efforts of the Carlists much longer, as the only heavy pieces were the mortars and the 18-pounder.

Being all wretchedly lodged, I went with two other officers, and took up my quarters about three miles up the bank of the river, in a large forge. The house adjoining was spacious and comfortable, and the owners apparently wealthy. Having ordered supper, we began to make acquaintance with our hosts; but a young lady seemed to be the mistress, and the others, superintendents, servants, and workmen. On inquiring the news, of course I gave them as favourable an account as possible of the Carlists, as generally the inhabitants took a lively interest in our success; and informed them that, unless Villafranca surrendered next day, preparations were making to storm it, and every living soul would be put to the sword. On this the lady of the forge burst into tears; and I gathered, with some difficulty, that her father and a brother were Urbanos, and then in Villafranca. We did our best to console her. We knew it was impossible for Valdes again to take the field, particularly to penetrate into the province, where, the valleys being narrower and the plains of trifling extent, every five minutes he was liable to be stopped either from advancing or retreating, by the Carlists. Moreover, since the defeat of the 2nd. and 3rd. January, they showed no desire to meet Zumalacarregui in the province; and the total discomfiture of Iriarte at Guernica by Gomez had added to this another fatal example. The main army of the Queen therefore made no further demonstration than advancing from Pampeluna towards the Borunda, whence, finding Ituralde there with his division, they speedily retreated.

In the first instance, our men had taken possession of some houses, not 50yds from the gate, during a dark night; Here they commenced mining. On their retiring from before the place, the Christinos sallied, and burned these houses. It was supposed that battering the place alone would suffice. Two mortars, one throwing shells of 175lb weight, played: incessantly, and did considerable damage, though each time à shell was seen in the air, a man, placed on the lookout in a steeple, struck the bell to give the inhabitants warning, so that they might rush into the houses, where they ran less risk. It seems surprising how our heavy pieces had ever, by the mere draught of oxen, been brought up the steep slippery road such a height, the soil of which was stiff clay soaked by the long rain. A breach was at last effected in the wall of two massive old houses, and, although-scarcely practicable, the General ordered the assault. As Villafranca is in the province of Guipuscoa, he gave the post of honour to the 1ˢᵗ. Battalion of Guipuscoa, and in particular to two companies, which were to lead the way. Three battalions of Navarre were to follow. They advanced silently with ladders to scale the walls. Having had two or three men killed, the two foremost companies fell back, and resolutely refused to be, led again to storm the place. When the officers of the companies signified this to the General his fury knew no bounds. He broke the commissioned and non-commissioned officers, and ordered the companies to draw lots for one man in ten to be shot, for cowardice according, to martial law. It was now too late to order on the battalions of Navarre to storm it, as the garrison had thrown out lights in the ditch all round it.

The next day, the cowardly behaviour of the Guipuscoans being known, Captain Lathchica, a very spirited officer commanding the 8th company of Guides, offered to lead the forlorn hope, a 120 men having volunteered for that purpose. Amongst the first were 18 French soldiers, all that were in the army; immediately after four companies of the 3ʳᵈ. battalion, or the *Requeté,* also volunteered; and also the four first companies of the Battalion of Guides. All those chosen for the assault were ranged all day along the bank of the river, drinking, singing, and merrymaking. The approach of danger seems to play the part in the soldier's thoughts of death when introduced in the old drinking-songs, reminding him of how short a time he may have to devote to pleasure and the bowl.

Lathchica deserves some notice in this memoir. Previous to the death of Ferdinand he had been in the horse grenadiers. His dwarfish but withal well-proportioned figure, scarcely higher than his fur cap, rendered him the butt of continual jokes, which his spirit was the last to have brooked, and occasioned continual affairs of honour, which are severely punished in the Spanish army. On one occasion, having struck an insolent trooper, who probably had drunk too freely, the man drew his sword, and made a furious cut at him; he parried this, and severed his head to the jawbone. According to martial law he was right; but he gave in his resignation, finding that his diminutive size occasioned continual quarrels, and excited a want of respect in the soldiers. He was placed on half pay, and had retired home to Andalusia. When, little by little, the Queen's government was obliged to send all their officers into the northern provinces, he received an order to join a regiment of lancers; being of Carlist opinions, he threw up his commission; but it was intimated to him that, unless he set out with a good grace, he should be conveyed to the corps to which he had been appointed by carabineros from station to station. He therefore resigned himself to his fate, determined to pass over to Don Carlos, which he did before he had been a week in Pampeluna. In our service he had been in the first instance in the cavalry, and thence exchanged to the Guides, where he much distinguished himself during the defeat of Valdes.

On obtaining leave to lead the forlorn hope, he begged, instead of any promotion, that he might gain by it the lives of the soldiers now at the prevention to be tried for cowardice, saying, that he had conversed with them, and he was willing to answer with his head that they would be the first to scale the walls with him. This the General readily granted; and the men were liberated. The storming party were all in the highest glee. Every one was talking of soon crossing the Ebro for good. This, however, might have been only conjecture; and as such I should have considered it, had I not heard it from the General's own lips, and he was always particularly guarded in announcing what his intentions were. Lathchica having kindly proposed to cede to me a part of his men, I went to Zumalacarregui to volunteer on the forlorn hope with him, the French soldiers having all offered to go with me. He refused, on the plea that I was a cavalry officer, "of whom," said he, "I shall soon be in want. We are going into the plains of Old and New Castille in a few days, and I reserve you for a service equally desperate and honourable, in your own arm."

As the breach had already been filled up, and it was intended to scale the walls, the ladders having been prepared, the place would not have been carried without some slaughter. The men remained all night without receiving the order to storm. Zumalacarregui, acquainted with a movement of Espartero to relieve it, and aware that the surrender of the place would follow his defeat, delayed the assault to save the lives not only of all the inhabitants, but of those of his own men, who must hare perished. Burgess arrived from the Bastan with another officer, where he had been attending on the eldest of the two sons of General Cuevillas, who, three weeks before, at the battle of Elzaburu, where, Oraa's column had been destroyed, had been mortally wounded, a bullet having fractured the spine. Burgess instantly pronounced that there was no hope of saving him. He was attended by his mother and sister. At Lecumberri, on returning, to headquarters, he saw 480 prisoners, who were afterwards sent to us; they had all been taken at Elzaburu. The capitulation effected by Lord Eliot had only been known the day previous, and to this circumstance they were indebted for quarter.

Espartero, assembling 7,000 men from the garrisons of Bilboa and St. Sebastian, resolved to attempt a *coup de main*, with a view to surprise the Carlist army and to relieve the place; during a dark and stormy night, he marched across the mountains to attack us with the above force. Zumalacarregui, however, whose vigilance never slept, acquainted with the movement, disposed of everything for his reception, and sent Eraso with eight companies, whose march could be more easily concealed, to attack him during his march in the darkness. Espartero could scarcely be blamed for making this desperate effort, or for the want of success that attended it. His design, once suspected by the Carlists, could produce nothing but a disastrous result. Although entirely routed by eight companies, the very numbers of his men increased their confusion; their inferiority on this point was a protection to the Carlists. The attack commenced on the heights of Descarga.

Espartero, leading his troops to surprise the besiegers along the narrow road, perishing with cold, and pierced through to the skin by the rain, slipping and falling every instant in the mud, was suddenly himself surprised by the discharges of musketry of the Carlists, who knew they had only to fire upon the road - and rending the air with their shouts of *"Viva el Rey! Viva Zumalacarregui! Hai quartel! Hai quartel* (There is quarter! there is quarter!) rushed upon them. So demoralized was at that time all the Queen's army by the successes of the Carlist leader, that, making one discharge, they dispersed and fled or surrendered, whole companies throwing down their arms. The son of Eraso behaved with peculiar gallantry on this occasion. Fortunately for the vanquished, the treaty of Lord Eliot and their late success considerably calmed the animosity of our men; and not 100 of the enemy were killed or wounded, although before daybreak 1800 prisoners were made; those who escaped reaching Bilboa in the most pitiable plight, without hats, without shoes, and covered with mud from head to foot. Espartero himself had had his cloak pierced by the thrust of a lance from one of Eraso's own escort; and Mirasol and all his staff were made prisoners in a house by the roadside. Mirasol, who is a little man, was fortunate enough to make his escape in the following manner: as the uniform of brig. general is only distinguishable in the Spanish army by the embroidered cuffs, he turned these up, and saying that he was a "tambor" - as all the soldiers were anxious to capture officers, and no one would condescend to secure a drummer - he received a sound kick, and was delivered to the custody of those without, from whom, having more prisoners than they could manage, he easily escaped.

The next morning a parlementary was sent into Villafranca, to inform the besieged that Espartero, coming to their relief, had been entirely defeated, and that, if they did not surrender immediately, the place would be stormed. Having sent out an officer to assure themselves of the veracity of this statement, by seeing and conversing with the prisoners, he returned with a confirmation of the fütility of any further hopes of succour. The place was accordingly given up: the same afternoon, at 3 o'clock, we took possession. The national guard were disarmed, and, as had been promised, their property was respected themselves being dismissed to their homes, with a hint that, if they in any way again interfered against Don Carlos, they would be treated with less gentleness. Amongst the Urbanos were the father and brother of our patrona of the forge, both unhurt.

A great quantity of stores of all kinds - 800 muskets, an 8-pounder, but only a small quantity of powder - was taken. The fortifications were immediately rased, and we marched to invest Bergara, where some of the fugitives from his column, and it was for a time supposed Espartero himself, had taken refuge. Altogether it contained 1,300 men in garrison, and nine pieces of artillery, great and small. As soon as the fall of Villafranca was known, the city of Tolosa was abandoned by the garrison with such precipitation, that they left behind them two 12-pound iron carronades, having previously spiked them; also a great quantity of flour, salt fish, and 25,000 cartridges. It was immediately taken possession of, so that we had not even the trouble of marching against it. What with the large garrison Bergara now contained, to consume the little provision within - the facility the surrounding heights afforded the Carlists to batter the place, and the total inability of any of the Queen's generals to relieve them - Valdes having been entirely defeated – Iriartes's column dispersed at

Guernica - that of Oraa at Elzaburu, and that of Espartero, of which they formed part, on their way to Villafranca - left them no alternative but to surrender. The soldiers, even if the officers had been disposed to resist when they knew that Zumalacarregui himself was under their walls, refused to fight. He offered to allow the officers to go when they pleased; but if it were not surrendered the same day, he gave them his word that he would storm it. Colonel Carvallar, the governor, having held a council of war, answered, that if the evacuation of Tolosa was verified, he was willing to surrender. Accordingly, two officers proceeded to the spot, and having satisfied them—although I believe this was only matter of form—the next day Bergara was surrendered.

As we were marching in, we met upon the road the officers of the garrison, all excepting the governor of Bergara, on foot, and without their swords. According to the capitulation, on their promise not to serve against the Carlists, they were allowed to go where they chose, and several were accompanied by their wives; one or two had children; they were followed by some carts drawn by oxen. Excepting the colonel, there was not one who had either a gentlemanly or a military aspect; one or two, round and fat fellows, had rather, indeed, the appearance of grocers or tallow chandlers than of soldiers. In the Carlist army this was comparatively rare: some had a stern and halfbrigand appearance; but, on the whole, the officers were much more *distingué* or more warlike in appearance. I must, however, explain that, generally speaking, a great difference was perceptible between the officers of the enemy made prisoners in the latter part of the war, and those in the early stages of it, who had all gone through the regular routine, and were many of them men who had served in the constitutional war; whereas latterly, to supply the losses they sustained, they seemed to have given commissions to any one. I was struck by hearing a Carlist, an old Castillian captain, who had followed the King to Portugal, repeating the day of the month several times with peculiar emphasis, to his comrade, as we passed

319

the prisoners; and, on inquiring the reason of it, he informed me, that exactly that day twelvemonth they had found themselves in the same humiliating situation in Portugal - disarmed, and passing on foot through the ranks of the victorious Pedroites: there was, however, this striking difference our men did not, even by a single expression, further than *Viva el Rey!* insult their misfortune; whereas they had been robbed, maltreated, and many of them - murdered.

The day following that on which Zumalacarregui took possession, Charles V made his triumphal entry: 1,300 men surrendered prisoners of war; the number of those we nor had in our hands became quite alarming; Oñate, Mondragon, and Villa-real were full. I spent a night at the latter town, where there were 1,500 prisoners, and only 800 men to guard them. They all loudly begged to be allowed to enter our ranks, declaring that they had hitherto been deceived by their officers, who declared that the Carlists never forgave those who had once served against them, and had put even the deserters to death in the most cruel manner.

Eybar, famous for its manufactories of arms, but which was only garrisoned by Urbanos, had been invested by several battalions of Guipuscoa. Zumalacarregui offered them, if they surrendered, to respect their property, and allow them to return unmolested to their houses, on giving up all arms, ammunition, and horses; if they did not, he would storm the place, and they should be treated according to the laws of war. Eybar surrendered, and the same night that the fall of Bergara was known the garrison of Durango escaped to Bilboa. The next night we slept in Durango.

The evacuation of Salvatierra was here confirmed; and we were also informed that all the heavy artillery, provisions, and stores had been sent out of Vittoria with only five battalions, and the Urbanos remained to garrison. There was no doubt but that this small force would have abandoned it on our approach; and Zumalacarregui was now determined to march upon that city, and thence upon Burgos, and either force the enemy to a battle, or move forward upon Madrid. His rapid successes had struck such terror and consternation into the Queen's army, that all the forces in Navarre and the provinces would neither have given him battle, nor have opposed, excepting as far as the garrisons along its banks might his crossing the Ebro; nor, if Ituralde had been left with only 10 battalions, have been able to follow him in the rear. Their men would not fight on any terms. Bets ran high in our army that in less than six weeks we should be in Madrid; and any odds would have been given that we should be there within two months. One thing only was wanting money; the coffers of Don Carlos were absolutely empty. When he had arrived in Navarre, he had relied for pecuniary resources on a contract with a Jew named Baron Maurice de Haber: this had been signed on board His Britannic Majesty's ship *Donegal*, on the 14th. June, for the loan of £5,000,000. Haber had been accredited, and recommended by the house of Gower and Co.; and when Don Carlos passed through Paris, Mr. Jauge, the Royalist banker, confirmed his hopes, and offered to undertake the negotiation of Haber's loan in France. Jauge was in consequence, when he attempted publicly to dispose of stock, thrown into prison. Other financial arrangements were proposed, but through a long series of mismanagements, and a succession of deplorable intrigues, this was neglected; and the government of Don Carlos found itself (as it had been all along, excepting a few thousands which had been sent by friendly powers) left entirely to its own resources, which, in a country already obliged to feed the contending armies, were necessarily very trifling. It was the more provoking, as Europe was full of speculators who would, it is true, on rather exorbitant terms, have furnished means: had it not been for the lack of resources, Charles V might at the present hour have been on the undisputed throne of Spain. Many who were heavily engaged in the loans of the Cortes and of the Queen would have purchased stock to protect themselves.

This want of pecuniary supplies was the reason why the great error of attacking Bilboa instead of crossing the Ebro and profiting by the panic of the enemy, was committed. The King declared that not only was he without money to pay the arrears, but he had not the immediate expectation of receiving any, and that Bilboa, a rich and mercan, tile city, which might furnish a temporary assistance, must be besieged and taken. This Zumala, carregui strongly opposed: Bilboa would take them several days; besides, it was entirely a false military movement: inconvenient as it might be, it was better to take advantage of the panic of the enemy before he could recover, and march on Vittoria, Burgos, and Madrid - advancing through districts hitherto untired by the constant passage of troops, and leading the army to feel that as they were approaching the terminatiou of their labours, money would have been less necessary.

On reaching Burgos the Queen's, government would probably have fled; the Carlist party in Madrid would have then raised their heads, and the capital once taken, all the resources of the kingdom would be in their hands, and Bilboa, Pampeluna, and all the garrisoned towns must naturally have fallen. Unfortunately the want of money made such an impression on those about the King, that he was advised, against his better judgment, almost to insist upon the taking of Bilboa, and he merely put the question, "Can you take it?" to Zumalacarregui. I know that I can take it, but it will be at an immense sacrifice, not so much of men as of time, which now is precious," was the reply of the General.

He spoke, unfortunately, too truly, though, perhaps, he never anticipated that his own life was to be wasted before its walls. The evil genius of the Carlists having prevailed, and the attack on Bilboa having been so fatally decided upon, sending tho rest of his artillery on to Bilboa, while batteries were erected there, with an 18-pounder and two mortars he marched at the head of three battalions on Ochandiano, where a garrison of 380 men of the Regiment of Provincials of Seville, commanded by the

Marquess of San Gil, had fortified the place. They did not, however, surrender on the first summons, consequently our artillery began to play. All the houses were crenelled, but the principal fortification was the church, round which tambours had been constructed.

We commenced the attack at eight in the morning, battering down some houses they were in. Eight or ten, whose vicinity to the church annoyed them, were set fire to by their own people. Our troops after that entering the streets drove them from house to house, by making holes in the wall with a pick-axe above their heads, and dropping through hand grenades. By 1 o'clock they were driven into the church and its vicinity. Four 13-inch shells fell successively into this edifice, which was crammed full, the last wounding twelve men, and killing two. As they found the mortar had now been brought to bear well upon it, they hung out a white flag. On this an officer and a serjeant stepped forward, but were immediately fired at from a house still in possession of the enemy - the former was wounded in the leg, the latter shot through the brain. At this piece of treachery Zumalacarregui swore he would put every soul to the sword, unless the authors of it were given up. When the garrison surrendered at discretion, the men who had fired proved, however, that they knew nothing of the white flag having been hung out, and consequently only remained prisoners of war.

Here, besides 380 prisoners, the band of the regiment, a quantity of provisions, 100,000 cartridges, and 500 muskets, all nearly new and of English manufacture, having the Tower mark upon them, and probably forming part of those sent by the Duke of Wellington pursuant to the treaty of the quadruple alliance, were taken. The band was very good, and as we had nothing but our trumpets, drums, and clarions in the army, proved an acquisition: they evinced their willingness to serve Don Carlos. As soon as Zumalacarregui knew, however, that they required a cart or a couple of mules to carry their instruments, he sent them off to the royal quarters.

On entering the church, it presented a scene which baffles all description: knapsacks, chakos, great coats, broken chairs, benches, and ornaments, were scattered in all directions: in the centre the flagstones had been taken up, and four of the killed were laid in a large hole which had not yet been filled up; the mouldering skulls and bones, turned up in digging, being thrown up with the earth all over the pavement. Early the next morning we returned to Durango, and thence marched on Bilboa, whither the artillery had preceded us. Ochandiano, invested at eight in the morning, had surrendered before nightfall. This was the last triumph of the Carlist chief; just as he was beginning to reap the fruit of all his labours, an untimely death dashed them from his grasp.

On a fine summer's afternoon, we formed beneath the huge trees of the shaded promenade, alongside of which is a magnificent fives-court[109], and commenced our march along the dusty road. This was the last time that I saw Zumalacarregui in the saddle; his stern but noble features I had never witnessed wear such a gloomy aspect, rendered more striking by the contrast of the merry faces around him: for in an army there are few who judge any farther than what they see immediately about them, or trouble themselves beyond the morrow; and the idea of entering a city like Bilboa, which was within a few leagues, and which they never doubted a moment of taking, was, perhaps, even more agreeable than a march on Madrid, which was many hundred miles away. There was in what I have stated no imagination, as it was observed by everyone: an officer in particular said to me, "Look at the General! one would say he was going to mount a scaffold, rather than to pounce upon such a prey as Bilboa." "He has not got over wearing his black coat," was carelessly observed. This was in allusion to his having substituted a dress coat, on his last visits to the King, for the zamara, or dark fur-skin jacket he always wore over a black waistcoat. He had latterly put on this black coat when he went to see his Majesty, it having been observed to him that his jacket was

---

[109] A *pelota*, or *jai-alai* court.

not a fitting costume to go to court in; for he always refused wearing the uniform of a Lt. General, and seemed to take a pride in his uncouth dress, which, excepting his red trowsers, was only military because he had rendered it so. The soldiers, unaccustomed to see him thus, and he probably being in rather severer mood than usual when they made the observation, had all imagined "That Uncle Tomas," as they expressed it, "was always in an ill humour when he had to put on a dress coat."

He never wore any of the several orders conferred upon him; even when at Oñate, after the battle of Vittoria, Don Carlos threw round his neck the grand cross of St. Ferdinand, an honour to which a subject can scarcely ever aspire - he only wore it as far as his camp. In his red cap and zamara, his whip slung across it, he had more than once signified his intention of entering Madrid at the head of his favourite Battalion of Guides, with their hempen sandals and cartridge belts.

That his death was a loss to Spain, all those that knew him are well persuaded. I might write a long chapter of his intentions in case of success - in prosecuting innumerable great and useful schemes, which would have gone farther towards the reforming and regenerating his country, than those of all the self-styled Liberals. If he had lived two months longer, to reap the fruit of his toil, such a chapter might have been as interesting as it would now be wearisome to the reader; and if he had lived, perhaps, as Mazeppa says

> "At this hour I should not be
> Telling old tales beneath a tree."

The building next to the Church of Our Lady of Begoña, in which Zumalacarregui was mortally wounded

CHAPTER XXII.

Bilboa – Portugalete - Siege of Bilboa - Failure of Ammunition - Zumalacarregui wounded - Effects of it - His Interview with the King - Activity of the Enemy - misunderstanding - Explanation- A Parley - Weakness of Don Carlos - Attempt to enter Bilboa - Death of Zumalacarregui.

Bilboa is about 17 miles north-west of Durango, along the banks of the river Ibaizabal, or Ivaizaval, as it is pronounced. On approaching the city the river winds a great deal. The country here, although level in comparison with the interior, is, notwithstanding, very hilly, and the road, which is macadamised, is cut through the rock in many places. On your right and left, approaching it by the road from Durango, all that is visible is the massive church of Begoña, which, surrounded by a few houses, rises outside the city. On your right are some plains, partly wooded and partly cultivated, formed by the sinuosities of the river, before you reach a wide and handsome bridge of stone, which spans the river, and over which passes the road to Bilboa, which is still concealed by a hill covered with vines. On the other side of this bridge are a few cottages, a tolerable house to the left, and on the right is a venta. This spot is termed Puente Nuevo, from the vicinity of the bridge, although, like the Pont Neuf at Paris, its antique appearance belies its name; and here, all through the siege the Carlist headquarters were fixed.

Bilboa, built in rather a straggling manner, chiefly along the right bank of the river, which, in passing through the city, where it continues to wind as far as the principal quay, is deeper bút-narrower than at Puente Nuevo, seems, as far as we could judge, as besiegers, to be a handsome city. The left bank is also built upon, but to a much less extent, and that part is called *Bilboa la vieja,* or Old Bilboa, which joins a suburb, and communicates with the right bank by a suspension bridge. The houses along the quays and in the squares seem all very high, regular, and well built-mostly of stone, with balconies, but all clean and well painted. On one square is the hospital, an immense building, but resembling, from its number of windows, a large green-house rather than an hospital, and seeming more picturesque than solid. It is perhaps, excepting Cadiz and Barcelona, the most commercial city in Spain, and is said to present a most gay and lively aspect. Of this we could judge but little, as even when the firing was suspended, there were but few that ventured from under the piazzas or through the streets. All around the city the soil is exceedingly fertile; and all the way to the sea, which is six niiles off, the banks are studded with villas and country houses. On the left bank, near the Bay of Biscay, is Portugalete, off which the larger vessels that cannot come up the river are obliged to anchor. This was fortified and garrisoned by the enemy. There were then lying at Olaveaga, a little out of Bilboa, at the foot of the monastery of San Mames, four or five French and English merchantmen, and three ships of war; the French government steamer, *Le Météore*, a French goëlette, and his Britannic Majesty's ship *Saracen*. The officers in command of these vessels had an interview with Zumalacarregui, who, according to the admission of the captain commanding on the river, behaved very politely, and gave a pass for the British Consul to be allowed to communicate freely with the *Saracen*.

Bilboa, in which were at that time 30 pieces of artillery, it would have been difficult to have taken by battering down the isolated forts, or rather fieldworks thrown up on terraces round the city, and joined by a wall with a deep ditch - that is to say, difficult for us, who had but two 18-pounders of battering-train; our brass pieces of six and eight doing little damage, and our batteries being dismounted by the number and heaviness of the enemy's guns, many of which were 32-pounders. To storm it was comparatively easy, and a loss certainly under 500 men would have made the town our own; and on storming it Zumalacarregui resolved. On the left bank of the river, on a height immediately overlooking the place where the hospital stands, were placed three mortars; and in front of Begoña, on the right bank, a battery of two 18-pounders was advanced to within a short distance of a terrace and wall, which commanded a great part of the city. In the church of Our Lady of Begoña, which, although without the walls, is the principal one of Bilboa, the Battalion of Guides was stationed; our ammunition being drawn up in carts by oxen, and ranged behind the church. To the left of this was a palacio. As it was found that the walls of this building were sufficiently solid, two embrasures were made, and pieces of cannon placed in them. Our batteries having at last opened fire, it was reported, by nightfall, that a breach was nearly effected. Lots had been drawn, and it had fallen on the 1st. and 2nd. companies of Guides to lead the way for the storming party. Zumalacarregui, in a few words, informed the men that the first 100 who entered the place should each receive an ounce of gold; if they fell, their families should be well provided for; and six hours' pillage[110] were to be given. He was answered by loud shouts, to send them on. At this moment our ammunition failed; messenger after messenger was despatched, but the fire having slackened, the breach that had been made was filled up with sandbags; and, having once had time to repair it, the breach became the most difficult place to get over, as probably they had placed *chevaux-de-frise*, and dug trenches on the other side. Zumalacarregui now delayed the storming till next night, and had preparations made for establishing a battery considerably on the left of Begoña, having now decided on the wiser plan of battering down the wall that united the separate forts, and entering the city; as, when that was taken, all the fortified points and terraces round it, although commanding it, could only burn it, and must eventually surrender.

The palacio next to the church of Bilboa afforded a most commanding view; and although not above a 100 toises from the enemy's work, early the next morning, notwithstanding the representation of his staff, Zumalacarregui, who would see everything himself, went out with a telescope into the balcony,

---

[110] The authorization of so-many hours' pillage was a standard practice of all parties, including the British Auxiliary Legion.

although the woodwork of the window was like a riddle, and all the bars excepting three were torn away by the grapeshot. The instant anyone appeared in sight, the enemy commenced their fire of musketry; so that, on seeing a man so exposed, and by his telescope and black fur jacket evidently a superior officer, all the men lining their batteries and the works commenced firing on him. It has been said that he was struck by one of the English marines, from the steamer in the Queen's service, then in the river; but this it is impossible to ascertain, and it was more than probable that it was a Spaniard that sped the bullet which occasioned his death (although a shot fired from behind a wall is scarcely a subject worthy of dispute), as the marines in the battery could not at most have been more than 20 or 30; and all agree that a discharge of at least 100 muskets took place. The General came slowly out of the balcony, but finding that he could not conceal his lameness, he at last admitted that he was wounded. A bullet, bounding from one of the bars of the balcony, struck him in the inner part of the calf of the right leg, passed without hurting the *tibia*, and fracturing the smaller bone, without having force to penetrate, as it is usual with spent shot, dropped two or three inches lower down in the flesh.

I had spent the previous night near Zornosa, about nine miles off on the road to Durango, and had received orders to join his staff, to which I had been appointed, early next morning. As I had already been before Bilboa, and the accommodation was wretchedly bad, on receiving a second summons at nine in the morning, having been all the preceding day on horseback, I did not hurry. On reaching the village of Zornosa, I was informed that I had been sent for thus early, because the General was wounded, to accompany Burgess, whose medical assistance was required, but who had difficulty in making himself understood. He had already been gone half an hour. I spurred away, but only reached Bilboa as the General was carried, bed and all, by twelve soldiers along the road. He seemed in some pain, but conversed and smoked his cigarillo all the way, as if nothing had happened. Burgess had not examined the wound, as he also had only been in time to join him; but from the description given by the surgeon that attended, it was very trifling. Notwithstanding this, the necessity of quitting the army, and being unable to direct the operations of the siege, seemed to prey upon his mind. All along the road where the news of Zumalacarregui being wounded had flown like wildfire, the peasants and soldiers thronged round his couch. He took chocolate twice on the road, saying, I suppose I must not take anything else?" which the doctors confirmed.

It was already, on account of the slowness of our march, nightfall before we reached Durango. One of the best houses in the town opposite the palacio, in which the King was lodged, was prepared for his reception. All the ministers were in waiting to receive him. As Zumalacarregui - which I believe I have already mentioned - had never been on cordial terms with those about the King, he received them rather bluntly. When they inquired whether he was in pain, he replied, abruptly, "Do you imagine that a bullet through the leg does not hurt?" On examining the wound, it was found as I described: he had a little fever, which augmented during the night. His first observation, when left by the King's people was, "The pitcher goes to the well till it breaks at last. Two months more only, and I would not have cared for any sort of wound." He was attended by the surgeon of his own staff a man who had deserted over from the Christinos a few weeks before, and in whom he seemed to place confidence the King's own physician, and Burgess. The two former were of opinion that in a month, so slight was the wound, he would be again on horseback: the latter stated a still shorter period for his recovery, and said that, in a fortnight or three weeks he ought, if properly treated, to be 6 able to resume his occupations. Burgess was also of opinion that the bullet should be instantly extracted this was opposed by the other two, and even dressing the wound was neglected till next morning: he also opposed their putting on any bandage, or a Samaritan balsam of wine and oil, which he said was unnecessary. They all three slept

331

in the same room, keeping watch by turns: for my own part, being unwell, and very tired, I ordered the alcalde to furnish me with a lodging, and early the next morning returned to the General's room. At 6 o'clock Don Carlos came to see Zumalacarregui, and they conversed at considerable length: the tears stood in the King's eyes, and the interview was highly affecting. Zumalacarregui looked very pale and exhausted, having slept but little all night. He read over and signed several papers. He then desired me to inform Mr. Burgess, that as his wound was of a most trifling description, and, besides his own senior surgeon, the King had sent his to attend him, he (Burgess) had better return to Puente Nuevo, where his services might be more useful to the wounded. He also dismissed me, to join Eraso's staff, who, *ad interim,* was commander-in-chief. He was carried on a litter to Segura, and thence to Cegama, a distance of about 30 miles, passing through the village of Ormaistegui. Thrice after a lapse of many years he had passed through the spot of his nativity, which he had quitted at an early age - once during the defeat of the enemy on the 3rd. January, when we had all gone through at full speed in pursuit; once after the defeat of Espartero, the surrender of Villafranca, and the evacuation of Tolosa and Salvatierra by the enemy, when he was marching to invest Bergara; and a third time, stretched on a litter by a wound that proved mortal, when he came to lay his bones within a short distance of his birthplace, which was only hidden from sight by a mountain that had been the scene of one of his early triumphs.

He died, if I remember right, the eleventh day after he received his wound. He was then delirious, and expired in a manner characteristic of his life: he seemed, in this temporary derangement, to fancy himself leading on his followers in some desperate action; and breathed his last calling his officers by name, and giving orders to his battalions to charge or retire, as if he had been fighting that last battle which must have decided the fate of Spain, and where we should have seen him fall with less regret.

332

With him, not alone the Carlists, but Spain, lost a man whose like she had not seen for long years, and which I hope she may soon look upon again.

When I parted from him at Durango I never anticipated this. We had seen him always escape so providentially, and he was so bound up with our cause, that we had never dreamed that he could die. It would have seemed less strange to us if earthquake had swallowed up one-half of our army. I returned to Puente Nuevo, but a languor was visible in all our operations. Zumalacarregui had battered in breach the second day. Although fresh pieces were brought up, this was never afterwards effected. The governor Mirasol, who had somehow gained intelligence of Zumalacarregui's being wounded, had given out to the garrison the prophetic falsehood of his death. Their loud and deafening cheers announced to the Carlists their exultation. "We have killed your barbarian leader! The terrible Zumalacarregui is no longer with you! Have you made sausages of his blood, brigands?" Our men answered by a very useless fire of musketry, and swore that the heart's blood of a Christino should flow for every drop that their chief had shed. From this moment, however, a great increase of energy and spirit was visible in the enemy. They strengthened their works, made two sorties, and fired with surprising vigour on our batteries. If the church of Begoña was not levelled, it was only owing to its massive walls. I was in the steeple when the largest bell was dashed to pieces by a 12-pound shot. Two or three houses, in which companies of our troops were on guard, were riddled like a sieve; but being built of framework and plaster, they were unable to knock half of them down. We had a gun dismounted in the palacio, and the large mortar broke one of its spokes. How it happened I know not, but their principal fire seemed directed to the left of the church, where they battered in breach a stone wall of great thickness, without any apparent use, doing no further damage than killing four oxen; one 24-pound shot going through those that were yoked to two carts laden with ammunition, which had somehow been left exposed. Two men were killed under the Piazza, beside the church, by shells. An artilleryman lost his head by a cannonshot, and six or eight were wounded by the splinters of the bell, but further I heard of no loss during the five or six hours their heavy fire lasted.

A sortie was made next morning, with a view to seize on some cattle on a hill beside the rope-walk. Our men feigned a retreat, to draw them away; but finding them too wary, they rushed upon them, and drove them in. A captain of marines, an Irishman, in the Queen's service, was killed in this sortie; his name was, I believe, O'Brien. Count Mirasol, in publishing the official account, remarked, "My horse was wounded; Captain O'Brien was also killed." This must be a satisfactory reference for the men under Evans[111], to know the estimation in which they will be held by those for whom they are about to shed their blood. An English captain may fight, if not for victory or a place in Westminster Abbey, for a place in the bulletin next to a Spanish brig. general's

---

[111] Colonel, soon to be General, Sir George de Lacy Evans, was best known for having burned the Capitol in Washington D.C. during the British-American War of 1812, as a consequence of which the charred building had to be painted white (hence White House). He commanded the British Auxiliary Legion of mercenaries which, along with the French, confusingly named "Spanish" Legion, were the forerunners of the International Brigades of a century later. Wellington opposed intervention on the grounds that it was impossible to win a war in a foreign country against the wishes of the people. The Whig government under Earl Grey (after whom the tea is named) backed down from military intervention despite a barrage of propaganda from the liberal press. Eventually it was agreed that a private legion of volunteers, paid by the Spanish government, could be raised by de Lacy Evans, and would receive some support from the Royal Navy.

The Liberals in England were not honest about the purpose of this Legion. In public they claimed that it was in aid of peace in Spain; yet they insisted that the officers should be Liberals. The politicization of the force meant that officers were not selected on merit – and it showed. The men were recruited in roughly equal numbers from England, Scotland and Ireland.

8,000 men were raised but, as a private force, were prevented by law from training in England. They arrived in San Sebastian and were let loose on the town as an undisciplined rabble with too mjuch money. The recruiting agents were paid for the numbers of recruits, not for quality. On arrival several hundred were found to be too old, too young or too sick for military purposes. De Lacy Evans instituted the very un-liberal Provost System (flogging without court-martial) and thus earned the nickname "Cat o'nine tails Evans" or simply "the Cat". After a humiliating reconnaissance at Hernani, they were moved to Vitoria where they bumbled about the countryside, dying of disease and, as winter set in, cold. However, after six months they had become a sufficiently well-disciplined force to be able to wreck the Carlist encirclement of San Sebastian and, eventually, to seize the coast as far as the French border, including the essential Carlist harbour at Pasajes.

horses. It was next day, I believe, that I was sent by the commander-in-chief *ad interim* - Benito Eraso with Lt. Colonel Arjona and another officer, on board his British Majesty's brig *Saracen*. Here we had a conference with the English and French naval officers, relative to a misunderstanding which had taken place. Zumalacarregui had given a pass to the British Consul to proceed up and down the river from the city, to communicate with the ships of his own government. Immediately after his being wounded, however, Giubelalde, who was in command of some battalions quartered along that bank of the river and about San Mames, had refused to acknowledge it, imagining it to have been given only for one day. The troops along the banks having been changed, and the orders to allow all boats with the French and English flag to proceed down the river not having been repeated to them, they had refused to allow any whatever to go either up or down the river to Portugalete. This of course was but a mistake; but it appears to have been an unwarrantable proceeding, as it was detaining French and English vessels against their inclination, and the blockade had only been declared from higher up the river than where they were lying, where a double row of boats and barges had been sunk across the river. The Captain commanding on the river, whose name has escaped my memory, and the Consul, declared, that on their interview with Zumalacarregui he had behaved in the most handsome manner; and had said that those British inhabitants who did not choose to leave the city, in case the place was taken by storm, on placing the British flag over their doors, should have their houses respected, to which effect the strictest orders should be given. He had also, without difficulty, given permission to the English and French consuls and the commanding officers to go from the city to Olaveaga, and vice *versa;* but, immediately after he was wounded, a great change took place. Not only they refused to allow the Consul to return to Bilboa, but to let his boat go down the river. On applying to Giubelalde, he said, "Do you wish me to compromise myself by acting contrary to my instructions?" The truth was, he had received general orders strictly to keep up the blockade; and as Eraso had not thought necessary to repeat to him the exceptions in favour of the consuls and French and English officers, he adhered to them to the letter. The mistake about the boats was immediately rectified, and we galloped on to Puente Nuevo to get the pass from Eraso for the Consul, which was immediately sent down; and the next morning was fixed on for an interview between the two consuls and Eraso.

Next day, the two consuls, their interpreters, and the captain, came down the road from the promenade of Miraflores, preceded by sailors carrying their flags, and were introduced to Eraso. Eraso commenced by apologising for the detention of their boats, for which he offered to suspend the general of the division who had been guilty of the aggression; and he furnished the consuls and captains with passes either for themselves or their responsible officer. The consuls, finding him thus far easy, demanded that all British and French subjects should be allowed free ingress and egress to and from Bilboa. This was insisted on in a very haughty manner by the French consul; and I doubt not, if it had not been for that circumstance, might have been obtained. He was, however, told, that if he was not aware of the laws of war, he must be made acquainted with them; that it was only by favour that the Carlists, having declared the place in a state of siege, allowed any communication whatever with it; and even that, having given the consul and inhabitants leave to quit the place, they were by no means bound to exempt them from any of the penalties of a place taken by storm. On this the demand was immediately abandoned.

We were rather amused by the English consul's begging, as "no doubt the General was not making war on the consuls and their families," to be allowed to send out a servant with a basket every day, to fetch a little fresh meat, which for some time they had not tasted. It appears it had become a very scarce article in the place; a pound of beef had been sold for 48 reals, or 12s., and a dozen eggs were worth 36 reals. Eraso smiled, but very politely said, that certainly he would not only permit it, but, if they would send out a servant with the English flag, he would order meat to be given for all of them. The French consul thanked him, but observed with *nonchalance*, I do not know how it is - my cook has always found meat." "Has he?" said his British colleague and the interpreter all in a breath, "I should like to know where it is to be had." This amused us exceedingly. The previous day, when on board the *Saracen*, one of the officers, whose name has escaped my memory, requested of me, if I could do so, to get a basket with provisions passed in to Bilboa, to a particular friend of his. The next day a basket containing fowls and ducks arrived, addressed to me. Having obtained permission, the only difficulty was to find some one to take them in; as the peasantry were afraid they would not be let out again, and it was a matter of considerable embarrassment to give orders to the posts, which were constantly ehanging, not to fire at them, in particular when they sallied. The thought immediately struck me, that it would be a good plan to send it in by the sailor carrying the union jack, whom I imagined, of course, to be an Englishman. He turned out to be a sailor from the French steamer Météore. I ordered the basket to be given to him, with a message that it was for his consul. On entering Bilboa it was delivered to the French consul's cook, who, deeming it as an ill wind that blows nobody any good, forthwith proceeded to spit them; and the officers of the Météore, who that day dined with his master, informed me afterwards that they had drunk a health over them to the providence of the English.

Unhappily, as soon as Zumalacarregui had given up the command, against the urgent representations of Eraso, his plan of storming the place was overruled. The King was persuaded that the giving up a city to the horrors that must follow this desperate resource of warfare would be a most unwarrantable act, as above a third of the population were Carlists, and innocent and guilty would all perish alike before the fury of the soldiery when once let loose. Struck with horror at the representations that were made him, the King, who is a remarkably conscientious man, and who, though he may often err in judgment, would not, to gain his crown, commit the slightest act which he considered wrong, gave positive orders that the extreme works only should be stormed, where only the military defending them would suffer from the fury of the victors.

This false mercy, or rather weakness, which the Bourbons have so often been guilty of, has caused oceans of blood to be spilled. Would it not have been better that a part of those lukewarm partisans within the city should have perished, than that hundreds of those who were armed around him, and had devoted their existence to his cause, should fall in successive combats. The consequence was, when the troops were informed that they were to storm the forts, and the forts only, to run all the risk and be cheated of the recompense which the soldier in all times and places has been taught to look upon as the reward of his desperate efforts, namely, to riot - in scenes of murder and rapine, which, to the disgrace of the nature of man, seem ito be the only allurements that can lead him over the bristling rampart, and into the very cannon's mouth - they naturally refused to mount, the walls, or, at least, from the observations that were made, it was known that they would have done so.

Many of the Colonels of battalions, and the Captains of companies, declared that they were willing to go but as simple volunteers, and unless their men were allowed the pillage, refused the responsibility of leading their corps to the assault. It was then decided that the town should be bombarded; but as Zumalacarregui had only ordered a certain quantity of ammunition to be brought up, well knowing that Bilboa was easy to be taken by storm, although impregnable to the Carlists by other means they were obliged to wait till fresh troops could arrive. All this was wasting precious time, and allowing the enemy to recover from their panic, and gather fresh confidence and strength; while in Bilboa they only

338

continued to increase their means of defence, where a few shells fell harmlessly, or tore off the roofs of a few houses.

An attempt was now made to throw auxiliaries into the city, by landing at night a force on the right bank near the seashore. Our troops stationed there, forced them speedily to reembark. Espartero, however, having collected 7,000 men at Portugalete, and knowing that nearly all the force their late defeats had left them, about 18,000 men, was advancing to effect a junction, and that the greater part of our troops had been sent to observe them, he determined on making a push to enter the city.

The news of Zumalacarregui's death, prematurely circulated, had wonderfully inspirited the enemy. All the time that he had been besieging, and taking garrison after garrison, not a step was made; from utter despondency they were roused by this intelligence to the fallacious hope that, Zumalacarregui dead, the Carlists would be dispersed on the slightest efforts, and immediately advanced.

Eraso had been left with only six battalions immediately round Bilboa; he was himself persecuted by the unpitying disease which since my departure has carried him to the grave. He got up from his bed to take command of three battalions, which were opposing the passage of Espartero who, from Portugalete, could not reach Bilboa without crossing the Salcedon, a river which runs into the Ibaizabal, considerably higher than the latter city. All the southern bank was lined by the Carlists and the houses fronting the stone bridge which traversed the river had been previously crenelled, so that they with little difficulty repulsed him in all his efforts to cross it. A desperate push to carry the bridge was made by a captain of the Queen's army; he advanced with a drummer, the drum beating, and 18 men; before they had reached the bridgehead, drum and drummer, and all the party that attempted to lead the way, excepting five, including the gallant captain, were rolling in the dust. The survivors precipitately retired. Espartero, acquainted with the march of Castor's Biscayan Battalion and two others to take him in flank, precipitately retired to Portugalete.

We had hitherto received the most satisfactory accounts of Zumalacarregui's convalescence, and we joined in the feeling of our soldiers, who replied to the shouts of the enemy, that we had lost our leader, "You will see, in a few days, whether we have lost him!" The next morning, like a thunder-stroke, came the intelligence of his death. Every one, when I returned from the monastery of San Mames, where I had been, was looking mysterious and gloomy. I saw directly that some mishap had happened, but never dreamed of the reality. They still endeavoured to conceal it from the men, but the news was flying, although only whispered, in every direction in their ranks. It seemed, however, to carry less discouragement than I should have imagined, though many of the officers and privates of the Guides, who were still stationed at Begoña, could not conceal their tears.

Little by little it was spoken of more openly, and the Navarrese battalions, but particularly the Guides, loudly demanded to be led to storm Bilboa to revenge his death. "We will go without pillage! - we will go without the 100oz! we will go even if h— were before us!" were their incessant exclamations.

If the enthusiasm of the troops had even then been taken advantage of, Bilboa might have been captured before the columns advancing to relieve it, and who came hesitatingly, and feeling their way, could have forced us to raise the siege. The consequences of this fresh success are incalculable. I saw one of the servants who had attended him all the while; it appears that, notwithstanding a continuation of fever, he had persisted in occupying himself with affairs. The surgeons had at last determined on extracting the bullet, but as it had fallen many inches lower, they kept cutting and cutting away, and performed the operation in so barbarous a manner, that he suffered most intense pain, from the effect of which he fainted; to lull this, they had given him opium, it appears, in too great a dose, for soon after the bullet was extracted he died in delirium, as I have already described. He was placed in a leaden coffin in the church of Segama, the little village on the banks of the Orrio where he breathed his last. A key was sent to his wife, a key to the king, and a third remains with the coffin.

All his fortune, which consisted of 14 oz. of gold, or £48, he left to his household. To his widow he bequeathed only the grateful remembrance of his Sovereign; and although he lies without even the tribute of the humblest monument to tell where he expired - in his poverty and his glory - his name is one that Spain will ring with for many years to come. If Don Carlos ever sit on its throne, to Zumalacarregui he will be indebted for his success. That Commander, when dying, left the King's affairs in a position very different from that in which they stood at the period of Ferdinand's death, and bequeathed to Don Carlos the means of triumph in the desperate struggle which at its commencement was so hopeless.

Zumalacarregui left a little box containing papers, supposed to be plans of a campaign for continuing the war.

**Zumalacarregui, mortally wounded,
is carried from the scene of battle on an old sofa**

CHAPTER XXIII.

Hopes of the Christinos after Zumalacarregui's Death - Siege of Bilboa raised - Execution of two Deserters – Christinos - Death of Eraso and Rena - Lopez Reyna - The Writer leaves the Army - Origin of the Work.

No sooner was the death of Zumalacarregui (rumours of which had been previously circulated amongst the enemy's troops by their leaders to encourage them) known in reality to have happened, than the whole of their force, which I have stated was in number 18,000 men, rapidly advanced to effect a junction with Espartero, and relieve Bilboa. Some of the officers of the *Saracen* and the French vessels came to dine with me the day after we had received the news of Zumalacarregui's death. Their names have all escaped my memory excepting Lieutenant Rogers. He spoke perfectly the French and Spanish languages, and seemed a very well-informed and gentlemanly man. In general, the officers of the Queen's army they met in Bilboa seemed to have made far from a favourable impression on them.

Mirasol, the governor, anxious to gain time, now sent a parlementary with a flag of truce, who stated that he was desirous of holding some communication with the besiegers. Lt. Colonel Arjona, son of the ex-governor of Seville, and Zaraitegui, Zumalacarregui's secretary, accordingly entered the place. The former had known Mirasol previously. They soon found, however, that he had no intention of surrendering. As far as regarded himself, he behaved very politeiy; they lunched with him, and on departing were escorted by several of his officers to the gates. A mob of the most outrageous of the inhabitants gathered, however, to insult them on their passage. They were chiefly from the commercial classes, or the very lowest of the rabble; and not content with crying out at a distance, at last pressed close on them. Arjona immediately stopped, and said he would not proceed amidst the insults of a set of miscreants. "We cannot prevent," said the Commandant, "the people from expressing their feelings."

343

Arjona said that if he could not impose silence, and make them respect a parlementary, which everywhere was held sacred, he would return to the Governor's house. "Oh," said the Christino, sneeringly, "fear nothing; they shall do you no harm." "No," said Arjona, who was a young and spirited officer, "I have no fear for myself. I might certainly be put to death, but tomorrow 150 of your officers would be dangling at the other end of Puente Nuevo, for Antonio Arjona." It was at the end of this bridge that the officers of the Provincials of Grenada were executed the preceding January.

The approach of the enemy, when too late, must have convinced the King's counsellors how erroneously they had advised him. Bilboa might have been taken by storm over and over again. With such artillery, disorganised as it was, which the Carlists possessed, and 30 heavy pieces within the place, to knock their batteries to pieces, it would have required six weeks to make any impression by bombarding it. Much precious time had thus been expended for no earthly purpose, while the enemy were daily recovering from their panic; the death of Zumalacarregui quite restored their confidence. It was now determined to attack the army advancing to its relief. Carlos himself assumed the command of his army, Moreno was appointed chief of his staff, and Eraso was left before Bilboa; but little by little so much of his force had been drawn off, that he was obliged to raise the siege, and we marched on Villareal de Alava. The Carlists were two hours too late to attack the enemy in positions under highly advantageous circumstances, and the Royalists having committed this blunder, both armies seemed afraid to engage, and passed each other, after a little hesitation, without firing a shot.

On joining again the Royal quarters in quest of my leave of absence[112], I was witness to the execution of two deserters. They

---

[112] After successfully crossing the frontier, Henningsen wrote the present account and returned to the army. He continued to fight under the Carlist

belonged to the 3rd. Castille, composed of the prisoners taken at Treviño, who had embraced the cause of Carlos. Having resolved to desert, they profited by a dense fog to abscond, and having met with a peasant, loaded their muskets before him, and, promising him ½ oz. of gold if he led them to the Queen's troops, swore that they would shoot him the instant they were betrayed. At a little distance, and particularly during a fog, the only distinction easily made between the troops of both armies, is in the round bonnets of ours and the shakos or foraging caps, or *gorras de quartel,* of the enemy. The peasant immediately recollected that several Carlist battalions of Alava wore also the foraging cap, and knowing the village where one of them was quartered, led them thither. On seeing them at a distance, the two soldiers fancied all was right, but when their guide had got them close upon the village, he shouted out with all his might, *Muchachos! Aqui hai dos traidores! (*Here, my lads! here are two traitors!) Perceiving that they were betrayed, they attempted, without even giving themselves time to punish him, to save themselves by a precipitate flight. They were, however, pursued, and as they did not know the country, they were easily recaptured.

The march of the greater part of the Carlist army was now directed on Salvatierra, which Zumalacarregui had previously forced the Christinos to abandon. Salvatierra, a very ancient town, situated on the left of the road from Vittoria to Pampeluna, was surrounded by an old wall of considerable height and solidity. Although strong at a time when artillery was either unknown, or in its primitive state, its walls flanked only by square turrets, afforded but an inadequate shelter against the engines of hostility employed at the present day. But it must be remembered, that in the commencement of the war the Carlists were in the state in which all armies were before the use of cannon was known, and even worse, for they had not the means which the warriors of former

---

banner until October 17th. 1837, but was immediately captured. By this time his book had become a best seller.

times had used in the absence of cannon-the catapult, the scorpion, and the battering-ram. Anything that would ward off a musket-shot thus became a fortification to their enemies, until, by the exertions and perseverance of a single artillery officer, they at last succeeded in manufacturing in the woods and mountains sereral of those formidable weapons, which, once obtained, enabled them to procure others; but that beginning was the difficulty.

On Salvatierra being evacuated by the enemy, the Carlists took possession, and, as usual, immediately began demolishing the fortifications. This, however, was a work of some time. We found here, chained together, labouring at them, 200 peseteros and chapelgorris, who, since Lord Eliot's convention, had received quarter, but were never intrusted with arms; indeed, if Zumalacarregui had been inclined to have made a trial of them, the soldiers would unanimously have refused to receive them into their company, so great was the hatred they always inspired. With the line, on the contrary, the instant they exchanged their shako for the beret, they were looked upon as brethren, and treated as such.

Amongst these prisoners was one old man whose appearance immediately indicated him to be of a superior class to the labourers about him. I was afterwards informed that he was a marquess. His name I have forgotten; but he had rendered himself notorious amongst the liberals, and was captured by the *partida* when sallying with a small escort from Vittoria, to levy a free corps for the service of the Queen: he was therefore treated as a pesetero. He seemed to undergo the change of circumstances with great fortitude. On the arrival of the King the hard labour was mitigated, and the next evening the marquess's son and another officer, with a flag of truce and a small escort, came from Vittoria to propose an exchange for the family of a superior officer held prisoner by the enemy. This was effected.

From Salvatierra, I followed the King through a tremendous storm to Eulate, in the Amescoas. The next day he took up his position with 14 battalions at Arrouniz, Eraso having

346

meanwhile laid siege to Puente la Reyna, to force Cordova to a battle. Here, learning that my passport had been sent on to Eraso, I joined him before Puente.

I found Eraso in a little village within gunshot of the town: this I reached at midday. Eraso, who was gradually dying of consumption, had just got up, and was at dinner. This man, who proved himself a skilful soldier, and ranked, in my estimation - although still at an humble distance next to Zumalacarregui, had fought through a most disinterested feeling of Royalism. It was to Eraso that Zumalacarregui offered to give up the command, on account of his seniority of rank; but he, as a partisan, frankly acknowledging that he believed Zumalacarregui's talents greater than his own, refused to accept it.

He was well aware that he was dying; he had even firmly entertained this conviction many months before, which may have confirmed the symptoms of his disease. He had, in consequence, behaved throughout his career like a man who, with the prospect of death almost face to face, saw the littleness of all worldly ambition. His last exploit was the defeat of Espartero on the heights of Descarga, and the capture of 1,800 prisoners. When I took leave of him, and expressed a hope for his recovery, he shook his head, and said, with a melancholy smile, "At the fall of the leaf I shall be no more." He prophesied truly; for about six weeks after he expired.

I observed that he had taken all Zumalacarregui's servants and household under his protection. These were mostly churlish peasants from the villages in which the hero of Ormaistegui had spent his early youth. Although he had evinced a preference for them as his immediate compatriots, they met with no places or promotion that it was in his power to bestow, beyond their slender merits. Eraso, before we parted, begged of me to give him a copy of the head of Zumalacarregui, which forms the frontispiece to this work: he pronounced it a striking likeness.

As it was my intention to depart for the frontier in a few hours, I went to dine with Colonel Goni, of the 1st. Battalion. During dinner, we were alarmed by a discharge of musketry. As his battalion was on duty opposite Puente, we immediately mounted our horses, which, fortunately, were ready saddled, and proceeded to the battery. Puente la Reyna stands on the declivity of a hill; on the further side the river Arga runs before it: this end was rendered unapproachable by two batteries on slight eminences. On advancing, we found that the enemy had made a sortie, and taken possession of one which we had erected opposite these. Having placed himself at the head of two companies, which were on guard about 100yds from it, we advanced, and recaptured it, with a trifling loss, Goni being wounded but very slightly in the thigh.

The first thing that met our sight on entering, was Reyna lying dead; he had received a bayonet wound through the heart, from which the yet warm blood was bubbling, and a shot through the throat; we next perceived Lieutenant Plaza with his brains blown out; and seven artillerymen, all killed by shots that had evidently been fired the muskets touching, as the clothes of two of them were burning like tinder. All this happened through the negligence of the sentinel, who had fallen asleep, and had first paid the forfeit of his carelessness. Tired with superintending the battery all night, Reyna was taking an hour's sleep between some shells, the rest were eating. It is supposed some spy must have crept through the vines, and given the enemy intelligence of this; for he so completely surprised them, that the artillerymen had not time to snatch their muskets up before they fled. From the evidence of these men, it appears that Reyna, Plaza, and seven artillerymen surrendered prisoners of war. "Quarter for those who surrender on their knees!" cried the Christinos. Reyna and the others obeyed this injunction. After an interval of 10 minutes, when they had pursued the rest, and spiked our pieces, they murdered those prisoners in cold blood; as it was after that time that the discharge was heard in the battery. Three of the bodies of their victims had their hands tied behind their backs by pockethandkerchiefs, and one by the strap of a cartouchbox, which had been cut up for the purpose. This was the first time since the Eliot convention that they were called on to apply it to the persons of Carlist officers, although so well had Zumalacarregui observed the treaty, that above 4,000 prisoners had been made during the last month. They had managed, as I have stated, to spike our pieces, and in a most complete manner, only with iron instead of steel nails; so that they were easily drawn out with pincers; and half an hour after the battery opened fire again. I could not get any of the soldiers, probably from some superstitious feeling, to lend me a knife or scissors to cut off a little of Reyna's hair to send to his brother, a chef d'escadron, under whose orders I had served, and with whom I was particularly intimate. I was obliged at last to use the sword of an artilleryman, which was very sharp. Reyna and his brother had been the means of saving the lives of many of the prisoners, and were as noted for their humanity as their valour.

Two days after, when I was near the frontier, the battle of Mendigorria took place, in which the Carlists were worsted, although the defeat led to no important results. Reyna, who had received the intelligence of his brother's death, and the melancholy token I sent him, distinguished himself by saving two battalions of Castille. Lopez, with 500 horse, was pursuing, when Reyna was allowed to charge with the 3rd. and 4th. Squadrons, in all 240 horse: he broke and routed the cavalry of Lopez, and, giving no mercy, made a great slaughter, to avenge the murder of his brother. I have heard from an eyewitness, who joined me afterwards at Bayonne, that all the 4th. Squadron came back with their lances dripping with blood.

Tomas Reyna, still a young man, was captain of cuirassiers of Ferdinand's guard. He had much distinguished himself, and was a great favourite with Zumalacarregui. No one more deeply lamented or endeavoured to assuage, as far as lay in his power, the horrors of civil war. Since then I have heard that he has become the Claverhouse of the Carlist army - having vowed never to spare foes who showed so little kindness to his own blood.

The last scene I witnessed before leaving the Royalist army was - as the first had been - one of bloodshed. Reyna was one of my earliest acquaintances. Few, very few of those I had known in the beginning of the war, a year ago, survived its vicissitudes - and the links of the friendships I had contracted had one by one been broken. Three days after, I re-crossed the frontier, and abandoned my red beret and sword for a round hat and walking staff.

My object in detailing a few passages of my campaign, mostly from notes made on the spot, has been to give some account of the difficulties with which a man whose exploits are worthy of some record had to struggle - and what he achieved - and to enlighten the public, by the history of what Don Carlos has hitherto contended with, as to the real chances of success which the devotion and energy of the Basque people give his cause.

CHAPTER XXIV.

Observations on the Quasi Intervention - Refutation of the Queen's right to it - Falsehood practised to deceive the Public demonstrated - Of Colonel Evans and the Auxiliaries - What they will probably meet with if they take the Field - The consequences if they remain in Garrison.

Great as the gullibility of John Bull is universally admitted to be, it is a matter of surprise how thoroughly a few of the rulers of the money market have, by bribery and intrigue, for so long a period contrived to keep him in total ignorance of what was going on in the northern provinces of Spain, and which, to many, was a question of very vital interest. The greater part of the vehement supporters of the Queen are so, because if the throne that has been usurped for her should flit away, their money would vanish with it. Of this they are perfectly aware, but as to the justice of the case, it neither enters into their calculations nor interests them. They find it just, because it is profitable, that a nation should have a government, however adverse they may be to it, crammed down their throats, even if necessary, by a parcel of strangers and mercenaries, to make the fortunes of a few individuals in the cities of London and Paris.

Of the intervention of the men gone out under Evans, useless as I believe it will be, I have but a few words to say. If the extensive stockholders in the city of London imagine that Spain is to be conquered, like Portugal, with their gold, they are miserably mistaken in their estimate of the Spanish character. I am talking in case of their supporting her as they did Don Pedro; for any 10,000 or 15,000 men would be like a drop of water in the sea, and will do the Queen's cause more harm than good. There is no limit to the injustice and falsehood they have been guilty of, in representing the affairs of the Peninsula, by which they have inveigled and ruined many, and will ruin thousands more whose utter ignorance of the rights of the question alone entitles them to our pity.

The public were led to believe that the majority of the nation was in favour of the will by which Ferdinand, in violation

351

of the established law, altered the succession to the throne, on condition of its being surrounded by *soi-disant* liberal institutions. On that consent hinged the rights of Isabella and the exclusion of Don Carlos. There was evidently no right, according to their own reasoning, without this majority; but, according to their statements, the majority of the people were in favour of government, which had also the army of 120,000 men, all the strong places, and all the *materiel* of the kingdom. How is it possible, if all this were true, that they should need the aid of strangers? And such as have been sent them the sweepings of a country, and of a country, too, in that particular resembling a hotbed, where noble fruits and flowers seem to spring amidst dung and filth, more prolific of the latter than any other in the world. If the majority were in favour of the Queen's government, it could have no need of auxiliaries - holding, as it does, every resource - and least of all such auxiliaries as have been sent them. If it be not so, the right of the Queen is at once destroyed, on their own principles, and it is a crying injustice to take any part against Don Carlos; for it is, then, clearly for the sake of lucre only[113].

How the stockholders - those I mean who are innocently blind - can still give faith, as they do, to the statements of those papers which have so palpably betrayed and deceived them, exceeds my comprehension. Let anyone take all the numbers of the greater part of these oracles for the last two years past, and they will find it repeatedly reported, that when the question first began to be agitated in England, "the Carlist faction, or rather the armed bands, represented as desolating parts of the kingdom, did not exist." Although they had never existed, we were subsequently informed that they were entirely destroyed. After being crushed and destroyed repeatedly, they met with constant and fatal defeats;

---

[113] Wellington made the same point in the House of Lords. Don Carlos issued the Durango Decree which said that the mercenaries would not be included under the terms of the Eliot Convention and could expect no quarter. Ludicrously, De Lacy Evans claimed that British subjects serving with the Carlists were taking arms against the British Crown, a claim hotly contested in parliament by Peter Borthwick M.P., later editor of the *Morning Post*.

and yet, when the intelligence of the defeat of Valdes came by the unquestionable authority of Lord Eliot, and the fact of Bilboa being besieged by Zumalacarregui was equally undisputed - which certainly was enough to convince the simplest minds of their falsehood, for which a retrospection of their own contradictory and absurd statements of Spanish affairs since the beginning alone should have sufficed - still, after all this, they were as much credited as before; so anxious are we to believe what we wish; and people naturally say, "Those who hold Spanish stock at least ought to know."

Regarding the Auxiliaries, we are told that the great knowledge Colonel Evans possesses of the country is to work miracles - a topographical knowledge at best; and what is that to the knowledge Mina, El Pastor, and 100 other officers on either side have, not only of the position of the mountains, roads, and villages, but of every path, rivulet, and almost the number of stones on every bridge[114]. Of Mina's talent as a leader he knows nothing, or at least has yet had no opportunity of developing it; and the oratorical powers he possesses, however useful among his constituents at Westminster, will be of little use among the mountains and peasantry of the provinces. Some boldly affirm that his plan to *bring the war to a conclusion* is, to seize on certain commanding positions. To those who know the country, this requires no comment. For the information of those who do not, I shall take the liberty of observing, that at the time the Queen's army was infinitely more numerous than it is at present - when the Carlist army, without a single gun, did not amount to 6,000 men, Rodil, being commander-in-chief, garrisoned every large town, and fortified every commanding military position in the country, as far as it was possible, and yet found that it was entirely fruitless. Now that the Carlists are 30,000 men, possessed of artillery, which

---

[114] On inquiring of a Carlist officer, who had served with Mina, whether this quality was exaggerated, he replied, "We are now on the bridge of Sumbillio - if you were to go to Mina at Cambaud, he could tell you how many inches it is long and wide, and how many stones there are along the parapet." (CFH)

no longer renders it possible to fortify mere houses and convents, what is Colonel Evans, who, after all, is in a subordinate capacity, to do with his 6,000 or 8,000 ragamuffins?

As far as regards the men, they are still perfectly undisciplined; and, natural as bravery and decision is to my countrymen, supposing this first obstacle already got over, I have no hesitation in saying, that of all troops in the world to contend in a guerrilla warfare, they are the most unfitted. Supposing that they could defeat the Carlist battalions, they will only reduce it to this. It then becomes no longer a stand-up fight, but a war in which their antagonists will be hunger, fatigue, disease, and the knife - and, worst of all, the sudden transitions from want to plenty. Are these, I demand, the antagonists the British soldier is calculated to battle with? And these, it must be remembered, are very far from being British soldiers. It has been fallaciously hoped that the name of these auxiliaries and the sight of redcoats alone would have a wonderful effect; but we must remember that the troops of the French empire had at least as wide a reputation at the period of their invasion, and struck, on account of their excesses[115], infinitely more terror than our own: yet this carried no discouragement into the hearts of the Spaniards; and the hundreds of thousands of these conquerors of Europe who perished without the glory of a single fight, fill an eventful page of Napoleon's history, and might have proved a useful lesson.

The mountains of Navarre are not the worst; the war would only recommence in Catalonia or Gallicia, if the King were to transport himself thither, and if it were possible to drive him out of the insurgent provinces. It became a saying amongst the French soldiers, that the Navarrese were like worms - cut them in two, and two Navarrese rose up against you. I know a lt. colonel in the French service, who, when Joseph was in Madrid, in leading his battalion from the frontier, without a single skirmish, had lost 3/5

---

[115] Here it appears the auxiliaries have proved themselves at least on a par with them. (CFH)

of his men. Spain was then deluged by an immense army. The aid the stockholders can send will be but an insignificant division. That they will be able to reduce it to a guerrilla warfare, I do not, however, for an instant anticipate, but believe that they will be vigorously opposed. In the first place, I am convinced that several of those battalions of Navarre, which, since the beginning have followed Zumalacarregui, and become inured to the greatest fatigues and hardships the human frame is capable of enduring - accustomed during nearly two years to daily skirmishes and engagements, are in other respects much better soldiers than the auxiliaries can possibly be made for many months to come. The Battalion of Guides of Navarre in particular, if ever they should meet them, may prove very different foes from what perhaps the men under Evans may imagine. In the next, every half hour of their road, while Don Carlos keeps in the provinces, the Carlists can take up a position, where, either they will repulse their foes entirely, or, if the latter carry the position, which is, after all, unimportant, they will find that they have three or four or six or eight times as many killed and wounded as the Carlists, and be obliged to make for the first fortified town, to repair their losses, subject to being harassed during their retreat. Or, on the other hand, the Carlists will retreat before them, leading them through places like the Ulzama or the Sierra de Andia, where, exposed to the hot sun or the piercing night wind, without being able to shelter one tithe of their force, they will be reduced to half rations, and often without one small pot per company to cook them in, unless they carry their kitchen utensils with them - a pleasant addition to the baggage, when obliged to march through 2ft of mud, or up and down a natural staircase of the rock. And then come the *partidas* cutting off all supplies and stragglers. After two or three days of such amusement, they will probably be attacked in earnest, when I know, by my own experience, that hungry, soaked through, and benumbed by the small piercing rain, and half dead by fatigue, men will let themselves be killed with sticks and stones without making any defence.

From these privations a day or two's march will lead them to a country where, for about the value of a farthing, the soldier can obtain his bottle of wine; and in such circumstances commend me to the sobriety of that respectable portion of my countrymen who have enlisted under the banners of her glorious Majesty! And mark, that within a gunshot there is always a merciless foe hovering round like the wolf, to make quick work with all who straggle from the fold. On the mules, or *baggages* as they are called in Spanish, it is with difficulty that the bare necessaries for a day or two can be carried without fear of their being cut off. For you cannot, if near a Carlist army, procure rations as they do; their *partidas* preventing the peasantry, nothing disinclined to being stopped, from bringing a single article to the Christinos. If you send out any force to escort them, they will be cut off, unless half your army marches to escort a few mule-loads from one place and a few from another, which of course is a downright impossibility, if you are combining any military operations. If you convey with you a sufficient number of mules and baggagehorses, when you get along the narrow roads where there are precipices and glens on one side, and high and steep rocks on the other, and your men cannot go two abreast - how are you to defend them? And yet everywhere, directly you leave a valley on the Camino Real, such are to be met with. If you detach *éclaireurs* to reconnoitre above you and below you, such are the obstacles they meet with, you could not advance a mile an hour; and otherwise, if you have many baggages, although they may be in the centre of a column of 10,000 men, a *partida* will rush down from the rocks above, cut the throats of your mules, and disappear in the ravine below, where you dare not pursue them, leaving the carcasses to embarrass the road. In the centre of an army of 50,000 or 100,000 men, it would be the same thing; your men, who can go but two by two between the baggages, can offer but a feeble resistance, although multitudes are before and behind them, but who cannot get up to give them succour.

If they are allowed, as some would propose in reply to these objections, to replace the garrisons, and remain behind the walls only, from what knowledge I have of the Spanish character, I shall be somewhat surprised. The jealousy of the Spaniards is proverbial, but we must understand it of strangers, much rather than of their women. Their consent to the acceptance of foreign aid has only been wrung from the liberal party and the army by downright necessity; and after the many hard blows they have met with, they will certainly not be got to fight while they are paying strangers to do their work for them, if those strangers are to remain in the garrisons. If such should be the ease; I can foresee nothing but dissensions between them and the Spanish troops; which probably will, at all events, terminate the affair. We must not suppose they will give the English credit for assisting them from any friendly impulse, for they are well aware that it is only from mercenary motives. I am not alluding to the employed, but to their employers. The liberal's class, too, and the population of the towns, are precisely the classes in Spain where a dislike to the English does prevail; they accuse us of things which are not worthy of refutation. They will tell you very gravely, that when the English were in Spain, they had orders, while wearing the mask of friendship, to burn all their manufactures, which they did; and that, at the battle of Toulouse, the Duke of Wellington placed the Spaniards, according to the instructions he had received, where they were sacrificed, because they were known to entertain liberal opinions. All over Europe it is certain we have met with the unfortunate fate, not only of having our real faults and errors severely commented on, but of being more calumniated and ill-used by fame than any people under the sun. The northern provinces of Spain, at least had retained, amongst the peasantry and all those classes which compose the Royalist party, a grateful recollection of the eminent services we had rendered them; and

357

although the same dislike of all born beneath a foreign sky prevails there as in the rest of Spain, the name of an Englishman was hitherto a high recommendation. As usual, we must undo all this to favour a party by whom we shall be none the better liked, and make ourselves deservedly the detestation of the inhabitants as much as the French have been since their invasion, and further to cover our name with disgrace in the eyes of Spaniards of all classes.

Thus far I had written before the mercenaries had sallied from St. Sebastian and Santander; and although some months have elapsed, and some trial has been given, I see no reason to alter a line of what I have recorded. In what I had ventured to predict, the event has fully borne me out. It is now more than six months since these British auxiliaries have entered Spain. Not their warmest advocates can pretend that they have reaped either glory or advantage to themselves or the government they went to serve; and according to the accounts of their adversaries, and even of totally impartial authorities, they have met with nothing but discomfiture and disgrace, which unhappily they will entail on the British name amongst the Spaniards, who will not discriminate between a nation and the refuse of a nation, a designation to which Evans's corps generally are entitled. Of course there may be, and I believe there are, some exceptions, but I also believe them to be few. Whatever my private judgment may be as to the accounts that are to be selected as most veracious from the contradictory statements that have been made of the three reconnoissances, skirmishes, or engagements in which the Anglo-Spanish legion[116] has been engaged at Hernani, Arrigoriaga, and on the road from Vittoria northward, I shall not here venture to give an opinion, as it has been my object throughout this work to confine myself to the narration of facts of which I was either an eyewitness or am enabled to speak with certainty.

---

[116] The British Auxiliary Legion commanded by de Lacy Evans.

The reader, by referring to the map, may however distinctly perceive that each of the two first movements was made to open a communication between the coast and the plains of Vittoria and the Ribera, by forcing a passage through the mountainous part of the country by the roads from St. Sebastian and Bilboa to Vittoria. Along the first of these the British Legion advanced to Hernani, where the first skirmish took place against the division of Gomez, composed of the rawest troops in the army of Don Carlos. This affair was differently represented by both sides[117]; but neither will dispute the fact, that the Anglo-Spanish garrison of St. Sebastian retired to its walls, from whence along that road they never sallied again, and that from St. Sebastian to Bilboa they went by sea, when they did quit for the latter place. From Bilboa they marched several leagues along one of the Vittoria roads, with the bulk of the Christino army. An affair took place at Arrigoriaga, also differently represented, but of which the result was again, that they retired back to the coast, or at least to Bilboa, from whence they had come.

These, we are gravely told, are reconnoissances, and for the city politicians and fundholders this may do very well; but every military man must in an instant see the humbug of pretending that reconnoissances are made with 4/5 of a garrison, or all the disposable force, and in such a manner that the safety of it is compromised, when 50 or 100 men would have answered all the same purpose.

When the junction with Cordova at Vittoria was effected finally, it was by making a considerable circuit to the west, not by the direct road from north to south; in attempting which they were twice driven back. Having joined Cordova, they again made the essay in this last affair of the 17th. January, by marching from Vittoria northwards, to open a communication between the plains of Vittoria and Ribera and the northern coast, through this tract of

---

[117] Modern historians agree that the Hernani affair was a British fiasco due to a failure by de Lacy Evans to conduct any sort of reconnaissance.

(as far as human foresight can penetrate) but in a French intervention, which is now very unlikely to take place.

The day is gone by when even a national intervention on the part of England would terminate the contest. Don Carlos may proceed but slowly; but he loses nothing by delay. The Queen's government runs the risk of going hourly to pieces by the breakers amongst which it is stranded. The civil war, which has so long desolated one of the fairest lands of the European continent, is not likely, therefore, to terminate very speedily, and all attempts that foreign powers can make, so far from accelerating its conclusion, would, at best, but smother a fire which will inevitably break out again, and which must and will, therefore, burn to its ashes, and come naturally to its end. If a French intervention had taken place, if the partisans of Don Carlos had been dispersed, and he himself killed or taken prisoner, those who imagine that this would put an end to the struggle, either err very much in their estimate of the Spanish character, or much misapprehend the state of the case.

It is not a mere war of succession, but of the conservative principle, throughout the country, against the destructive one; and of the whole edifice of Spanish nationality against a small, though powerful faction. There is too much pride in the Spanish people, of which the immense majority are Carlists, to abide by the decision of foreigners; and that determined spirit which beat back the Moor, and baffled the efforts of the great modern conqueror, is still easily to be disturbed from its slumbers in the most lukewarm, when the national jealousy is in any way awakened.

Under these circumstances, it must be a matter of deep regret to every Englishman who views the question in the same light as myself, that the belligerent parties had been in any way interfered with, except as the Duke of Wellington interfered, by a mission of peace, to the success of which, in saving the lives of 5,000 of the inhabitants of that country which he had once liberated by his sword, I myself was witness, during the few months only that I remained after the Eliot convention. The Administration

361

which has succeeded that of his Grace has only added fuel to the flame, and fresh elements to the chaos of civil discord.

THE END.

APPENDIX

Zumalacarregui and Mina (From the Paris Correspondent of the *Standard*) PARIS. Dec. 9th. 1834.

I have received from a very distinguished Spanish Liberal officer (whose name I have communicated to you) the following important letter. I do not concur in all his views; but as no one can be placed in a better position than himself for knowing all that is passing in his native country you may place the fullest reliance on his statements." Pampeluna, Nov. 26. "My Dear Sir—I redeem the promise I voluntarily made you when last we parted, of writing to you from my native land: and I offer you many apologies for my tardiness, and apparent but not real forgetfulness. I remained a long time on the frontiers before I entered Spain. When Mina returned to Spain I crossed the frontiers and after many marches and counter-marches, am at Pampeluna, where the cholera has once more made its appearance. Mina is greatly dejected. His wife is dangerously ill. He no longer finds his standard when planted the rallying point of the Navarrese and Basques. From other provinces and from distant shores he is obliged to draw his resources; and the name of Mina, instead of being a tower of strength and a shield from oppression, is now the signal to the inhabitants to rise up and oppose him. You know my opinion of Mina. Fortune has done more for him than talent. When, as in former times, all the country was for him his march was triumphal, and he proceeded from victory to victory. But now as the people are arrayed in these provinces against him, and so well founded is his apprehension for his life that he does not dare to leave himself alone for an instant, and takes every necessary precaution as to his food. It is very easy, my dear friend, to make war in a country where the peasants, proprietors, women, and children are with you, and where you are looked upon as the liberator and the supporter of the rights and privileges of the inhabitants. But it is a very different thing to make war in a country where streams are poisoned, where grain is burnt rather than that you should take it, where cattle are driven away leagues and leagues off at your approach, the cattle owners preferring to lose them rather than you should have them, and where in every man, woman, and even child you see a foe. You would not in dear Old England look with greater horror upon a band of robbers suddenly appearing in the midst of some tranquil hamlet than do the Basques and Navarrese look upon us, the servants or soldiers of Christina. We can obtain nothing but at the edge of the sword or at the point of the bayonet. Mina has scoured the country for provisions, but we obtain none, I mean none but of the worst possible description, And do not imagine that money is of any use to Mina. It is of no use whatever. We could not get a thousand head of cattle for all the riches of the Indies. The loan which is making at Madrid will do us no good. We know the best system of warfare. I admit this. But it is no use knowing when we cannot practise it. Do we make a forced march in order to surprise that wonderful Zumalacarregui, we are prevented from succeeding, because some peasants perceive our object, cut across the country by lonely and unknown paths, and acquaint him hours beforehand of our intentions. Do we take guides, pay them well, threaten them well, and flatter them well, it is of no use. Our guides deceive us, and either take us the longest way round, to afford time for the rebels to be informed of our approach, or else they do still worse - they conduct us into the very teeth of our enemies. This has happened many times lately in several skirmishes. If we enter a town or village we can find nothing. The money and valuables are hidden. There is no food, there is no forage. Our officers are poisoned, our men are betrayed. We make no advance.

Now all this is wholly irrespective of the merits of either Generals. I do not think that Mina, at his time of life, with his wretched state of health, and with his numerous infirmities, is capable of fulfilling the duties of Commander-in-Chief. And yet I admit that Mina is a brave and an honourable man and was a very good general officer. I think that Zumalacarregui is more daring and bold than Mina; and this is something; and that he has a better knowledge of the localities than has Mina. This is a great point. But let us admit that they are both equally good as soldiers and officers; and yet all the circumstances are for Zumalacarregui, and all against Mina; for not only are the inhabitants against us, but the soldiers of the Queen are dispirited. They do not dare to traverse a pass. They are afraid of Zumalacarregui popping down upon them just when they are least prepared; and the good star of Mina has forsaken him. The soldiers being dispirited they will not undertake any enterprise requiring great daring, but wish always to see a league or two before them. We have obtained no victories. The defeat of our troops under the walls of Vittoria has done us incalculable injury. The name of Zumalacarregui strikes terror into the hearts of our soldiers. Add to this, that the inhabitants and soldiers of the Pretender fight for a popular cause, viz., for themselves and their own local privileges, so dear to every Basque; whilst we fight for a cause which changes every day; for now, if we are to have such institutions and such Ministers as will please the Duke of Wellington and you English Tories, we may just as well take Don Carlos at once without any more bloodshed. The cause of the Queen is not the same cause as it was months ago, and I suspect we shall soon find out that it will be a very different one if the Tories shall be successful in your country. We have no confidence in the Queen. She was Royalist to please King Ferdinand, she was Revolutionary to please and serve herself; she was anti-Revolutionary to please the Government of Lord Grey, she was Liberal again when the wind set that way in England and France a few weeks ago, and now she will turn back again to Zea and his Party, or to any other party, if the Duke of Wellington will but recognise her.

You will then ask me, perhaps, "Why do I serve her?" My answer is, because I am a soldier, and because I think that in the course of time some revolution to overthrow her and establish a democratical government may take place. If I did not feel and hope

365

this I would leave the cause tomorrow, and get back once more to the banks of the Thames. I am not however at all sure that although I hope for a revolution and a democratical government that such a one will be established. I remain here, and I fight on, hoping that something will turn up in favour of my views and wishes; but if the French should enter Spain to assist us I would declare tor Don Carlos tomorrow. In saying this I speak not for myself alone. I express the sentiments of Mina and of all honourable men. I would prefer to assist at the triumphal entry of Don Carlos into Madrid than to witness the "tri-colore" floating amidst the Spanish flags. Do not entertain any apprehensions of a French intervention. Harispe knows too well all our sentiments upon this subject to attempt or counsel such a measure. I have told him myself that it three French soldiers and a corporal should appear in Spain to take cause with the Queen against Don Carlos I would instantly pass over with all my men to the opposite side. In conclusion. What will be the issue of this contest? I cannot answer this question.

CHRONOLOGY UP TO HENNINGSEN'S DISCHARGE ON PAROLE

1812	King Joseph Bonaparte issues the radical Cadiz Constitution
1813-14	Restoration of Ferdinand VII and repeal of 1812 constitution
1815	Birth of Henningsen in Brussels
1820	Liberals seize power to restore 1812 constitution
1823	Sacred Alliance restores Ferdinand VII
1830	Henningsen's first published work (poem); Ferdinand issues Pragmatic Sanction disinheriting Don Carlos; Belgian Revolution breaks out
1831	Henningsen's family flees to London; he publishes account of his experiences of the Belgian revolution.
1833	Ferdinand VII dies in September; Don Carlos proclaimed King on 6 October at Tricio. Santos Ladron shot on 15th.

OUTBREAK OF FIRST CARLIST WAR			
Battle	**Commanders**	**Numbers if known**	**Won**
1833			
Oct 30	Zumalacarregui joins the Carlist revolt		
Nov 3	Vargas	Ibaraloa & Villalobos	120	L
		Uriarte	180	
Dec 29	Nazar &Asarta	Zumalacarregui	3000	draw
		Lorenzo	5000	
1834			
Apr 10	Maials	Carnicer		L
		Carratala & Breton	2000	
Apr 22	Alsasua	Zumalacarregui	3200	C
		Quesada	3200	
Jun 18	Gulina	Zumalacarregui		C
		Quesada		
Aug 19	Peñas de San Fausto	Zumalacarregui		C
		Carandolet		
Sept 4	Viana	Zumalacarregui	240	C
		Carandolet	900	
Oct 27	Alegria de Alava	Zumalacarregui		C
		O'Doyle	7500	
Oct 28	Venta de Echavarri	Zumalacarregui	3200	C
		Osma	5200	
Dec 12	Mendaza	Zumalacarregui		L
		Cordova		
Dec 15	1st. Arquijas	Zumalacarregui		C
		Cordova & Oraa	2000	

1835				
Jan 3	Ormaiztegui/Segura	Zumalacarregui	2000	C
		Espartero	8000	
Feb 5	2nd. Arquijas	Zumalacarregui	8500	C
		Lorenzo	14000	
Mar 9	Larraga	Zumalacarregui	6000	L
		Soane	4000	
Apr 22-24	Artaza (las Amescoas)	Zumalacarregui	5000	C
		Valdes	22000	
Apr 28	Eliot Convention			
Jun 2	Descarga	Espartero		
		Eraso		
Jun 18	Death of Zumalacarregui			
Jun	British Auxiliary Legion begins recruiting			
Jul 16	Mendigorria	Moreno	24000	L
		Cordova	36000	
Aug 17	4,000 French Foreign Legion intervene to support Liberals			

1836				
Jan 16-17	Arlaban	Villareal		draw
		Cordova, Evans	8000	
Feb	Henningsen's book published by John Murray, Albemarle St. 2 vols Price 18 shillings			
Apr 26	Tirapegui	Garcia	3500	L
		Bernelle	1100	
Aug	8,000 men of the British Auxiliary Legion arrive in San Sebastian to support Liberals			
Aug 8	Escaro	Gomez Damas[118]	3000	L
		Espartero	6000	
Aug 13	La Granja Revolution: Queen Christina forced at gunpoint to sign the 1812 Constitution			
Aug 30	Matillas	Gomez Damas	3000	C
		Lopez	6000	
Sept 20	Villarrobledo	Gomez Damas	6850	L
		Alaix Fabregas	10000	
Nov 23	Majaceite	Gomez Damas		L
		Narvaez	3 divisions	
Dec 24	Luchana (Bilbao)	Villareal	10500	L
		Espartero	14000	

---

[118] For a superb and entertaining short account of Gomez Damas' Long March in 1836, see Peter Missler's paper published in the George Borrow Bulletin (2002) currently also on their website.

1837				
Mar 16	Oriamendi	Don Sebastian	5900	C
		de Lacy Evans	8300	
Mar 24	Huesca	Don Carlos	8000	L
		Iribarren	8000	
May 17	Behobia (Irun)	Sagastibeltza	500	
		de Lacy Evans	12000	
Aug 24	Villar de los Navarros	Don Carlos	12500	C
		Oraa	7800	
Sep 14	Andoain	Uranga	3000	C
		O'Donnel	7000	
Sep 19	Aranzueque	Moreno	12000	
		Espartero	25000	
Oct 17	Henningsen leaves the Carlist army for good			
Oct 21	Henningsen captured by Liberals of the National Guard of Munilla near Zornosa.			
Dec 11	Release of Henningsen from prison with Mr. Gruneisen of the Morning Post			

Printed in Great Britain
by Amazon

66757623R00210